LIFE APPLICATION® BIBLE COMMENTARY

1 TIMOTHY
2 TIMOTHY
TITUS

Bruce B. Barton, D.Min.
David R. Veerman, M.Div.
Neil Wilson, M.A.R.

Series Editor: Grant Osborne, Ph.D.
Editor: Philip Comfort, Ph.D.
Associate Editor: Linda K. Taylor

Tyndale House Publishers, Inc.
WHEATON, ILLINOIS

Contributing Editors: James C. Galvin, Ed.D. and Ronald A. Beers

---

Library of Congress Cataloging-in-Publication Data
Barton, Bruce B.
    1 Timothy, 2 Timothy, Titus / Bruce B. Barton, David R. Veerman,
Neil Wilson.
        p.   cm. — (Life application Bible commentary)
    Includes bibliographical references and index.
    ISBN 0-8423-2832-7 (pbk.)
    1. Bible.   N.T.   Pastoral Epistle—Commentaries.   I. Veerman,
David.   II. Wilson, Neil S., 1950- . III. Bible.   N.T.   Pastoral
Epistles.   English.   1993   IV. Title   V. Title: First Timothy,
Second Timothy, Titus.   VI. Series.
BS2735.3.B27   1993
227'.8307—dc20   93-4926

Printed in the United States of America
99 98 97 96 95 94 93
8   7   6   5   4   3   2   1

CONTENTS

FOREWORD

The *Life Application Bible* Commentary series provides verse-by-verse explanation, background, and application for every verse in the New Testament. In addition, it gives personal help, teaching notes, and sermon ideas that will address needs, answer questions, and provide insight for applying God's Word to life today. The content is highlighted so that particular verses and phrases are easy to find.

Each volume contains three sections: introduction, commentary, and reference. The introduction includes an overview of the book, the book's historical context, a timeline, cultural background information, major themes, an overview map, and an explanation about the author and audience.

The commentary section includes running commentary on the Bible text with reference to several modern versions, especially the New International Version and the New Revised Standard Version, accompanied by life applications interspersed throughout. Additional elements include charts, diagrams, maps, and illustrations. There are also insightful quotes from church leaders and theologians such as John Calvin, Martin Luther, John Wesley, A. W. Tozer, and C. S. Lewis. These features are designed to help you quickly grasp the biblical information and be prepared to communicate it to others.

The reference section includes a bibliography of other resources and an index.

INTRODUCTION TO THE PASTORAL EPISTLES

The wise coach gives his junior quarterback valuable game time—the experience will prepare the young athlete for the starting role next fall . . . or sooner. The wise employer watches for promising young employees, then helps them learn new skills and assume greater responsibilities. Wise parents nurture and teach their children, helping them mature and grow into responsible adults. Wise leaders serve as mentors to emerging, potential leaders.

The next generation holds a vital position in every family, institution, movement, or church—for leadership, vision, life . . . for its future. The apostle Paul knew this truth.

Paul began to follow Christ as an adult. Through a dramatic confrontation on the way to capture and imprison the hated believers in Jesus, Paul's life changed dramatically (Acts 9:1-19). Soon he became known as a fearless champion of the Christian cause, a peerless evangelist, and a pioneering missionary. With strong commitment, deep courage, and boundless energy, Paul went to the ends of his world, preaching and teaching the Good News of Christ to all who would listen. Although thousands had responded to the gospel message and churches had been planted and were growing, Paul knew that the future of the Christian movement would depend on new leadership. Given the hostile environment of the Roman world and the advancing age of the apostles, in a short time the first generation of Christian leaders would be gone. Then who would direct, guide, evangelize, and spread the Word? So Paul encouraged younger coworkers like Timothy and Titus to "teach others those things you and many others have heard me speak about. Teach these great truths to trustworthy men who will, in turn, pass them on to others" (2 Timothy 2:2 TLB).

Paul followed his own advice as he worked closely with younger believers, Timothy and Titus, helping them deepen their faith and developing them for leadership. Timothy was a second-generation Christian; his mother, Eunice, and grandmother Lois were Jewish believers who helped lead him to Christ (2 Timothy 1:5;

3:15). A young Greek man, Titus was converted to Christ through Paul's ministry. In fact, Paul presented him to the leaders of the church in Jerusalem as a living example of the ministry among the Gentiles (Galatians 2:1-3). Because of the tremendous potential Paul saw in these two men, he groomed them for leadership in the church. And he gave them detailed instructions on how to choose other church leaders, specifically elders and deacons.

Paul's instructions to his protégés are included in three letters, preserved as the Bible books 1 Timothy, 2 Timothy, and Titus. Although these letters are known as the "Pastoral Epistles," Timothy and Titus were not pastors of individual congregations. Rather, they served as apostolic representatives sent to Ephesus and Crete, respectively, to help organize the churches under the leadership of other trained elders and deacons.

Some scholars have proposed that the Pastoral Epistles were not written by Paul but by a later admirer of Paul who imitated Paul's writing style and attached Paul's name to them. This theory arises from the difficulty of matching the events mentioned in these letters with the book of Acts. And if, as had been surmised, Paul's Roman imprisonment ended with his execution, it seems impossible to date these letters prior to his death. In addition, some believe that the writing style in these letters differs from the other Pauline Epistles. The content seems to differ as well, with little or no emphasis on Christ's return (contrasting greatly with 1 and 2 Thessalonians). Instead, the local congregation of believers is central in the Pastoral Epistles—the writer is concerned with church organization and theological purity.

The arguments against authorship by Paul seem quite subjective, especially when balanced against the strong affirmation of Paul as author by the early church fathers (Ignatius, Polycarp, Justin Martyr, Clement of Alexandria, Tertullian, and Iranaeus). In addition, the possibility of *two* imprisonments separated by a few years during which Paul traveled extensively answers most of the objections to the timing of the books (see the possible itinerary under "Date" in the introduction to 1 Timothy).

As you study these letters of the great missionary apostle to his young pastors, watch Paul develop leaders of the early church. Follow his example by passing the faith and leadership to the next generation. And learn how to help your church through Paul's instructions to his friends and coministers.

1 TIMOTHY

INTRODUCTION TO
1 TIMOTHY

AUTHOR

Paul: the great apostle and missionary of the church.

The first line of this letter to Timothy names Paul as the author (1:1). Paul and Timothy probably met on Paul's first missionary journey (Timothy accompanied Paul on his second journey) when Paul preached at Lystra (Acts 14:6-7). Timothy's grandmother and mother had come to faith first and had been a great influence on him (2 Timothy 1:5; 3:14-15). Their faithful witness and instruction in the Scriptures prepared Timothy also to follow Christ. In addition, Timothy must have seen Paul stoned at Lystra for his faith, dragged out of the city and left for dead, and then return to life after the prayers of the believers. All of these factors must have had a profound effect on Timothy, convincing him that Jesus was, in fact, the promised Messiah. Paul calls Timothy his "child" or "son" (1 Corinthians 4:17; 2 Timothy 2:1), implying a relationship as Timothy's spiritual father.

Beyond leading young Timothy to Christ, Paul became Timothy's mentor, bringing him along as a fellow missionary and appointing him to a leadership position in the church. Ever since meeting in Lystra, Paul and Timothy were close, as friends, brothers in Christ, and partners in the ministry. In fact, Paul's last known message is his second letter to Timothy, in which he asks Timothy to visit him in prison as soon as possible (2 Timothy 4:9). Paul's letters to Timothy stand as a powerful witness to the close relationship these men enjoyed as Paul gave Timothy encouragement, guidance, and strong instruction.

SETTING

Ephesus and the surrounding area.

The gospel had come to Ephesus through Apollos, an outstanding orator and young believer (Acts 18:24). But when Paul visited the city for the first time (on his third missionary journey), he found many who had an incomplete faith, having received only the "baptism of repentance" (Acts 19:4). So Paul told the Ephesians about Jesus (Acts 19:5). They responded to his teaching and received the Holy Spirit (Acts 19:6). Paul stayed and ministered in Ephesus for more than two years, first in the synagogue, and then in the lecture hall of Tyrannus (Acts 19:8-10). After a riot ensued, instigated by Demetrius the silversmith, Paul gave final words of encouragement to the believers and left for Macedonia (Acts 19:23–20:1). A few months later, before leaving the area, Paul met with the Ephesian elders at Miletus. During this meeting, Paul warned the Ephesian elders about false teachers who would try to draw believers away from the truth (Acts 20:28-31). After a time of challenge and prayer and an emotional farewell, Paul sailed to Jerusalem (Acts 20:13–21:1). Paul had a very warm and close relationship with the church at Ephesus, and he was concerned for their spiritual well-being.

Although nothing more is said about Ephesus in the book of Acts, Paul probably visited the city after his release from his first Roman imprisonment (see his possible itinerary below). During this visit (with Timothy), he discovered that a number of spiritual problems had arisen during his absence. Paul and Timothy stayed in Ephesus for a while to teach and to straighten things out. When Paul had to leave for Macedonia, he left Timothy there as his representative to lead the church (1:3).

The area surrounding Ephesus probably had a number of young churches, not just one, with each church led by an elder. Thus Paul did not appoint Timothy as the "elder," "bishop," or "overseer" of the churches, but rather as his representative, carrying his apostolic authority to order worship (2:1-15) and appoint elders and deacons (3:1-13).

AUDIENCE

Timothy and the church at large.

Timothy was born and reared in Lystra in Lycaonia. Timothy's mother, Eunice, and grandmother Lois were devout Jews who had come to faith in Christ (Acts 16:1; 2 Timothy 1:5), but his father was a Greek. Evidently the father was not a Jewish proselyte or a convert to Christianity, since Timothy had not been circumcised (Acts 16:3). Timothy's mother and grandmother had carefully taught him the Old Testament Scriptures (2 Timothy 3:15), so he was open to the gospel when he heard Paul preach on his first visit to Lystra (Acts 14:6-7).

Because of Timothy's growth in the faith and his spiritual gifts, Paul chose him to become a partner in spreading the gospel on the second missionary journey (Acts 16:1-3). Paul also may have seen Timothy as one who was free from the prejudices of many Jews—Timothy had a mixed family (a Jewish mother and a Greek father). To avoid a problem with the Jews in the area, Paul circumcised Timothy before they left (Acts 16:3). Paul also ordained Timothy at this time (4:14).

Although Paul trusted Timothy completely and expected him to be a strong leader in the church, Paul also was very aware of Timothy's weaknesses. Timothy was very young and, evidently, was shy and hesitant. So Paul warned him against being intimidated by his opponents and their teachings (4:12; 2 Timothy 1:5, 7; 3:10; see also 1 Corinthians 16:10-11). In addition, Timothy may have had stomach problems (5:23).

As requested, Timothy left his family in Lystra to travel with Paul. On that journey Timothy helped establish the churches at Philippi, Thessalonica, and Berea (Acts 16:1–17:14). When Paul left Berea early to go to Athens, he left Timothy and Silas behind. But Paul sent word for them to join him as soon as possible (Acts 17:13-15).

Soon after Timothy arrived at Athens, Paul sent him to Thessalonica to strengthen the faith of the believers there (1 Thessalonians 3:1-2). Later, Timothy rejoined Paul at Corinth and helped establish that church (Acts 18:5). The Bible doesn't say whether Timothy traveled with Paul from Corinth to Ephesus and then to Caesarea, Jerusalem, Antioch, and back to Ephesus (Acts 18:18–19:1). We do read, however, that Timothy worked with Paul at Ephesus (Acts 19:22). Then Paul sent him (and Erastus) to Greece to minister to churches there and to prepare the way for a possible visit by Paul, while Paul stayed at Ephesus (Acts 19:22; 1 Corinthians 4:17; 16:10). Before Paul left Ephesus, however, Timothy rejoined him (Romans 16:21; 2 Corinthians 1:1). Then they traveled together to Macedonia, to Achaia, back to Macedonia, and on to Asia (Acts 20:1-5).

The book of Acts makes no mention of Timothy during the record of Paul's trip to Jerusalem, arrest, two-year imprisonment at Caesarea, and voyage to Rome (Acts 21:1–28:16). We know that either Timothy was with Paul during those years or he rejoined Paul at Rome during the early months of imprisonment, because we read that he was with Paul in Rome (Philippians 1:1; 2:19; Colossians 1:1; Philemon 1).

During Paul's first imprisonment, he planned to send Timothy to Philippi (Philippians 2:19-23). Paul may not have done this, however, because of his early release. After Paul's release from prison, Timothy traveled with Paul to Ephesus, where he was left to care for the church (1:3—see the possible itinerary on page 5). Although Paul asked Timothy to visit him in prison during the second imprisonment, there is no evidence that Timothy made it there before Paul was executed.

Because of the reference in Hebrews to Timothy being out of prison (Hebrews 13:23-24), there is speculation that Timothy had been imprisoned in Rome and then later released. According to tradition, Timothy was martyred during the reign of either Domitian or Nerva.

OCCASION

False teachers and potential divisions at Ephesus and a possible delay in Paul's arrival to the area.

Having been released from his first Roman imprisonment and apparently on his way to Asia Minor, Paul traveled to the island of Crete and left Titus there to finish organizing the churches (Titus 1:5). Then Paul went to Ephesus, where he was joined by Timothy, who evidently had returned from Philippi (Philippians 2:19-23). Paul and Timothy discovered that heretical teachers were spreading false teachings, just as Paul had predicted would happen (Acts 20:29-30). These false teachers were preying especially on women, new believers who were enjoying unprecedented freedom in Christ to study the Bible and be involved in worship.

As he left Ephesus, Paul left Timothy behind as his representative to reorganize the church there (1:3). Evidently Paul had planned to see Timothy again, where he could have instructed him in person. But Paul was delayed, so he wrote his instructions in the epistle we know as 1 Timothy (3:14-15).

PURPOSE

To encourage and instruct Timothy about the organization of a local church and to help him deal with false doctrines.

Although 1 Timothy is addressed to one individual, undoubtedly the contents of the letter were meant for the church at large. The epistle is filled with exhortations for the whole church, not just personal matters. Paul warned about false teachers (1:3-7; 6:3-10), gave instructions for worship (2:1-15) and how to deal with various groups in the church (5:1-21), and explained how to choose elders and deacons (3:1-13). Paul gave special instructions about how women should behave in the church because they were susceptible to the false teachings and because many were flaunting their new Christian freedom (2:9-15).

First Timothy is also a letter of encouragement for a young pastor who must have been intimidated by older and more mature members. Paul told Timothy not to let his age limit his ministry (4:12) and to boldly exercise his gifts (4:14-16).

DATE

About A.D. 64, from Rome or Macedonia (possibly Philippi).

Identifying when the Pastoral Epistles were written is not an easy task because, unlike other epistles, they don't seem to correspond with the chronology of the other New Testament books, and they contain no references to events in Acts. Most scholars believe, therefore, that these letters fit in the time between Paul's two Roman imprisonments. The itinerary for Paul, outlined below, is consistent with references in the epistles and explains when and where these letters to the young leaders were written.

1. After his appeal to Caesar, Paul traveled to Rome as a prisoner (Acts 25:11; 28:15-16).

2. Paul remained under house arrest for two years, during which he ministered to many of the Roman believers (Acts 28:23-30).

3. Apparently having been released from prison in about A.D. 62, Paul traveled for about four years. These travels included:

   - A trip to Crete, leaving Titus to carry on the ministry (Titus 1:5)
   - A trip to Ephesus and then Macedonia, leaving Timothy to minister at Ephesus (1 Timothy 1:3)—then, perhaps, a visit to Spain
   - A visit to Ephesus as Paul had intended (1 Timothy 3:14)
   - A stay at Nicopolis during the winter (Titus 3:12)
   - A visit to Miletus, where Trophimus was left sick (2 Timothy 4:20)
   - A visit to Troas, where a cloak and parchments were left (2 Timothy 4:13)
   - A visit to Corinth (2 Timothy 4:20)

4. During this time, Paul wrote 1 Timothy and Titus (approximately A.D. 64–65).

5. Paul was taken prisoner again and returned to Rome (2 Timothy 1:16-17).

6. During this final imprisonment, Paul wrote 2 Timothy, his last letter and farewell address (approximately A.D. 66–67).

7. Paul was beheaded in Rome (approximately A.D. 67).

There is evidence in the Bible text for two imprisonments. Clearly Paul expected to be released from prison (Philippians 1:25-27; 2:24; Philemon 22—both of these letters were written from prison). The book of Acts also seems to imply that Paul would be released, not executed (Acts 23:12-35; 28:21, 30-31). There is also evidence in other historical writings: Clement of Rome and Eusebius both wrote of ministry by Paul in the west, possibly Spain (mentioned by Paul as a desire of his—Romans 15:24), which could only have taken place after the imprisonment recorded in Acts.

MESSAGE

Sound doctrine; public worship; church leadership; caring church; personal discipline.

Sound doctrine (1:3-11; 4:1-10; 6:3-5). Paul's first challenge to Timothy and the Ephesian believers was to combat the false teachers who had infiltrated the church. Paul warned Timothy about these heretics three times in this letter. After each warning, Paul exhorted Timothy to cling tightly to the faith, to be strong, and to live rightly (1:18-19; 4:9-16; 6:11-21).

The exact nature of the heresy is unclear from the text, but Paul referred to endless genealogies (1:4), a strain of legalism (4:3), "unhealthy interest in controversies" (6:4 NIV), and teaching for personal, financial gain (6:5). Paul urged Timothy to combat the false teachings by confronting the false teachers (4:6; 6:12) and by having nothing to do with them or their ideas (4:7). Paul also urged Timothy to have love (1:5; 6:11), a sincere and strong faith (1:5, 19; 6:12), a clear conscience (1:5, 19), and a godly life (4:7; 6:11). The greatest weapon against heresy is sound doctrine (1:10; 4:16; 6:3)—holding to the truth and living it. Sound doctrine is also high on the list of qualities needed in elders and deacons (3:9).

Importance for Today. The only way to identify what is false is to know the truth. God's truth is contained in his Word, the Bible. Thus our theology (that is, our doctrine, what we believe) should be consistent with what the Bible says. Unless we are grounded in the Word, we will be susceptible to any number of false teachings. In addition to being well grounded, we also should avoid anyone who twists the words of the Bible for his or her own purpose. And we should confront and expose false teaching and teachers whenever we find them.

Unfortunately, there seems to be a tragic absence of theological awareness among Christians today. With little understanding of sound, biblical doctrine, many are "blown here and there by every wind of teaching and by the cunning and craftiness of men in their deceitful scheming" (Ephesians 4:14 NIV). This can happen when individuals read passages out of context, read into Scripture their own interpretations, or listen to false teachers.

How well do you know God's Word? Be a student of the Bible, reading, studying, and applying it. And pay careful attention to "sound doctrine" so that you will be able to identify false teaching and stand against it.

Public worship (2:1-15). Beyond the issue of false teachers, Paul's next area of concern for church life was worship. Paul began by emphasizing the necessity and centrality of prayer. Prayers should be made for everyone, including "kings and all those in authority," because God wants everyone to be saved (2:1-4 NIV). In fact, all Christians, wherever they gather, should pray together (2:8).

Next, Paul discussed the conduct of women in worship. Evidently the actions of some women had been disruptive. Paul explained that although they were enjoying new freedom in Christ to study the Bible and to worship with men, women should not rush into leadership or flaunt their freedom (2:9-15).

In both issues (prayer and women in worship), Paul's focus was unity. The implication is that there were potential or real divisions in the Ephesian church that threatened to disrupt worship.

Importance for Today. People attend worship services for many reasons: some come out of habit; others make it a social occasion; some simply want to be seen; a few are so eager to teach and lead that they eagerly follow false teachers with hollow promises. But any motive that does not flow from sincere devotion to Christ holds potential for trouble in the church. Women and men should worship with humility and submission, praying together for God's direction and for the needs of others.

What draws you to worship? How often do you pray with your brothers and sisters in the faith? Keep your focus on Christ, the "one mediator between God and men . . . who gave himself as a ransom for all men" (2:5-6 NIV).

Church leadership (3:1-16). Paul gave specific instructions concerning the qualifications for church leaders so that the church might honor God and operate smoothly. Again, the fact that this section has such prominence in the letter seems to imply that less than qualified men were leading the various congregations (or were aspiring to be leaders). In fact, it is likely that the false teachers were former and current leaders in the church. As Paul's representative and with apostolic authority, Timothy was to make sure that church leaders had spiritual maturity, specific spiritual gifts, sound theology, a solid family life, and a good reputation.

Importance for Today. There is no more important role than church leadership; therefore, those selected to fill leadership positions in local churches must be of the highest caliber, wholly committed to Christ and strong in their faith. If you are a new or young Christian, make developing your Christian character your first priority, and don't be anxious to hold a church leadership position. May your motive be to seek God, not to fulfill your own ambition.

Caring church (5:1-20; 6:1-2, 17-19). Jesus told his disciples that the world would know that they were his followers by their love for each other (John 13:35). The greatest witness the Ephesian believers could make for Christ in their world would be as a caring church. But the command to love must result in specific actions. So Paul outlined for Timothy the way the church should treat older men (5:1), younger men (5:1), older women (5:2), younger women (5:2), widows (5:3-6, 9-16), and church elders (5:17-20), and how slaves should repond to their masters (6:1-2). In addition, Paul encouraged Timothy to challenge rich members to invest their wealth in helping others (6:17-19).

Importance for Today. The church has a responsibility to care for the needs of all its members, especially the sick, the poor, and the widowed. Caring must go beyond good intentions. Caring for the family of believers demonstrates our Christlike attitude and exhibits genuine love to nonbelievers. What plan does your church have to care for members in need? What can you do to help those who are suffering and struggling? Look for ways to put Christ's love into action in your church and community.

Personal discipline (4:11-16; 5:21-25; 6:6-16, 20-21). Paul knew that it took discipline to be an effective church leader. Timothy, like the elders, had to guard his motives, minister faithfully, and live righteously. Paul told Timothy to do what God has called him to do despite his young age. In fact, Timothy should set an example of spirituality and right living (4:11-12). Paul also told Timothy to diligently exercise his spiritual gifts, preaching, teaching, and leading (4:13-16). As God's man and Paul's representative, Timothy must keep himself pure, avoiding worldly temptations, especially the love of money (5:21-25; 6:6-10). Finally, Paul urged Timothy to be disciplined by keeping his eyes on Christ (6:11-16) and refusing to become sidetracked by endless, empty discussions (6:20-21).

Importance for Today. All church leaders must keep morally and spiritually fit. To stay in good spiritual shape, you must stay focused on Christ and on your calling, discipline yourself to study God's Word and to obey it, and put your spiritual abilities to work. What distracts you from serving Christ wholeheartedly? What has God called you to do to serve him? Be an example to others of how a mature Christian should live.

VITAL STATISTICS

Purpose: To give encouragement and instruction to Timothy, a young leader

Author: Paul

To whom written: Timothy, young church leaders, and all believers everywhere

Date written: About A.D. 64, from Rome or Macedonia (possibly Philippi), probably just prior to Paul's final imprisonment in Rome

Setting: Timothy was one of Paul's closest companions. Paul had sent Timothy to the church at Ephesus to counter the false teaching that had arisen there (1:3-4). Timothy probably served for a time as a leader in the church at Ephesus. Paul hoped to visit Timothy (3:14-15; 4:13), but in the meantime, he wrote this letter to give Timothy practical advice about the ministry.

Key verse: "Don't let anyone look down on you because you are young, but set an example for the believers in speech, in life, in love, in faith and in purity" (4:12 NIV).

OUTLINE

1. Instructions on right belief (1:1-20)
2. Instructions for the church (2:1–3:16)
3. Instructions for leaders (4:1–6:21)

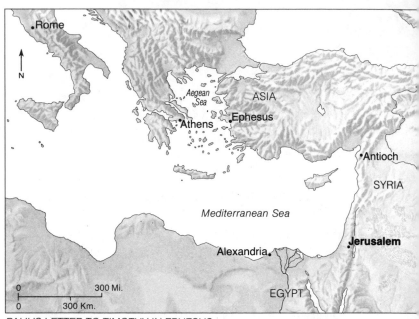

PAUL'S LETTER TO TIMOTHY IN EPHESUS
Paul wrote to Timothy, who was taking charge of the Ephesian church.
The city of Ephesus was a strategic city, ranking in importance with
Alexandria in Egypt and Antioch in Syria as a port on the Mediterranean
Sea. It lay on the most western edge of Asia Minor (modern-day Turkey),
the most important port on the Aegean Sea on the main route from Rome
to the east.

1 Timothy 1

Paul wrote this letter to Timothy in A.D. 64 or 65, after Paul's first imprisonment in Rome (Acts 28:16-31). Apparently Paul had been out of prison for several years, and during that time he had revisited many churches in Asia and Macedonia. When Paul and Timothy returned to Ephesus, they found widespread false teaching in the church. Paul had warned the Ephesian elders to be on guard against the false teachers who inevitably would come after he had left (Acts 20:17-31). Paul assigned Timothy to remain in the Ephesian church while he moved on to Macedonia. From there Paul wrote this letter of encouragement and instruction to help Timothy deal with the difficult situation in the Ephesian church.

The more we know about Timothy, the more we can appreciate what Paul's letters must have meant to him. He followed Paul for years. At this point he represented Paul as leader of a local church. He was probably lonely and intimidated. How could he consider himself a capable replacement for Paul? As is the case with some churches, he undoubtedly had among his congregation those who did not hesitate to point out his inadequacies. Paul's letter was as welcome to Timothy as a guiding light penetrating the fog on a stormy night.

Effective delegators keep track of those they entrust with responsibilities. Paul knew he had given Timothy a challenging assignment. He also knew Timothy very well. Their travels together enabled Paul to understand how much pressure Timothy could handle. He also knew how much encouragement Timothy would need along the way. Paul kept in touch through his letters. From his opening words in this letter, Paul blended encouragement with direction for his "child in the faith" (1:2 NRSV).

1:1 Paul. Unlike most personal letters of today, ancient letters often began with the writer's name instead of adding it at the end. So, although what follows is a personal letter to Timothy, Paul identified himself in a formal manner. Anyone else who would read

this letter would recognize it as personal, but not private. Paul
intended his words to be heard by a greater audience.

DON'T HOLD BACK
It's easy to be stingy with encouragement. Each day we have
many opportunities to support and inspire family members, fellow workers, and even total strangers. People need help and
affirmation all along the way. In his letter to Timothy, Paul modeled for us six important principles to help us encourage others:
1. Begin with encouragement. People who know we will
   encourage them will cooperate more than those who feel
   they must "earn" every morsel of affirmation.
2. Expect of others only what you expect of yourself. People
   will resist being held to unfair standards.
3. Develop expectations of others with consideration for their
   skills, maturity, and experience. People will reject or fail to
   meet expectations that do not fit them. Be patient with dis-
   tracted or slow learners.
4. Monitor your expectations of others. Changing circumstances sometimes require revised or reduced expectations.
5. Clarify your expectations with others. People are not likely to
   hit a target that no one has identified for them.
6. End with encouragement. People feel used when their
   efforts go unnoticed.

Paul wrote these instructions to Timothy, a young pastor who
was also Paul's associate. But they were certainly directed to a
wider audience. Paul wanted the believers in Ephesus to comply
with his commands through his representative, Timothy. Because
Paul addressed the requirements of various roles within the local
church, his directions continue to apply to church leaders today.

An apostle of Christ Jesus. *Apostle* comes from the Greek word
apostolos, meaning "one who is sent." The word was used to
describe an envoy (a person sent out with a message) or an
ambassador (a person sent out to represent a country and leader).
In a broad sense, all believers are apostles, for all are "sent" with
the message of the Good News to unbelievers, and all are "sent"
to represent their King, Jesus Christ.

But New Testament usage of the title *apostle* was stricter. Paul
was an apostle called personally by Jesus Christ himself. His
commission to this position came directly from God on the road
to Damascus (see 1 Corinthians 9:1; 15:8). The title *apostle* was
reserved for certain followers of Christ who had accompanied
Jesus and had seen the risen Lord. Paul used this title in all of his
letters except Philippians (cowritten with Timothy, with the salutation "Paul and Timothy, servants of Christ Jesus" NIV), 1 and

2 Thessalonians (cowritten with Silas and Timothy, who would not, in the strict sense, be designated as apostles), and Philemon (also cowritten with Timothy, where Paul described himself as "a prisoner of Christ Jesus" NIV). Paul presented this important credential of apostleship in most of his letters as a foundation for his instructions. He was not writing suggestions or opinions, but what Peter classified along with "the other Scriptures" (2 Peter 3:16 NIV). Paul expected to be heard because he represented Jesus Christ.

AUTHORITY
The Bible is the written form of what God expects us to know and do. God chose Paul to carry out one phase of the plan. Through Paul, the inspired teaching was written down. As such, it was passed on to Timothy. Then, it was passed on to others. Later, it was passed on to us. Times have changed, but the original authority remains. Because the Bible is from God, it must be studied seriously, understood thoroughly, and applied faithfully. Paul did not intend for Timothy to skim this letter. It requires no less attention from us.

By the command of God our Savior and of Christ Jesus our hope.NRSV How was Paul an apostle? Although he was not one of the original twelve disciples, Paul met Jesus personally. Before his conversion, Paul, a devout Jew, had pursued and imprisoned Christians, sincerely believing that they were a threat to Judaism and should be destroyed. But he was sincerely wrong—and Jesus appeared to him on a road to Damascus and told him so. At that time, Paul was temporarily blinded and had to be led into Damascus to await God's orders (see Acts 9:1-9).

God chose Paul for special work: "He is an instrument whom I have chosen to bring my name before Gentiles and kings and before the people of Israel" (Acts 9:15 NRSV). In Acts 13:2, the Holy Spirit, through other believers, said, "Set apart for me Barnabas and Saul [Paul] for the work to which I have called them" (NRSV). Paul did not seek this missionary apostleship, rather, God appointed Paul. By God's *command,* Paul served as "one sent" with the gospel to the Gentiles. He served under direct orders from the King of kings.

Paul calls God *our Savior.* Paul used the phrase "our Savior" six times in the letters to Timothy and Titus (see 1 Timothy 1:1; 2:3; 4:10; Titus 1:3; 2:10; 3:4). Although Jesus Christ came to earth to die on the cross for our sins, God can also be called "Savior" because he "so loved the world that He gave His only begotten Son, that whoever believes in Him should not perish but have everlasting life" (John 3:16 NKJV). God in his fullness (Father, Son, and Holy Spirit) authored salvation.

Paul also may have used this particular Greek word, *soter,* because, at the time, the cruel emperor Nero applied it to himself. The apostle would not have hesitated to repudiate Nero's claim. Paul reminded his readers who the true Savior was—not any human leader (most certainly not Nero!), but God himself, through his Son, Jesus Christ.

Paul calls Christ Jesus *our hope.* The psalmist wrote, "Why are you cast down, O my soul? And why are you disquieted within me? Hope in God . . ." (Psalm 43:5 NKJV). Paul wrote to the Colossians: "God willed to make known what are the riches of the glory of this mystery . . . which is Christ in you, the hope of glory" (Colossians 1:27 NKJV).

What does it mean to call Christ "our hope"? Our hope rests in Jesus Christ. He is the embodiment of our faith, the basis for our eternal life. When we place our hope in Christ, we are not pacified with vague "maybes," rather we are given certainties. We "hope" for what we already know is ours. Our union with Christ provides our salvation now. Our hope is our belief that one day our salvation will be realized—final and complete—when he returns for us. Where have you placed your hope?

1:2 To Timothy. Paul addressed many of his letters to churches across the Roman Empire, and these letters were meant to be read aloud to all the believers. This letter, although addressed to Timothy, was also meant to be read to the entire congregation in the church at Ephesus (and beyond) (see 1:3). First Timothy has

> Mercy is not for them that sin and fear not, but for them that fear and sin not.
> *Thomas Watson*

been called the first of the "Pastoral" Epistles (1 and 2 Timothy and Titus). All of Paul's letters express pastoral concerns, but these three relate specifically to local church issues.

Timothy grew up in Lystra, a city in the province of Galatia. Paul and Barnabas visited Lystra on Paul's first missionary journey (see Acts 14:8-21). Most likely, Paul met the young Timothy and his mother, Eunice, and grandmother Lois (see 2 Timothy 1:5) on this journey, perhaps even staying in their home.

On Paul's second missionary journey, he and Silas went to several cities that Paul had already visited, including Lystra, "where there was a disciple named Timothy, the son of a Jewish woman who was a believer. . . . He was well spoken of by the believers in Lystra and Iconium. Paul wanted Timothy to accompany him" (Acts 16:1-3 NRSV). So began an incredible adventure for the young disciple, Timothy, who would travel the empire with Paul, preaching and teaching the Good News. He became Paul's assistant—traveling with him and sometimes for him, as Paul's emissary.

ADVENTURE HIGHLIGHTS FROM TIMOTHY'S LIFE
Before beginning his travels, Timothy submitted to being circumcised by Paul. Paul felt this was important "because of the Jews who were in those places [where Timothy lived], for they all knew that his father was a Greek" (Acts 16:3 NRSV).

When Paul escaped to Athens from upheaval in Berea, Silas and Timothy remained behind, undoubtedly to continue to teach (Acts 17:10-15). Silas and Timothy later rejoined Paul in Corinth (Acts 18:1, 5).

Paul remained in Ephesus, but sent Timothy and Erastus (another assistant) on ahead into Macedonia (Acts 19:22).

Timothy was in Corinth with Paul when Paul wrote his letter to the Romans (Romans 16:21).

Paul sent Timothy to Corinth (1 Corinthians 4:17; 16:10), and Timothy was with Paul when Paul wrote 2 Corinthians (2 Corinthians 1:1, 19).

Paul sent Timothy to Thessalonica (1 Thessalonians 3:2); Timothy was also with Paul when Paul wrote to that church in response to the good news that Timothy had brought regarding the Thessalonians' faith (1 Thessalonians 1:1; 3:6).

Timothy was with Paul when Paul wrote to the church in Philippi, and Timothy went as Paul's emissary to that church (Philippians 1:1; 2:19).

Timothy was with Paul when Paul wrote his letters to the Colossians and to Philemon (Colossians 1:1; Philemon 1:1).

My true son in the faith.[NIV] Paul and Timothy had developed a special bond, like father and son. Paul wrote of Timothy, "As a son with his father he has served with me in the work of the gospel" (Philippians 2:22 NIV). This father/son language primarily reflects the fact that Paul led Timothy to Christ during his first missionary journey while Paul was at Lystra. Second Timothy 1:5 and 3:15 show that Timothy had known the Old Testament Scriptures and had been influenced by his mother and grandmother. Probably Paul led all three to the Lord. Timothy was a *true* son; that is, his faith was genuine. But he was also a *son* (*teknon,* "child") to Paul, indicating their intimate friendship. This has repercussions for today. If people felt the same parental love and responsibility for people they lead to Christ, there would be very few follow-up problems.

Timothy was an important leader in the early church and, like Paul, was imprisoned for his faith. The writer of Hebrews mentioned Timothy at the end of that letter: "I want you to know that our brother Timothy has been released. If he arrives soon, I will come with him to see you" (Hebrews 13:23 NIV).

THOSE UNIQUE PASTORAL LETTERS
In the past decades, computer studies of the Pastoral Epistles have revealed that they differ significantly in vocabulary from the rest of Paul's letters. Their style is also "calmer" and more polished than the rough-and-tumble of Paul's earlier letters. These discoveries have led some to the conclusion that Paul may not have written the Pastorals. Different language has been taken to indicate different authors. But there is another equally acceptable conclusion: Different language can also indicate different audiences.

In the Pastoral Epistles, Paul used a number of technical phrases that are not found elsewhere in the New Testament. One example, *pistos ho logos* ("The saying is sure" NRSV or "Here is a trustworthy saying" NIV), serves as both a unique and technical term in the Pastorals (see 1 Timothy 1:15; 3:1; 4:9; 2 Timothy 2:11; Titus 3:8). Critics have labeled this phrase "too advanced" to have been Paul's. A statement doesn't become "a saying" until it has been used a while, or so the theory goes. But long-standing friendships often develop unique phrases or language that affect conversation. Also, the "summarizing" tone of much of these letters indicates that they were written to reinforce lengthy verbal instructions Paul had given Timothy and Titus. Students have nothing to gain by doubting Paul's authorship of these letters.

Grace, mercy, and peace from God our Father and Jesus Christ our Lord.^NKJV Paul used *grace and peace* as a standard greeting in all of his letters. However, it is only in his letters to Timothy that he used *mercy.* "Mercy" carries with it the Old Testament picture of God's loving-kindness. God's mercy helps us day by day. Paul knew that Timothy was facing a difficult situation in Ephesus, so he added the word *mercy* to reassure Timothy of God's protection and guidance.

God as *our Father* also is a key Old Testament concept. For example:

- "Is He not your Father, who bought you? Has He not made you and established you?" (Deuteronomy 32:6 NKJV)
- "I will be his Father, and he shall be My son. . . ." (2 Samuel 7:14 NKJV)

Many people come from fatherless homes or from dysfunctional families with an abusive father. Perhaps the role of father has been underplayed. However, Christians should not delete references to God as "our Father." Instead of seeing God as similar to our pictures of imperfect fathers, we understand true fatherhood through knowing God the merciful and gracious Creator.

By using the phrase *Jesus Christ our Lord,* Paul pointed to Jesus as a full person of the Godhead. Both God the Father and Christ the Lord are coequal in providing the resources of grace, mercy, and peace. Paul recognized the full deity of Jesus.

PAUL WARNS ABOUT FALSE TEACHERS / 1:3-11

After communicating volumes with his brief greeting, Paul abruptly turned his attention to one of the immediate reasons for his letter—Timothy's struggle with false teachers.

Paul had left Timothy in Ephesus as a personal deterrent to those who were promoting their own brands of religion. To help Timothy, Paul reminded him of the central points in the conflict, then followed with a personal comparison between himself and the false teachers (1:12-16). Among the issues surrounding the false teachers were the following:

- False teachers taught what was wrong (1:3).
- False teachers engaged in trivial but divisive arguments (1:4).
- False teachers were more interested in controversy than in faithfully spreading the gospel (1:4).
- False teachers had turned away from the personal evidences of God's presence in their lives and had taken up "meaningless talk" instead (1:6).
- False teachers desired the position and prestige of teachers, but they had nothing of value to communicate (1:7).
- False teachers set the law and the gospel against each other, although each has its own place in the plan of God (1:8-11).

IT'S URGENT!
Urgency implies action, but in Timothy's case, the required action meant he had to stay where he was, doing his job. Urgency doesn't necessarily mean doing something new; it may mean renewed effort or perseverance under pressure. Our responsibilities in life require an occasional "urgency check." Marriage, parenting, being a church leader, or other long-term tasks can easily become halfhearted efforts. Do you have someone in your life who urges you to stay faithful? Meet regularly with that person or group to encourage one another.

1:3-4 I urge you.^{NRSV} Paul wanted Timothy to remain in the important role he had been given. The same urgency that caused Paul to leave him in Ephesus was still Paul's concern.

Ephesus. Paul first visited Ephesus on his second missionary journey (Acts 18:19-21). Later, on his third missionary journey, he stayed there for almost three years (Acts 19). Ephesus (along with Rome, Corinth, Antioch, and Alexandria) was a major city in the Roman Empire. Ephesus was a center for the commerce, politics, religions of Asia Minor, and the location of the temple dedicated to the goddess Artemis. It is unclear whether Paul had just left Ephesus or was traveling in the vicinity. In either case, he left Timothy in the troubled Ephesian church while he traveled on to Macedonia, and then wrote to his young protégé from there.

> Serve Christ; back Him; let His cause be your cause; give not an hairbreadth of truth away, for it is not yours but God's.
> *Samuel Rutherford*

Remain . . . so that you may instruct certain people not to teach any different doctrine, and not to occupy themselves with myths and endless genealogies.NRSV Paul gave Timothy a difficult task. It seems that the rather timid disciple may have been reluctant, for Paul gave strong commands and loving encouragement to young Timothy in this letter (see, for example, 4:11-16). Paul allowed Timothy to learn leadership by experience, directing him to come down hard on the false teachers. Paul was confident that Timothy could handle the assignment (see 4:14). The Greek word for *instruct* can also be translated "charge," "command," or "to give strict orders." Timothy was to be undaunted and unintimidated by those teachers (who were probably older men, see 4:12) who taught a *different doctrine*; that is, a doctrine other than the teaching of Jesus, the apostles, and the Old Testament.

The English word *doctrine* is a transliterated Latin word for "teaching" (*doctrina*). It came to mean the central truths, or principles, of a philosophy or religion. Words related to the root Greek word (*didaskalia,* translated "doctrine") occur frequently in the Pastoral Epistles (see, for example, 1:3, 10; 4:16; 6:3; 2 Timothy 3:16; 4:3; Titus 1:9; 2:1). Paul used the term in writing to Timothy to refer to the unchanging truths of the gospel. The positive application of this command can be found in 2 Timothy 2:2: "And the things you have heard me say in the presence of many witnesses entrust to reliable men who will also be qualified to teach others" (NIV). No one was at liberty to change that doctrine.

But what did these *myths* and *genealogies* have to do with anything? There are two possibilities:

TRUTH OR CONSEQUENCES
The problems faced by Paul and Timothy continue to plague the church. In every age, there have been those who would soften the teachings of Christ to make them more palatable to people. Some have been willing to say whatever would gain them a following. Others, out of curiosity, pursue novelties of theological debate. But serious problems arise, as Paul pointed out, when anything is substituted for the Good News. The challenge for believers will always be to communicate the unchanging truth of the gospel in a constantly changing world.

(1) The church at Ephesus may have been troubled by the same type of heresy that threatened the church at Colosse—the teaching that to be acceptable to God, a person had to discover a certain hidden knowledge and had to worship angels (Colossians 2:8, 18).

(2) Thinking that it would aid in their salvation, some Ephesians constructed mythical stories based on Old Testament history or genealogies. Perhaps they placed too much emphasis on Jewish writings such as the Book of Jubilees.

The "myths and endless genealogies" only served to promote speculation and lead to discussion about ideas that did not come from Scripture but from the minds of the false teachers. This, in turn, took valuable time away from teaching the truth of Scripture and spreading the gospel. The believers got caught up in these false ideas and had no energy left to study the truth.

Therefore, Paul urged Timothy to remain in Ephesus, instead of traveling on with him, in order to stifle the false teachers, who were motivated by their own interests rather than Christ's.

DON'T BE DECEIVED
The damage that false teachers cause is not limited to the cults, nor to past days in church history. Some of the characteristics of false teachers show up in churches and ministries professing to be faithful to the true gospel. Many leaders and authorities today demand allegiance; some would even have us turn from Christ to follow them. Because they seem to know the Bible, their influence can be dangerously subtle. How can you recognize false teaching?
■ It promotes controversies instead of helping people come to Jesus (1:4).
■ It is often initiated by those whose motivation is to make a name for themselves (1:7).
■ It will be contrary to the true teaching of the Scriptures (1:6-7; 4:1-3).
To protect yourself from the deception of false teachers, you

should learn what the Bible teaches and remain steadfast in your faith in Christ alone. Doctrine is right and true only to the extent that it agrees with God's Word.

These promote controversies rather than God's work—which is by faith.[NIV] These false teachings embroiled the Ephesian church in endless and irrelevant questions, controversies, and speculation. Paul was amazed at the controversies flying around the Ephesian church over utter nonsense. These distractions took precious time away from God's work—teaching the gospel. The *work* (Greek *oikonomia*) mentioned here can also mean "nagement"; our word *economy* is derived from it. Under God's economy, or management, controversies are settled and the gospel is proclaimed. Getting involved in controversies might heighten someone's ego, but it quickly becomes a substitute for the work that matters, work done not for ego, but *by faith*. Christian work requires the power of faith to complete it. These false teachers were basing their authority on the law (1:7).

"DON'T CONFUSE ME WITH THE FACTS"
When people refuse to see beyond their own interests, conflicts inevitably follow. For instance, when a person expresses a very strong opinion against every version of the English Bible other than the one he uses, his position tends to be informed by hearsay rather than specific facts. But that line of thinking can easily become hardened into a standard to measure other believers: "If you don't read the Bible translation I read, there's something wrong with you!" That person has replaced honest questions and responses with harsh judgments. Most Christians can relate painful events in their past when someone determined to have his or her own way no matter who was injured in the process.

Worthless and irrelevant discussions can quickly crowd out the life-changing message of Christ. Religious speculation and theological arguments about minute details may seem harmless at first, but they have a way of sidetracking us from the central message of the gospel—the person and work of Jesus Christ. They waste time we should use to share the gospel with others. Avoid anything that keeps you from doing what God wants you to do.

1:5 The purpose of the commandment is love from a pure heart, from a good conscience, and from sincere faith.[NKJV] The noun *commandment* (*paraggelias,* "charge or instruction"), which Paul used here, can also be found as a verb in verse 3 ("instruct"). Paul expanded his directions to Timothy by reminding him and

PAST, PRESENT, AND FUTURE
Our present, past, and future are all intimately affected by God's Word. When we have a right relationship with God, we will experience him, and we will want to please him. As for the past, our conscience will be clear, cleansed by confession and forgiveness. As for the future, we will face life with the confidence that faith provides. When we live under God's instructions, we not only avoid the pitfalls of error, we also make progress in love.

anyone else who would read the letter that the correction of the false teachers would do them good, not harm.

The false teachers were motivated by mere curiosity and a desire to gain prestige as intellectuals. In contrast, genuine Christian teachers are motivated by *love,* that is, love in its purest form. There are three sources of real love:

(1) In Matthew 5:8, Jesus said, "Blessed are the pure in heart." A pure heart is devoted to God and free from guilt and corruption. We must keep ourselves morally straight. God purifies us, but there is action we must take to keep morally fit. Daily application of God's Word has a purifying effect on our heart and mind. It enables us to love freely.

(2) In order to love properly, our conscience must be clear. First, it must be clean from unconfessed sin so that guilt doesn't hinder us. Second, our motives must be free from pride and personal gain. Then we can love openly.

(3) When we attempt to love others without our faith sincerely based in Christ, our efforts to minister become hollow and self-serving. Sincere faith enables us to love genuinely.

The commands and instructions in this letter to Timothy reveal Paul's desire to maintain the purest truth in all the church's teachings. As a mother nourishes her child with pure foods, so Paul nourished the infant church with only pure teaching—the truth of God's Word. He focused on the truth and love of the gospel (see 1 Corinthians 13).

1:6-7 Some people have deviated from these and turned to meaningless talk, desiring to be teachers of the law, without understanding either what they are saying or the things about which they make assertions.^NRSV Paul wrote against those who wanted to be *teachers of the law.* These men taught strange philosophical theories and ideas loosely based on the Pentateuch (the first five books of the Old Testament). These men were either Gentiles who were impressed with Judaism or Jews who did not

WAX ELOQUENT
Paul reminded Timothy that a sincere faith provides one source from which real love can flow. *Sincere* literally means "without hypocrisy." The ancient Latins had a marketplace expression (*sin cera*) from which we derive our word *sincere.* When pottery makers wanted to advertise the quality of their wares, they labeled them *sin cera,* which meant "without wax." Dishonest potters were known to trick customers by filling the cracks in their pottery with wax to hide the flaws. When the pots were heated, both the cracks of the pottery and the hypocrisy of the potters were revealed.

Sincere faith displays its cracks. The man who said to Jesus, "I believe; help my unbelief!" (Mark 9:24 NKJV) was exercising sincere faith—without hypocritical wax. In spite of its imperfections, it is sincere faith that catches the world's attention.

know much but wanted to gain respect. The false teachers at Ephesus had constructed vast speculative systems, and then they argued about the minor details of their wholly imaginary ideas! They wandered away from the gospel, the truth, and love and slipped into meaningless drivel that helped no one and, in fact, hurt the church.

Paul's composite picture of these men takes on lifelike proportions. These were real know-it-all types who made people feel intensely stupid by intimidation, and who looked down on the simplicity of the truth as something for only "common" people. They wanted "to be teachers of the law" but did not understand anything they were talking about. Not only were they terribly mistaken about God's Word, they were not even able to make their own teaching understandable.

We should allow nothing to distract us from the good news of salvation in Jesus Christ, the main point of Scripture. We should know what the Bible says, apply it to our lives daily, and teach it to others. When we do this, we will *not* be deviating from the truth; we will *not* be degenerating into meaningless talk or slipping into a shallow treatment of Scripture. Rather, we will be able to evaluate all teachings in light of the central truth about Jesus, and we will be able to tell others the simple truth of salvation.

1:8 We know that the law is good, if one uses it legitimately.NRSV
The false teachers wanted to become famous as teachers of God's law, but they misunderstood the law's purpose. The law was not meant to give believers a list of commands for every occasion, but to show unbelievers their sin and bring them to God. God's

law is also important for believers. To use the law *legitimately* means understanding several facts about the law:

> The preaching of the law does not make us more sinful, but reveals those sins unto us which before we discerned not; as the sun shining upon some filthy place does not make it so filthy, but only makes it manifest which was not seen in the dark.
> *George Downame*

- God's law gives us direction for living a holy life. In Exodus 20, God shows his people the true function and beauty of his laws. The commandments were designed to lead Israel to a life of practical holiness. In these commandments people could see the nature of God and his plan for how they should live.
- Galatians 2:11-21 shows us that God's law offers direction, not justification. Paul wrote in Romans 7:12, "The law is holy," but following the law can never make us acceptable to God.
- The law still has an important role to play in the life of a Christian.
- The law guards us from sin by giving us standards for behavior.
- The law convicts us of sin, leaving us the opportunity to ask God's forgiveness.
- The law drives us to trust in the sufficiency of Christ and the strength of the Holy Spirit, because we can never keep the Ten Commandments perfectly.

For more of what Paul taught about our relationship to law, see Romans 5:20-21; 7:7-16; 13:9-10; Galatians 3:24-29.

1:9-11 This means understanding that the law is laid down not for the innocent.NRSV The law exists not for the innocent (also translated "righteous" NIV), but for lawbreakers; not for those who have recognized their sin and turned to Christ, but for those who continue in their sin. "The law is good" (1:8) because it can bring about conviction of sin.

The list Paul includes follows the order of the Ten Commandments in Exodus 20. The first set of sinners corresponds to the first four commandments (Exodus 20:1-11). These sins have been committed directly against God: **lawbreakers and rebels**NIV who cannot be taught or disciplined; the **godless and sinful**NRSV show no reverence for God, and indeed oppose him because they are **unholy and profane.**NKJV

The second set represents violations of the next six commandments (Exodus 20:12-16): **Those who kill their father or**

mother,^{NRSV} the ultimate act of dishonoring parents; **for murderers,**^{NRSV} clearly breaking the command not to murder; **adulterers and perverts,**^{NIV} dealing not just with adultery, but with all sexual sin.

"ALTERNATE" LIFE-STYLES
"Perverts" (*arsenokoitai*) refers to those who practice homosexuality. Some attempt to legitimize homosexuality as an acceptable alternative life-style. Even some Christians say that people have a right to choose their sexual preference. But the Bible specifically calls homosexual behavior sin (see Leviticus 18:22; Romans 1:18-32; 1 Corinthians 6:9-11). We must be careful, however, to condemn only the practice, not the people. Those who commit homosexual acts are not to be feared, ridiculed, or hated. They can be forgiven, and their lives can be transformed. The church should be a haven of forgiveness and healing for repentant homosexuals without compromising its stance against homosexual behavior.

Slave traders.^{NRSV} Also translated "kidnappers" (NKJV). Kidnapping is the worst form of theft. **Liars, perjurers**^{NKJV} are those who violate the commandment not to bear false witness.

And for whatever else is contrary to the sound doctrine that conforms to the glorious gospel of the blessed God.^{NIV} In case anything might be missed, Paul's final statement includes any other behavior contradicting *sound doctrine* or teaching. *Sound* means "healthy," "whole," "clean." It comes from the Greek word similar to our word *hygiene*. Christian doctrine is not to be sickly or unhealthy, like the teaching of the false teachers. *Doctrine* refers both to proper beliefs and teachings, and also to right behavior (see 1 Timothy 6:1 and Titus 2:1). Here Paul stressed the importance of moral Christian conduct coming from orthodox Christian teaching.

Which he entrusted to me.^{NRSV} Paul had been entrusted with this Good News (Acts 9:15-19; 1 Thessalonians 2:4; Titus 1:3). This call became Paul's life mission as he preached the gospel across the Roman Empire, including Ephesus, where this letter was directed (Acts 20:17-27). All who hear, believe, and accept this "sound doctrine" have also been *entrusted* with it.

In short, the law is meant to reveal our sin, but using it as guidelines for our response to God leaves us no better off than the false teachers. The law has a descriptive, not a prescriptive, role. It brings us face-to-face with our problem but does not tell us how to solve it. The gospel challenges us to respond in faith to

God, who, through Christ, will forgive us our sins. Then, as believers entrusted with the Good News of Jesus Christ, we are to tell the truth ("sound doctrine") of the gospel, share its effect on our lives, and offer the message of eternal salvation to those who are still as lost as we once were.

GOD'S MERCY ON PAUL / 1:12-17

If the law fulfills its purpose by convincing people they are sinners; mercy fulfills its purpose by convincing people they can be saved! As Paul proceeded to compare himself with the false teachers, he was anxious, not so much to point out how he was different from them, but to make it clear that he was just like them. In fact, Paul claimed, in the category of sinners, "I am the foremost" (1:15 NRSV).

In the previous paragraph Paul included a hard listing of sinful behaviors. But his reason was not for self-righteousness—pointing out other people's sins to make himself look better. In the face of our tendency to despair when confronted with our own sinfulness, Paul could cheerfully say, "Well, just look at how desperate I was, and what God's mercy has done for me!" Paul was convinced that if God could save him, then God could save anyone.

The brief doxology that closes this paragraph flows naturally from the ideas that Paul was writing. The God whose mercy would include even us deserves the highest expressions of praise we can compose.

1:12 I am grateful to Christ Jesus our Lord, who has strengthened me, because he judged me faithful and appointed me to his service.NRSV His catalog of common sins reminded Paul of his own sin (he called himself the worst of sinners, 1:15). But instead of allowing that memory to overwhelm him, he overflowed with gratefulness that God had *strengthened* and *appointed* him to serve in spreading the Good News of salvation to his fellow Jews and to the Gentiles (see Acts 9:15; 11:25-26; 13:1-3).

Paul's gratefulness extended to three specific areas:

(1) God *strengthened* Paul. The Greek word here is *endunamo-santi,* which literally means "empowered." The former can imply the idea that God added strength to what Paul already possessed, while the latter conveys the thought that Paul considered any power that he might use to have originated in God. Paul used the same verb in Philippians 4:13 when he wrote, "I can do everything through him who gives me strength" (NIV).

(2) God *judged* Paul *faithful.* "Judged" translates *hegesato* (considered) and conveys a more relational idea than "judgment." Paul did not think he had earned God's favorable judgment, but that being called faithful was itself part of God's grace. The idea might be paraphrased, "because he gave me the benefit of the doubt in considering me faithful" (see also 1 Corinthians 4:2).

(3) God *appointed* Paul for service. Paul was not a passive receiver of God's power and grace. He saw himself as a channel through whom God could work. As he wrote almost immediately (1:16), the results of God's work in his life were demonstrated in the way God was able to bring about belief in others.

Express your thankfulness to God for his strength, for his regard for you as a faithful worker, and for his appointing you to do his work.

RINGING CLEAR
The picture of all that God can do to us remains incomplete as long as we fail to let him work through us. Paul not only expressed his gratitude to God; he demonstrated it. Is it possible to appreciate all that God has done in your life and not feel compelled to tell someone else? The part of the gospel that says, "This is what God will do for you" rings more clearly when preceded with, "This is what God has done for me."

1:13 I was once a blasphemer and a persecutor and a violent man.[NIV] Paul did not exaggerate his past performance. Scripture first reveals Paul as an archenemy of Christians (all verses are quoted from NIV):

- As Stephen was stoned to death for believing in Jesus, "Saul was there, giving approval to his death" (Acts 8:1).
- "Saul began to destroy the church. Going from house to house, he dragged off men and women and put them in prison" (Acts 8:3).
- "Saul was still breathing out murderous threats against the Lord's disciples" (Acts 9:1).

Paul also testified against himself:

- "Many a time I went from one synagogue to another to have [the Christians] punished, and I tried to force them to blaspheme" (Acts 26:11).
- "I persecuted the followers of this Way to their death, arresting both men and women and throwing them into prison" (Acts 22:4).

- "I too was convinced that I ought to do all that was possible to oppose the name of Jesus of Nazareth" (Acts 26:9).
- "I persecuted the church of God and tried to destroy it" (Galatians 1:13).

As a *blasphemer,* Paul denied Jesus as Lord, and he tried to get the Christians to renounce their faith or face persecution.

I received mercy because I had acted ignorantly in unbelief.^{NRSV} Paul persecuted Christians because he sincerely believed that he was serving God by stamping out this distortion of his beloved Jewish faith. Despite all of his knowledge as a learned Pharisee (Acts 23:6), Paul remained in ignorance about Jesus' true identity and stubbornly remained in unbelief, even after seeing the unwavering faith of Stephen and the other Christians whom he persecuted and perhaps even killed. Paul had the chance to believe, but missed it. Yet God came to Paul even as he set out to capture more Christians, offering grace, mercy, and a new start. Paul knew from personal experience the words he wrote to the Romans: "God demonstrates His own love toward us, in that while we were still sinners, Christ died for us" (Romans 5:8 NKJV).

PAST AWAY
People can feel so guilt ridden about their past that they think God could never forgive and accept them. But consider Paul's past. He had scoffed at the teachings of Jesus and had hunted down and imprisoned God's people before coming to faith in Christ (Acts 9:1-9). God forgave Paul and used him effectively for his kingdom. No matter how shameful your past, God can also forgive and use you.

1:14 **The grace of our Lord was exceedingly abundant, with faith and love which are in Christ Jesus.**^{NKJV} Paul had blasphemed Jesus Christ, denied the Christian faith, and hated Christians; but God's grace had overcome it all, filling Paul with the conviction of the "sound doctrine" of the Christian faith and with love for believers and unbelievers alike. God supplied what Paul lacked, and not only supplied it but gave it to him in exceeding abundance. In order to express the overwhelming sense of God's grace, Paul coined a compound word, *huperpleonazein,* meaning "to superabound." God's undeserved favor toward us is always greater than any words we may use to describe it.

Grace is an important concept throughout the Pastoral Epistles as well as in all of Paul's writings. Here grace is shown gener-

ously. Grace comes to us through our relationship with Jesus
Christ (2 Timothy 2:1). We find grace nowhere else. It is not
based on anything we have done, but on God's love and mercy
(2 Timothy 1:9). Even our salvation is based on it (Titus 3:7).
When grace operates in a person's life, it results in faith and love
(see Ephesians 1:15; 1 Thessalonians 1:3).

OVERWHELMING EXAMPLE
Paul's boldness in Christ can be intimidating. We may feel that
our faith in God and our love for Christ and for others will
always be inadequate. We will experience times of failure. But
we can remain confident that Christ will help our faith and love
grow as our relationship with him deepens. Paul's prayer for
the Philippians applies to us also: "Being confident of this, that
he who began a good work in you will carry it on to completion
until the day of Christ Jesus" (Philippians 1:6 NIV).

1:15 This is a faithful saying and worthy of all acceptance.NKJV
Nowhere outside the pastoral letters does Paul use this phrase.
The term *pistos ho logos* also occurs in 1 Timothy 3:1; 4:9; 2 Timothy 2:2; and Titus 3:8. Because the expression is always used to
introduce what appear to be formulas or theological summaries,
some are convinced the letters reveal a long-developed Christian
faith dating much later than Paul. However, the phrase was used
in the Pastoral Epistles much like the "Amen" sayings in the Gospels; both point to especially important truths.

In Paul's writing, a *faithful saying* confronts us with nonnego-
tiable truth. We are not asked to consider, but to fully accept. We
are invited to submit rather than question. Pride demands full understanding before there is acceptance; humility bows before the
God who has made himself known in Jesus. God's Word stands
firm.

That Christ Jesus came into the world to save sinners.NKJV
Paul summarized and personalized the Good News: Jesus came
into the world to save sinners, and no sinner is beyond his saving
power. Jesus said, "I have not come to call the righteous, but sinners, to repentance" (Luke 5:32 NKJV; see also Luke 19:10; John
1:9-12). Jesus didn't come merely to show us how to live a better
life or to challenge us to be better people. He came to offer us salvation that leads to eternal life. No matter how entrenched your
sin, Christ can save you. Have you accepted his offer?

Of whom I am the worst.NIV Although Paul was a deeply religious Jew, zealous for his faith, he realized that in his ignorance,

unbelief, and desire to destroy the Christian faith, he was indeed "the worst" of sinners. We think of Paul as a great hero of the faith, but Paul never saw himself that way because he remembered his life before he met Christ. If Paul meant to emphasize the present tense "I am the worst," it would mean the more Paul understood God's grace, the more he became aware of his own sinfulness (see also 1 Corinthians 15:9-10; Ephesians 3:8). Some people teach that we should never speak of ourselves as sinners, but as saints. Yet Paul recognized both that he had been a sinner and that he was now saved by grace. He recognized his past, but did not wallow in it. Humility and gratitude should mark the life of every Christian. Never forget that you too are a sinner saved by grace.

1:16 I received mercy, so that in me . . . Jesus Christ might display the utmost patience, making me an example to those who would come to believe in him for eternal life.^{NRSV} Jesus came to this zealous persecutor, not striking him with judgment (as some might expect), but offering him mercy. Looking back, Paul realized Jesus' great patience in dealing with him; and what an example of mercy Paul gave to us! Jesus offers us mercy; we too can come to him and receive forgiveness and eternal life.

LOWERING THE GUARD
Paul was not nearly as interested in creating an image as he was in being an example. He did not hesitate to share his past, because he knew his failures would allow others to have hope.

There are times when we hesitate to share our past struggles with others because we are afraid it will tarnish our image. This, however, creates an immediate paradox. For their knowledge of us is incomplete. They don't know us, and we are not sure they would still accept us if they did know us. But these problems are image problems; they are difficulties we encounter in trying to manage what others know of us.

Paul demonstrated that lowering our guard can be an important step in communicating the gospel. People will not believe the gospel is important if they can't see that it is crucial in our lives. How has Christ shown patience with you? Did he stay with you when you doubted and rebelled? Did he remain faithful when you ignored his prior claim on your life? Did he love you when you disregarded his help and his church? Remember that his patience is unlimited for those who love him.

1:17 Now to the King eternal, immortal, invisible, the only God, be honor and glory for ever and ever. Amen.^{NIV} Reflecting on how good God has been to him, who was a blasphemer and persecutor, caused Paul to praise God. This verse is a typical doxology

given by Paul as a natural, emotional response to these reflec-
tions about the mercy of God. When Paul realized all that God
had done for him, he was left with no other words than praise.
God, our King, is *eternal* and *immortal*—that is, he can never
cease to exist. He is *invisible*—we cannot see him or touch him;
he is Spirit. He is *the only God*—not one of many, but "the only."
The word *wise* appears in some translations (such as NKJV) but is
not in the best Greek manuscripts; it may have been borrowed
from Romans 16:27 and added later.

Commentators usually attribute these phrases to an ancient lit-
urgy. The unspoken assumption credits poetry or rhythmic writing to some shadowy and impersonal past—letters are written,
while liturgies and poems "evolve." But people are the source of
this kind of material also. This doxology had an author. Why not
Paul? He was certainly able to compose a hymn of this depth and
perhaps use it over and over as he formed groups of believers on
his missionary journeys. Perhaps it was a formula statement in
which Paul was quoting himself!

CLING TIGHTLY TO THE FAITH / 1:18-20

From the high point of praise to God, Paul turned his attention
back to Timothy. The young disciple faced a difficult situation in
the church at Ephesus, but Paul knew he could handle the
challenge. What Timothy needed in the meantime was encouragement and helpful instructions. Like a coach preparing his eager
young fighter for the match of his life, Paul put an imaginary arm
around Timothy's shoulders and passed on a few last-minute
instructions.

1:18 I am giving you these instructions.NRSV *These instructions* (see
1:3, 5) refers to the job Timothy was sent to do in Ephesus—that
is, quieting the false teachers. Paul was expressing again his confidence in entrusting Timothy with an important ministry. Further
instruction for Timothy's work in the church is given in the
remainder of this letter.

Timothy, my child.NRSV Paul kept in mind the relationship he
shared with Timothy and assured young Timothy that the elder's
instructions were based on his love for him.

**In accordance with the prophecies made earlier about
you.**NRSV Paul made it clear, however, that his choice of Timothy
was not made solely on the basis of their friendship or his
hunches about Timothy's abilities. Other believers had noted

qualities in Timothy that Paul was happy to affirm and to put to work for the gospel.

Scholars have suggested two possibilities for these previous *prophecies* about Timothy: (1) These were Old Testament promises prophesied by the prophets, promises that Timothy claimed. (2) These were prophetic utterances at Timothy's ordination (Acts 14:23; 1 Timothy 4:14).

It seems likely that the "prophecies" refer to Timothy's ordination. Paul highly valued the gift of prophecy (1 Corinthians 14:1). Through prophecy, important messages of warning and encouragement came to the church. Timothy had been set apart for ministry when elders laid their hands on him (see 4:14). This was not an ordination service as we think of it today. This was probably a "commissioning" for missionary activity rather than an ordination into a church office. Apparently at Timothy's "commissioning," several believers had prophesied about his gifts and strengths. These words from the Lord must have encouraged Timothy throughout his ministry. We can only guess who gave the prophecies and what they said; in any case, Paul reminded Timothy of these statements to encourage him.

So that by following them you may fight the good fight.^{NRSV} Timothy had two immediate sources of reinforcement as he carried out his tasks: Paul's instructions and the prophecies from other believers. Paul employed a military metaphor to describe Timothy's work in Ephesus; it would indeed be a fight, but victory would achieve the good of the believers and the church—

> Moral collapse follows upon spiritual collapse.
> *C. S. Lewis*

it was the worthwhile fight of the faith. We are reminded of Paul's words to Timothy as Paul neared death, "I have fought the good fight" (2 Timothy 4:7 NRSV). Paul often used military language to refer to our spiritual struggle (see Ephesians 6:11-16; 1 Thessalonians 5:8; 2 Timothy 2:3).

CLEAR CONSCIENCE
How can you hold on to a good conscience? Treasure your faith in Christ more than anything else and do what you know is right. Each time you deliberately ignore your conscience, you are hardening your heart. Over a period of time your capacity to tell right from wrong will diminish. As you walk with God, he will speak to you through your conscience, letting you know the difference between right and wrong. Be sure to act on those inner tugs so that you do what is right—then your conscience will remain clear.

1:19 Holding on to faith and a good conscience.NIV One's faith and one's morals cannot be separated. To hold tightly to the Christian faith, and live by it, results in a good (peaceful) conscience. Faith and good conscience are like armor for the Christian. They keep us from giving in to temptation and to debilitating spiritual and moral sidetracks.Some have rejected these and so have shipwrecked their faith.NIV Rejecting the faith and refusing to listen to one's conscience will end in destroyed faith. This deliberate action reflects heresy, not just backsliding.

1:20 Hymenaeus and Alexander. Apparently these two men had been members of the church (because Paul had put them out of the church). We don't know who Alexander was—he may have been an associate of Hymenaeus, or the coppersmith mentioned in 2 Timothy 4:14 who hurt Paul. But he was not the Alexander mentioned in the riot at Ephesus (Acts 19:33). Hymenaeus's error is explained in 2 Timothy 2:17-18. He weakened people's faith by teaching that the resurrection had already occurred.

> Some want to live within the sound of church or chapel bell; I want to run a rescue shop within a yard of hell. *C. T. Studd*

Whom I delivered to Satan that they may learn not to blaspheme.NKJV To be *delivered to Satan* means that Paul removed these men from the fellowship of the church and back into the world—Satan's domain. Paul did this so that they would see their error and repent. The ultimate purpose of this punishment was correction. (See also 1 Corinthians 5:1-5; 2 Corinthians 2:5-8; 4:4; 2 Thessalonians 3:14-15.) The church today is often lax in disciplining Christians who deliberately sin. Deliberate disobedience should be responded to quickly and sternly to prevent the entire congregation from being affected. But discipline must be done in a way that tries to bring the offender back to Christ and into the loving embrace of the church. The definition of discipline includes these words: *strengthening, purifying, training, correcting,* and *perfecting.* Condemnation, suspicion, withholding of forgiveness, or permanent exile should not be a part of church discipline.

1 Timothy 2

The next two chapters cover Paul's thinking on the expected character and behavior of believers when they are functioning as a church. Included are some significant principles for worship. Key leadership roles are discussed, but the emphasis is clearly on the kind of people who should be chosen for certain roles, rather than what the roles themselves involve. For example, Paul did not spell out what a deacon should do. He was clearly more concerned with the kind of person a deacon should be. This section has been frequently taught as a handbook on church structure, but the specific forms of church life that can be derived from these passages vary greatly.

INSTRUCTIONS ABOUT WORSHIP / 2:1-15

Among the most hotly debated passages written by Paul, this one begins with guidelines for prayer (2:1-8) and moves on to what appear to be rigid restrictions placed on women (2:9-15) within the church. The range of interpretations varies from those who would still forbid women from teaching in the church to those who would write Paul off as presenting views not applicable to today.

If Paul's purpose in writing this letter was to guide Timothy in his confrontations with the false teachers (1:3), then that purpose must be used to understand Paul's instructions. What Paul told Timothy to do in the volatile environment in Ephesus may not be what he would have directed a church to do where peace and harmony prevailed. We must understand the problem that Paul was addressing within Timothy's situation before we conclude what applications might be made to our own. We must remember that Paul shares God's desire for everyone to be saved (2:4). To that end, he wants Christian men to pursue holiness and Christian women to conduct themselves appropriately in the church.

The entire spectrum of church government, from the hierarchical episcopacy of Roman Catholicism, through the mediating expression of Presbyterianism, to the extreme congregationalism of the Plymouth Brethren, all find support for their polity in these letters. *Gordon Fee*

2:1 First of all, then, I urge that supplications, prayers, intercessions, and thanksgivings be made for everyone.NRSV Paul's
urge echoed his original mission for
Timothy (1:3). False teaching had to be
challenged, and right actions needed to
be reinforced. Paul placed primary
importance on prayer; thus he
addressed this issue *first of all.*

> The wider the subjects
> for prayer, the larger
> becomes the vision of the
> soul that prays.
> *Donald Guthrie*

The different words used for prayer
focus not so much on different types of prayer as on the beautiful
scope of prayer—that we can come to God with requests, needs,
and desires for ourselves *and* for others. But often we forget the
last word—*thanksgivings* (*eucharistias*). This Greek word comes
into English as a term for the Lord's Supper, reminding us that
the most appropriate response, when we partake of the elements,
is thanksgiving. In practice as well as in teaching, Paul insisted
that prayer should always include thanksgiving (see, for example,
Romans 1:8-10; Ephesians 1:15-16; Philippians 1:3-6; 4:6).
Many are good at asking God for action, but not very good at
remembering to thank God for his answers.

Although God is all-powerful and all-knowing, he has chosen
to let us help him change the world through our prayers. How
this works is a mystery to us because of our limited understanding, but it is a reality. This verse highlights the words *for
everyone*. Readers often miss the inclusiveness of the word and
focus instead on the examples that Paul immediately gave. A
common application of this verse, therefore, urges prayer for government leaders. Paul's purpose, however, was most likely to
broaden the possibilities for prayer rather than narrowing them.
Paul's examples may well have caused Timothy to think of the
very persons with whom he was in conflict—the false teachers.
Both "kings" and "those in authority" were enemies of the early
church. False teachers were people in authority (2:2) who were
promoting error and creating controversies in the Ephesian
church. Yet Paul urged Timothy to pray for everyone, including
his opponents.

In situations of personal conflict, one of the ways to test our
objectivity is whether or not we can honestly pray for those with
whom we disagree. Jesus was quite clear—"Love your enemies
and pray for those who persecute you" (Matthew 5:44 NRSV).

2:2 For kings and all those in authority.NIV Paul's command to pray
for kings was remarkable considering that Nero, a notoriously
cruel ruler, was the current emperor (A.D. 54–68). When Paul
wrote this letter, persecution was a growing threat to believers.

Later, when Nero needed a scapegoat for the great fire that destroyed much of Rome in A.D. 64, he blamed the Roman Christians so as to take the focus off himself. That triggered severe persecution throughout the Roman Empire. Not only were Christians denied certain privileges in society; some were even publicly butchered, burned, or fed to lions. But believers were taught to support the government, not rebel against it (Romans 13:1-6; 1 Peter 2:13-25).

ROOM AT THE TOP
If we live in a country with a good government, our lives move along peacefully and quietly, making it difficult to remember to pray for those in authority. We take good government for granted. But we should pray for those at the top—whether we agree with them or not, whether we voted for them or not. In this way, we Christians *can* make a difference in the course of our nation. We should also pray for world leaders so that other cultures will be open to the gospel. Pray for your leaders, not just in times of national crisis, but every day—thousands of decisions are made daily that affect everyone. And beyond praying for those decisions that will affect you, also pray for the conversion of your leaders.

So that we may lead a quiet and peaceable life in all godliness and dignity.NRSV Paul did not explain *what* to pray, but his list in verse 1 was broad enough to include whatever prayer might be appropriate to any situation. He also gave the purpose behind his command to pray.

Prayer provides the Christian's ultimate armor for defense and weapon for offense. With the Roman government deteriorating under Nero and persecution of Christians increasing, Paul told Christians to pray. God sets up and removes all rulers; he is ultimately in control (see Psalm 2). Praying for the salvation of the rulers in Rome (and for the return of the noninterfering policy against Christians) would help restore the *quiet and peaceable life* the Christians had enjoyed prior to the persecution (see 1 Peter 2:12; 3:9).

Even in nations where Christians do not face persecution, they still need to be constantly praying for their leaders. Every day decisions are made in the halls of government that shape the policies, the future, even the morality of the nation. Constant prayer can be a mighty weapon against Satan's domination, helping the nation to remain "quiet and peaceable" so believers can continue with their work of spreading the gospel *in all godliness* and *dignity*. Godliness means true reverence and religious devotion that leads to exemplary conduct. Dignity means serious purpose, moral earnestness. These descriptive words do not imply private spiritual living. Rather, they convey a public faith consistent with God's purpose to achieve the salvation of persons and bring them "to a knowledge of the truth" (2:4 NIV).

HOT SPOTS
For Timothy, the area of greatest danger to the maintenance of peace and quiet was within the church itself. The church's prayers would balance the tensions that came as the church confronted error.

In our efforts to maintain a prayer life to include everyone, we must not overlook the "hot spots" around us. Do you pray for leaders of both parties in government? Do you pray for the leaders of the Gay Rights movement or other proponents of issues you oppose? Do you pray for local government and educational leaders? The threats of evil may be close or distant, but they ought to receive our concentrated efforts of prayer.

2:3 For this is good and acceptable in the sight of God our Savior.NKJV It may be difficult to pray for the salvation of civil leaders, but these prayers are *good and acceptable* to God, who alone is *Savior* (Philippians 1:28; 1 Thessalonians 5:9; and notes on 1 Timothy 1:1). The immediate context for Timothy included the conflict within the church with the false teachers. But even in this confrontation, the goal was to bring about their salvation. The recent mention of Hymenaeus and Alexander (1:20) illustrates the importance of redemptive discipline. While these men had been "turned over to Satan" (1:20 NRSV) and were therefore outside the church, the door of repentance still would have been open to them (see, for example, 1 Corinthians 5:3-5 and 2 Corinthians 2:5-11). In the meantime, they were among the subjects for prayer by the gathered church.

2:4 Who desires everyone to be saved and to come to the knowledge of the truth.NRSV Both Peter and Paul wrote that God wants everyone to be saved (see 2 Peter 3:9). Paul fought against two forms of elitism. The first was the Jewish belief that God "willed" the destruction of sinners. This idea caused some Jewish believers to not want to associate with Gentiles. The second was rooted with the Gnostic teaching that salvation was only for the spiritually elite. *Everyone* does not mean that all *will* be saved— the Bible affirms that many people reject Christ (Matthew 25:31-46; John 12:44-50; Hebrews 10:26-29). But God's desire is that all people would be saved, and he has provided in Christ the means to salvation. First Timothy 4:10 shows that the guarantee of salvation applies only to those who receive it. Paul was not teaching about election here; rather, he was showing God's intent that the gospel go to all people.

The gospel message (here called *the knowledge of the truth*) has a universal scope; it is not directed only to people of one race, one sex, or one national background. Because God loves the whole world, he sent his Son to offer salvation to every sinner. No one is outside God's mercy or beyond the reach of his offer of salvation. This knowledge goes beyond intellectual awareness. It requires deep spiritual discernment and full experiential knowledge. It is not enough to know that Christ is Savior; we must fully participate in that knowledge by loving and serving him.

> Christian theology has at times gone astray by taking as the basis for our understanding of the nature of God other sources—Greek philosophy, natural knowledge—and failing to take as seriously as it should the tremendous assertion of the New Testament that it is in Jesus that we see God. *Stephen Neill*

EVERYONE
Paul based his instructions about prayer for *everyone* on his conviction that God's invitation for salvation extends equally to all people. The word *everyone* itself captures the universal/particular nature of the gospel. The world that God loves includes every person (John 3:16). He loves us as individuals whom he knows intimately (Psalm 139:13-18).

God loves every person we will meet today. When we lack compassion for those who have not yet responded to the gospel, we show that we do not highly value the salvation God has given us. When we really pray for others, we will find ourselves telling them the truth.

2:5-6 Verses 5 and 6 cite three foundational truths of the gospel:

1. For there is one God. Judaism and Christianity shared the common belief that there is only *one God* (in direct opposition to the Greek and Roman pantheons and to the polytheism of the surrounding nations). The foundation for this teaching is Deuteronomy 6:4-9 (see also 1 Corinthians 8:4). There is only one God, who "desires everyone to be saved" (2:4), not just one little group.

2. There is also one mediator between God and humankind, Christ Jesus, himself human.[NRSV] Jesus said, "I am the way, the truth, and the life. No one comes to the Father except through

CHRIST OUR MEDIATOR

God chose the Lord Jesus to be the mediator between God and people. The Son of God, the second person of the Trinity, is the eternal God—equal with the Father. But he willingly took on himself the nature of a man; yet, he was without sin. These two complete, perfect, and distinct natures—Godhead and manhood—were inseparably joined in the person of Jesus without being altered or jumbled. Jesus is truly God and truly man.

The following verses show that Jesus was both God and man (quoted from NIV):

Matthew 16:27	"For the Son of Man is going to come in his Father's glory."
Matthew 22:42-45	"'What do you think about the Christ? Whose son is he?' 'The son of David,' they replied. He said to them, . . . 'If then David calls him "Lord," how can he be his son?'"
Matthew 25:31-40	"When the Son of Man comes in his glory, and all the angels with him, he will sit on his throne in heavenly glory."
Mark 14:61-62	"'Are you the Christ, the Son of the Blessed One?' 'I am,' said Jesus."
Luke 9:42-44	"But Jesus rebuked the evil spirit, healed the boy and gave him back to his father. And they were all amazed at the greatness of God."
John 3:35	"The Father loves the Son and has placed everything in his hands."
Romans 5:15	"For if the many died by the trespass of the one man [Adam], how much more did God's grace and the gift that came by the grace of the one man, Jesus Christ, overflow to the many!"
Romans 5:21	"Just as sin reigned in death, so also grace might reign through righteousness to bring eternal life through Jesus Christ our Lord."
1 Corinthians 15:49	"And just as we have borne the likeness of the earthly man, so shall we bear the likeness of the man from heaven."

Me" (John 14:6 NKJV). Muslims also believe that there is only "one God," but they differ in how he makes himself known. For the Muslims, God is Allah, and Muhammad is his prophet. The Jews believe in one God yet still await their Messiah; they believe in Moses as this mediator. Some of the Jews in Ephesus as well as the Gnostics may have regarded angels as mediators. The Romans were praising Caesar as their God. The Christians understand that there is one God and *one mediator . . . Christ Jesus.* Christ Jesus is our mediator because he is God and because he came from God, became fully human, experienced the trials, temptations, and tragedy of humanity (death), and now lives to intercede for us with the Father (see Hebrews 4:14-16; 7:23–8:2; 9:15).

Three elements interplay in this verse:

1. We have a mediator. There is a bridge between God and human beings, so we have hope.

2. God wants to reach out to all human beings.

3. Jesus as *man* reached all humans.

As the second Adam, Jesus was the prototype of the new creations we are to be (Romans 5:12-21; 1 Corinthians 15:21). As both God and man, he could be the perfect link between the eternal God and sinful people.

CHRIST OUR MEDIATOR
God chose the Lord Jesus to be the mediator between God and people. The Son of God, the Second Person of the Trinity, is the eternal God—equal with the Father. But he willingly took on himself the nature of a man; yet, he was without sin. These two complete, perfect, and distinct natures—godhead and manhood—were inseparably joined in the person of Jesus without being altered. Jesus is truly God and truly man.

---

3. Who gave Himself a ransom for all, to be testified in due time.[NKJV] Jesus also said, "For even the Son of Man did not come to be served, but to serve, and to give His life a ransom for many" (Mark 10:45 NKJV; see also Matthew 20:28). God is holy, sinless, morally perfect. People are, by nature, sinners. A holy God cannot embrace sinners any more than light can embrace darkness. For hundreds of years, the Jews sacrificed animals to God in order to maintain a right relationship with him. The sacrifices reminded them that sin has consequences and that only spilled blood would be enough to cover the people's sins. Yet, even that wasn't God's complete plan, for *in due time* he sent his Son to become the final sacrifice, to pay for the sins of all people (past, present, and future) with his own blood.

What is the "due time"? The phrase is literally, "The testimony in his own times." Several views have been proposed:

(1) It was the announcement of Christ himself in his life and before the Ascension (John 6:13; 18:37).

(2) It refers to the future preaching and teaching that Paul and all Christians would do (1 Corinthians 1:6; 2 Thessalonians 1:10).

(3) It refers to the whole chain of witness from Old Testament prophets to New Testament people and reflects God's timing in this process. This view seems best, for it shows God's fulfillment of his promises.

God's moral nature could not allow him to just overlook our sins and forgive them—the penalty for sins had to be paid. But "God so loved the world that He gave His only begotten Son, that whoever believes in Him should not perish but have everlasting life" (John 3:16 NKJV). Because Christ paid the price, the *ransom,* he mediates between us and God, allowing us to have access to God the Father and allowing us to experience God's forgiveness and love. "Ransom" (*antilutron*) means the exchange price for freeing a slave or redeeming a prisoner of war. It illustrates that Christ exchanged his life for ours.

Jesus gave himself as a ransom *for all*; thus there is room for "everyone to be saved" (2:4).

ONE WAY
Though some people think there are many ways to God, in practice, each person must choose a single way. We can stand on one side of a gorge and discuss the possibility of many bridges across the abyss. But if we are determined to cross, we will have to commit to one bridge. Those who insist there are many bridges to God usually fit one of the following categories:
- They have not personally committed to any "bridge." They are surprised that their belief in multiple ways does not automatically exempt them from having to choose one.
- Their belief in "many ways to God" hides their true belief that finding God doesn't really matter at all.
- They are convinced that arguing for "many ways to God" will insure that they won't be wrong. If there is only one right way, their generalized belief will presumably have included it.
- They have decided that believing in "many ways to God" requires less work than going to the trouble of actually considering the claims and histories of various religious systems.
  Jesus claimed to be the only Way. Those who are serious about believing in him can endorse no other bridge to God.

Christians can respect other beliefs and religions, but we must hold firmly to the three beliefs stated above without the slightest change. Although Christianity may appear "narrow" or "intolerant," it is willing to embrace everyone who believes. There is only one God; there is only one Mediator; that Mediator gave himself as a ransom—he paid the price. There is nothing more to do except believe.

The gospel invitation to believe is centered in Jesus Christ. Believing in something or someone other than Jesus may be faith; but it is not the Christian faith.

2:7 And for this purpose I was appointed a herald and an apostle ... and a teacher of the true faith to the Gentiles.[NIV] This *purpose* is "heralding" the Good News as summarized in the three basic tenets outlined in verses 5 and 6. Paul had been appointed as a *herald* or preacher. A "herald" was one who brought important news, much like our announcers at important events or like political ambassadors. He was also an *apostle*. He operated with a sense of divine commission (see comments on 1:1; see also 1 Corinthians 15:7-11). He had been given the special privilege of being a *teacher* of the *true faith*—the gospel—*to the Gentiles*. Paul's special commission went beyond that of the twelve apostles because he traveled to Gentile territory with the gospel. Paul emphasized his role as a teacher to Timothy, who was lax in his teaching duties.

I am telling the truth, I am not lying.[NIV] Obviously Timothy did not need reassurance of the truthfulness of Paul's words. Paul wrote this not for Timothy's sake, but for the church in Ephesus.

2:8 I desire, then, that in every place the men should pray, lifting up holy hands without anger or argument.[NRSV] *Then* shows that Paul connected verses 1-7 with the next section. Continuing the theme of prayer (begun in 2:1), Paul focused on public worship in the church. The word *desire,* following after Paul's explanation of his authority, should be rendered "I will" or even "I command"; not "I wish."

> When thou prayest, rather let thy heart be without words, than thy words without a heart.
>
> *John Bunyan*

Prayer in the congregation should be given by *men* (Greek *andras*). The *lifting up* of hands and the prayers offered by men only may appear somewhat unusual, but it was, in fact, the accepted way of prayer among Jews and the earliest Christians. In Old Testament times, prayers were made with the face pointed toward heaven and palms turned upward with hands outstretched. This conveyed supplication and longing for God's blessing. Quite often, hands were used symbolically to show the humble attitude of the person praying.

But these men who prayed needed *holy hands;* in other words, they had to be "clean" before God. In Timothy's context, the outward forms of prayer needed to be authenticated by the absence of *anger or argument.* Paul's concern indicates that the spiritual life of the Ephesian church was being undermined by ineffective prayers and divisive teaching. If individuals should be free from anger and quarreling while they prayed, how much more should those who offered prayer on behalf of others!

EFFECTIVE PRAYER
In addition to displeasing God, anger and arguments make prayer difficult. Jesus instructed us to interrupt our prayers, if necessary, to make peace with others (Matthew 5:23-24; Mark 11:25; see also Matthew 6:12; 1 Peter 3:7). An unforgiving or spiteful attitude disconnects our spirit from the Father's: "If I regard iniquity in my heart, the Lord will not hear" (Psalm 66:18 NKJV).

Not only does prayer given with anger in our heart reveal hypocrisy, it also insults God. Anger fuels the fiery quarrels and debates that so easily rob the church of love. Paul may have been referring to the practice of the false teachers in Ephesus (1:4-7; 4:1-3; 6:3-5). Mouthing the right words in prayer while holding sin in our hearts is disobedience. God wants us to obey him immediately and thoroughly. Our goal should be to have a right relationship with God and also with others. When we pray, we must first resolve our anger and forget our differences.

Paul's desire that men alone should pray seems to contradict 1 Corinthians 11:5, where he stated that women who prayed or prophesied should do so with their heads covered. There are two ways to reconcile these differences:

(1) Some scholars find evidence for two services in the early church: one service for evangelism, and then a private service for believers. Women could pray publicly in the believers' service but not in the evangelistic service.

(2) Other scholars think this problem of women leading in prayer and teaching applied specifically to the Corinthian and Ephesian situations. In these churches, recently converted and emancipated women tended to interrupt the service with improper questions or remarks. Paul urged them to defer to the men. But he was not generally refusing to let women participate in public prayer (see also the discussion on 2:11).

The second view seems most likely. It should also be noted that this verse does not limit prayer to the clergy or the elders, but encourages prayer from laymen. It wasn't until later in the church that some wrongly restricted prayer to clergymen.

No person can have truly *holy hands* or even be perfectly clean before God; but this phrase means that the person's spiritual life is up to date, sins are confessed, his or her relationship with God is not hindered in any way. As the psalmist wrote: "I will wash my hands in innocence; so I will go about Your altar, O LORD" (Psalm 26:6 NKJV; see also Ephesians 4:24).

2:9-10 In like manner also, that the women adorn themselves in modest apparel, with propriety and moderation.NKJV As the men were to show their right attitudes with "holy hands," so the

women in the Ephesian congregation were to show their holy attitudes with a modest outward appearance. Paul emphasized that their internal character was far more important than their outward adornment. Women's standard for dress was to be characterized by modesty. Paul's appeal here was to good taste and good sense within the culture. Women believers were to "dress" their behavior in a manner that complemented rather than clashed with their character. Women who worshiped in

> There is no act, no sermon, no parable in the whole Gospel that borrows its pungency from female perversity; nobody could possibly guess from the words and deeds of Jesus that there was anything "funny" about woman's nature.
> *Dorothy Sayers*

the Christian church should not be given to ostentation, costly attire, and excessive adornment. Neither was seductive or sexually suggestive clothing appropriate. They were not to detract from the worship by drawing attention to themselves.

That the Christian women in Ephesus dress **not with braided hair or gold or pearls or costly clothing**NKJV meant again that their emphasis should not be on how they looked, but on who they were.

ACCESSORIZING
Paul added to his instructions on the behavior of women in the church a list of wardrobe taboos. We must view these specific prohibited items as examples of impropriety in the Ephesian context. Contemporary application of Paul's teaching must appeal to modesty. Paul had in mind the attitude and character of Christian women and men. Those who hold today's women to this list often stay embarrassingly silent about insisting that all men be required to raise their hands while praying.

Today, to what degree would wearing braided hair, gold, pearls, or costly clothing by a Christian woman limit her ability to represent Christ by her life? Her answer must be an honest reflection of Christ, not the culture where she attends church. The general rule for both women and men emphasizes that both our behavior and dress must express our submission to and respect for Jesus Christ.

To understand these instructions, we must look at them in light of the whole Bible. Jesus set women free. He treated them as human beings. He recognized and responded to their needs as human needs. He taught women and included them as his followers. He proved himself to be their Savior, too. The accepted view of women in the time of Christ was as property rather than persons. Jesus personally shattered that conception. The gospel offered to women the gift of personhood—they were worthy of salvation.

Paul's instructions to the Christian women in Ephesus must be read in both their immediate and larger contexts before applying them. The immediate context was the church in Ephesus, which was suffering from the effect of false teachers who used women as their prime targets (see 2 Timothy 3:6-9). These women were also affected by their personal experiences within Ephesian culture. They would have struggled as much with cultural conditioning as we do.

The larger context includes what Paul taught elsewhere about the role and place of women in the church. One key statement occurs in Paul's letter to the Galatians: "There is neither Jew nor Greek, slave nor free, male nor female, for you are all one in Christ Jesus" (Galatians 3:28 NIV). Note also Peter's speech at Pentecost: "'In the last days, God says, I will pour out my Spirit on all people. Your sons and daughters will prophesy, your young men will see visions, your old men will dream dreams. Even on my servants, both men and women, I will pour out my Spirit in those days, and they will prophesy'" (Acts 2:17-18 NIV). Women were not being singled out, nor should these instructions be binding outside of the church. Modesty and self-restraint are for everyone at all times, but these specific prohibitions applied to the church in Ephesus.

Possibly, some Christian women in the Ephesian church were trying to gain respect by looking beautiful rather than by becoming Christlike in character. Some may have thought that they could win unbelieving husbands to Christ through their appearance (see Peter's counsel to such women in 1 Peter 3:1-6). In addition, Paul may have been referring to particular styles in Ephesus that were associated with prostitutes in the local temples. Artemis (also called Diana) was the goddess of Ephesus (see Acts 19:28). Considered the goddess of fertility, she was represented by a carved figure with many breasts. A large statue of her (the rock for which was said to have come from heaven, Acts 19:35) was in the great temple at Ephesus. That temple was one of the wonders of the ancient world. The festival of Artemis involved wild orgies and carousing. Obviously, Christian women should not look like or even copy the styles of the prostitutes in the temple of Artemis.

While there is nothing wrong with Christian women wanting
to look nice, each woman must examine her own motives.
Today's world places great emphasis on beauty—exceptionally
perfect women stare at us from magazine covers. Christian
women, while they can dress nicely and take care of their appearance, must at the same time not let their appearance become all-
encompassing, and they must not enhance their appearance
merely for "sex appeal" or attention getting.

**With good works, as is proper for women who profess rever-
ence for God.** NRSV A carefully groomed and well-decorated
exterior is artificial and cold without inner beauty. Scripture
does not prohibit a woman from wanting to be attractive.
Beauty, however, begins inside a person. A gentle, modest, loving character gives a light to the face that cannot be duplicated
by the best cosmetics and jewelry in the world. Christian
women are not to try to be unattractive; instead, Paul called
them to reject the world's standard for attractiveness. A Christian's adornment comes not from what she puts on, but from
what she does for others.

GOOD WORKS
While Paul placed at least temporary limits on women's freedom to teach in Ephesus, he also encouraged them to be
active in the practice of their faith. The context indicates that
both the church and the family provided great opportunities for
unlimited "good works."

Because Paul characterized the current teaching in Ephesus
with terms such as "false doctrines" (1:3), "myths and endless
genealogies" (1:4), "meaningless talk" (1:6), and "contrary to
the sound doctrine" (1:10), his instructions to the women were
actually a detour around the mire of the power struggle in that
local church. By keeping clear of the mess, they could quietly
go about the significant work of serving God.

Does Paul's emphasis on good works contradict his teaching
that salvation is by faith and not by works? No, because the
Pastoral Epistles encourage good works for all the believers
(Titus 2:4; 3:8, 14), for leaders (Titus 2:7), for the wealthy
(1 Timothy 6:18), and for widows (1 Timothy 5:10). Paul does
not teach that those good works were needed for salvation.
Jesus himself stressed good works based on love. Paul did,
however, stress the practical side of the Christian faith,
expressed by good works, in other letters (Romans 2:7; 2 Corinthians 11:8; Ephesians 2:10; Colossians 1:10).

In our churches today, as in the Ephesian church, there are
always temptations to pursue worldly agendas. We will stay on
track better if we regularly face the question, How much of my
time this week was spent in ways that will count for eternity?

While the church should not regulate what can or cannot be worn inside its doors (indeed many who need to know the Lord might not be able to enter if specific standards had to be met), those who *profess reverence for God* ought to dress sensibly and modestly. Even those words could be subject to disagreement among believers—one dressing in a manner that others deem not sensible or modest at all. Here the command of love applies, and believers must accept God's standard for appearance: "For the LORD does not see as mortals see; they look on the outward appearance, but the LORD looks on the heart" (1 Samuel 16:7 NRSV).

2:11 A woman should learn in quietness and full submission.^{NIV}
Many women have read these verses and been distressed. However, to understand these verses, we must understand the situation in which Paul and Timothy worked. In first-century Jewish culture, women were not allowed to study. Jews and Gentiles regarded it disgraceful for women to discuss issues with men in public. The Jews were stricter, not even allowing women to teach the male children past the age of five. (After male children reached the age of five, the Jewish men taught them.) In Greek philosophy, Plato granted women equality with men. Aristotle severely limited their activities, and his view was more widely accepted.

When Paul said that women should *learn* in quietness and full submission, he was affirming their recognition as teachable members of the church. Christian women were given "equal rights" with men when it came to studying the Holy Scriptures. This was an amazing freedom for many of the Jewish and Gentile women who had become Christians.

There were several problems in the Ephesian and Corinthian churches that made teaching in this area difficult. Some women, converted Jews, had grown up in an atmosphere repressive toward women. Suddenly these women experienced their freedom in Christ. They overreacted, flaunting their freedom and disrupting the church service. In addition, some of the women may have been converts from the cult of temple prostitution, so wide-

> The special gift and ability of each creature defines its special limitations. And as the bird easily comes to terms with the necessity of bearing wings when it finds that it is, in fact, the wings that bear the bird ... so the woman who accepts the limitations of womanhood finds in those very limitations her gifts, her special callings—wings, if fact, which bear her up into perfect freedom, into the will of God.
> *Elisabeth Elliot*

spread in these major cities. These women were immature in the faith and doctrine of Christianity. They needed to learn, not teach. Against this backdrop, we have the influence of the false teachers who emphasized elitism and special knowledge. A third group would be widows or weak-willed women (identified in 1 Timothy 5:3-16 and 2 Timothy 3:5-9) upon whom the false teachers were preying. These women should not be put up front to pray or teach until their doctrine had been straightened out.

Such women were to learn at home from their fathers or husbands; they were to maintain silence and not disturb the worship services (1 Corinthians 14:35). They were to speak, pray, or prophesy only when it was from the Spirit (1 Corinthians 11:5). Paul's prohibition was not against women in general. In several places Paul wrote about women in the church who were coworkers—helping him (Romans 16:1-3) and contending beside him for the faith (Philippians 4:2-3). Paul thought that women were coheirs of the image of God in Christ, that they were full members of the body of Christ, and that they fully shared in the responsibilities and gifts of serving.

Women's learning was to be *in quietness and full submission.* Other versions render this as "in silence" (NKJV). "Quietness" is clearer, for the Greek word used here (*hesuchia*) and in verses 2 and 12 means "settledness, calmness, undisturbed, implying voluntary restraint." Another Greek word, *sigao,* means "to be silent," as used in Luke 18:39 and 1 Corinthians 14:34.

"Submission" doesn't imply that women surrender their mind, conscience, or moral responsibility to obey God rather than men (Acts 5:29). This submission warns against presumptive and inappropriate grasping after authority.

2:12 I do not permit a woman to teach or to have authority over a man; she must be silent.^{NIV} This statement is part of a series of present commands in this chapter ("I urge," or "I am urging," 2:1; "I want," or "I am wanting," 2:8 and unspoken in 2:9; and "I do not permit," or "I am not permitting"). Unfortunately, the translation reads as if Paul actually wrote, "I never permit a woman to teach." Also, the grammatical order in Greek for this phrase carries less force than the English one ("To teach, a woman I am not allowing") and completes the thought about attentive learning in verse 11. The women in the Ephesian church were allowed to learn, but not to teach. Given the tension between the influx and recognition of women as fellow heirs of Christ within the church on the one hand, and the serious problems being caused by the false teachers on the other, Paul was affirming one right (to learn) while withholding another right (to teach) because of the condition of the church at the time. They did not need more teachers; rather, they all needed to return to the foundational truths of the gospel (2:3-7).

Some interpret this passage to mean that women should never teach in the assembled church; however, other passages point out that Paul allowed women to teach. Paul's commended coworker, Priscilla, taught Apollos, the great preacher (Acts 18:24-26). In addition, Paul frequently mentioned other women who held positions of responsibility in the church. Phoebe worked in the church (Romans 16:1). Mary, Tryphena, and Tryphosa were the Lord's workers (Romans 16:6, 12), as were Euodia and Syntyche (Philippians 4:2).

More likely, Paul restrained the Ephesian women from teaching because they didn't yet have enough knowledge or experience. The Ephesian church had a particular problem with false teachers. Both Timothy's presence and Paul's letters were efforts to correct the problem. Evidently the women were especially susceptible to the false teachings (2 Timothy 3:1-9) because they did not yet have enough biblical knowledge to discern the truth. Paul may have been countering the false teachers' urging that women should claim a place of equality for prominence in the church. Because these women were new converts, they did not yet have the necessary experience, knowledge, or Christian maturity to teach those who already had extensive scriptural education. In addition, some of the women were apparently flaunting their new-found Christian freedom by wearing inappropriate clothing (see 2:9). Paul was telling Timothy not to put anyone (in this case, women) into a position of leadership who was not yet mature in the faith (see 5:22). This deeper principle applies to churches today (3:6).

The women were not to *have authority over* the men, but instead were to be *silent* (meaning quietness and composure, see 2:11 above). The expression "to have authority" (*authentein*), found only here in the New Testament, implies a domineering, forceful attitude—an abuse of authority. Of course, no one should exercise abusive authority over anyone. The danger Paul was counteracting included a competitive struggle for power within the church as women took their rightful place. But conversely, Paul nowhere teaches male authority over women expressed in harsh domination.

Paul's instruction to the women of Ephesus displayed his missionary strategy. Because his desire was to reach the people of Ephesus with the gospel, he called for moderation and restraint against the potential misuse of freedom. Both Jews and Greeks in

Ephesus would be scandalized by women usurping authority over men. This would have created confusion and resentment among the pagans whom the Ephesian Christians were trying to reach. So Paul was giving a local strategy of restraint, not issuing unchanging rules of organization.

The women who became Christians may have thought that their Christian freedom and equality with men before God gave them the right to question or "lord it over" men in public worship. This disrupted worship and could have caused dissension in the church. Remember that equality of worth between the sexes was a completely foreign concept in both Hebrew and Roman cultures. It was not expected nor was it offered. The equality given by Christ was radical (see Galatians 3:26-28).

2:13 **For Adam was formed first, then Eve.** In previous letters Paul had discussed male/female roles in marriage (Ephesians 5:21-33; Colossians 3:18-19). Here he talks about male/female roles within the church. Some scholars see these verses about Adam and Eve as an illustration of what was happening in the Ephesian church. Just as Eve had been deceived in the Garden of Eden, so the women in the church were being deceived by false teachers. Just as Adam was the first human created by God, so the men in the church in Ephesus should be the first to speak and teach, because they had more training. Eve should have turned to Adam for advice about Satan's words to her because Adam had more experience with God's instructions. It was also necessary to simplify the task of weeding out the false teachers, also men, who were destroying the church from within. This view, then, stresses that Paul's teaching here is not universal; rather, it applies to churches with similar problems.

Other scholars, however, contend that the principles Paul points out are based on God's design for his created order—God established these roles to maintain harmony in both the family and the church (see Genesis 2:18). God assigned roles and responsibilities in order for his created world to function smoothly. Although there must be lines of authority, even in marriage, there should *not* be lines of superiority. God created men and women with unique and complementary characteristics. One sex is not better than the other. In designating Eve as "a helper suitable" for Adam (Genesis 2:18 NIV), the words imply another *like* him—signifying similarity and supplementation, but not dominance. We must not let the issue of authority and submission become a wedge to destroy what can be excellent working relationships, with men and women using their varied gifts and abilities to accomplish God's work.

WOMEN AS TEACHERS
Three views held by Christians on the role of women hinge on how each interprets 1 Timothy 2:9-15.

Nonauthoritative	These people see Paul as expressing his own opinion, not God's, or believe that this passage of Scripture was added later by someone other than Paul. They see these words as not the Word of God—or as irrelevant to modern practice.
Authoritative and absolute	This view holds that women should not be in authority over men in roles such as pastor, elder, or deacon. Some hold that women should not pray, give sermons, or even read Scripture aloud in public worship, and that women should not teach men in adult Sunday school. There is some variety of application as to limits of women's privileges in teaching, such as in Christian schools or in missionary roles.
Authoritative, but culturally limited	This view holds that Paul targeted the Ephesian culture and limited the role of women for this situation and others like it. The general principle to apply today is that we must not hinder the gospel.

2:14 And Adam was not the one deceived; it was the woman who was deceived and became a sinner.^{NIV} Paul was not excusing Adam for his part in the Fall (Genesis 3:6-7, 17-19). On the contrary, in his letter to the Romans, Paul placed the primary blame for humanity's sinful nature on Adam (Romans 5:12-21). Eve had not been told directly by God about the trees—Adam had instructed her. In turn, God instructed Adam about the trees before Eve was created. For Eve, the struggle was over whether to submit to Adam's command or to the serpent's words that seemed to offer her knowledge and understanding. But when Adam ate of the fruit, he directly disobeyed God. He was not deceived; he sinned outright. By then, however, Eve had already sinned.

This verse should not be taken to prove that women are more gullible than men in general. In Ephesus, due to the persuasiveness of the male false teachers, some women *were* gullible. Paul didn't use this verse to say women were easily deceived, but to point out that Eve should have submitted to Adam in her particular situation.

Likewise, this verse is not meant to be an echo of the curse in Genesis 3:16, "He shall rule over you" (NKJV). In Christ, this curse has been lifted (see Galatians 3:13-14, 28).

2:15 Yet she will be saved through childbearing.NRSV The phrase
saved through childbearing has been understood in several ways:

(1) The childbearing mentioned here refers to the birth of Jesus
Christ. Women (and men) are saved spiritually because of the
most important birth, that of Christ himself. This argument is
based on a very obscure reference to Christ and the Incarnation.
It would be unlikely for Paul to be so indirect.

(2) Man sinned, so men were condemned to painful labor.
Woman also sinned, so women were condemned to pain in childbearing. Pain caused a serious complication, but childbearing
was not the curse. Both men and women, however, can be saved
through trusting Christ and obeying him. Although this is true, it
does not seem as forceful in light of the context.

(3) From the lessons learned through the trials of childbearing,
women can develop qualities that teach them about love, trust,
submission, and service. Although this is true, it hardly seems to
be the main point.

(4) Women who fulfill their God-given roles of childbearing
and child rearing are demonstrating true commitment and obedience to Christ. One of the most important roles for a wife and
mother is to care for her family. This seems to be the most legitimate interpretation in light of the larger context and also in reference to 5:3-15. The women in Ephesus were abandoning their
God-given purpose because of the false teachers. So Paul was
telling them that caring for their families, or remarrying if they
were younger widows, was one way for them to remain effective
and to live faithful lives of service. By means of bearing children,
raising them, and fulfilling their design, women would be saved
from the evils of Ephesian society and maintain a pure testimony
to the lordship of Christ.

**Provided they continue in faith and love and holiness, with
modesty.**NRSV This expresses the goal that Paul placed before the
women of Ephesus. The women are called to faithfully carry out
their role as "childbearers" while pursuing "godliness and dignity" (2:2 NRSV) and coming toward "the knowledge of the truth"
(2:4 NRSV).

Scholars have written many volumes to present various
views of the role of women in worship and leadership. There
seems to be enough evidence and divided opinion to conclude
that the complete answer cannot be derived from 1 Timothy.
Church bodies have to decide the issue for their own congregations. Nonetheless, we would do well to consider the following statements:

- Scripture must be regarded in context. Paul gave other teachings about male/female relationships; all must be considered.
- Paul's clear teachings must be used to clarify what seems less clear.
- Though Scripture is not bound to culture, it is definitely targeted to culture. Paul was focusing on the Ephesians' problem.
- Remember Paul's missionary strategy. His local strategy for Ephesus may not be normative for all time.
- We must be consistent. If we allow women to wear jewelry but do not permit them to teach, we may be guilty of selectiveness.
- We must not let culture define how the church is run. If culture dictated a militant feminism, we should be against it. But if culture dictated a view of women more subordinated than the Bible suggests, we should oppose that as well.

1 Timothy 3

The list of qualifications for church office, which is similar to other lists in the Jewish and Greco-Roman world, is not a rigid judgment list for disqualifying certain people. Rather, it serves as a barometer for spiritual maturity. Those who aspire to a church office must realize that living a blameless and pure life requires effort and self-discipline. All believers, even if they never plan to be church leaders, should strive to follow these guidelines because they are consistent with what God says is true and right. The strength to live according to God's will comes from Christ.

> You are to follow no man farther than he follows Christ. *John Collins*

3:1 Here is a trustworthy saying: If anyone sets his heart on being an overseer, he desires a noble task.[NIV] The word *overseer* (*episkopes*) referred to a pastor, elder, or anyone who exercised an overseeing position. The word was borrowed from general culture and could refer to almost any kind of overseeing responsibility over others. The New Testament uses several words for church leaders; the most common are *apostle, overseer* (bishop), *elder,* and *deacon.* At first, the office of "apostle" referred only to the Twelve and to Paul, but it came to be used in a less technical sense for church representatives (see 2 Corinthians 8:23; Philippians 2:25). Pastors and elders were leaders in specific congregations, and the words were used interchangeably in Paul's letters. They were the teachers. Deacons were the administrators in these early churches—handling people, administration, finances, etc.

There apparently was a *saying* regarding church leadership, and Paul cited it here as a *trustworthy,* true and sure, saying. It is good to desire to be a spiritual leader. *Desire* means "to set one's heart on something." Leadership is a *noble task,* or excellent occupation. Paul stressed its importance. However, as Paul would point out, the standards are high.

Students of ancient culture have noted many similarities between Paul's list of leadership requirements and those commonly

GREAT ASPIRATIONS
Christians sometimes set the terms *service* and *leadership* in opposition to each other. Jesus defined leadership *as* service: "If anyone wants to be first, he must be the very last, and the servant of all" (Mark 9:35 NIV). A believer unwilling to consider how God might accomplish anything great through his or her life suffers from false humility or apathy. We should pursue leadership roles in the church, as long as our desires focus on pleasing Jesus and serving others.

We can clarify our desires for leadership/service in several ways:

- By making ourselves available to God in prayer and seeking his will;
- By taking note of those activities and roles that naturally appeal to us;
- By imagining ourselves in significant roles;
- By asking other believers how and where they see us serving in the church.

used to measure people's aptitude for various civic roles. This should not be surprising. God has created all people with a desire for ethical behavior. We may readily excuse and deny our own ethical failures, but we expect those who lead us to be above reproach. Because the church contains a cross section of human beings, the same high standards for leaders must be in place for effective life together. Paul's list treats accountability differently. Societal structures require accountability to the governed from those who govern. Within the church, accountability ultimately must be given to God.

3:2 Now the overseer must be above reproach, the husband of but one wife, temperate, self-controlled, respectable, hospitable, able to teach.NIV See 3:1 for notes about *overseer.* Paul enumerated fifteen qualifications for a church leader.

To be *above reproach* means this man must have no flaw in his conduct that would be grounds for any kind of accusation. He must be blameless. The term serves as a general opening summary of character. A leader within the church should have a good reputation among believers. Leadership sets the tone. What follows are the building blocks of that reputation.

He should be a married man, *the husband of one wife.* This expression has been interpreted in several ways:

(1) He should not have more than one wife. This does not make sense because polygamy was rare in the cultures Paul visited, and it is never mentioned elsewhere as a problem in the early church.

(2) He should not be remarried after a divorce. Some scholars have argued strongly that this is the meaning Paul intended. Others have allowed that the Bible regards divorce as permissible in some conditions (Matthew 19:9; 1 Corinthians 7:15).

> Would that our pulpits were all in the power of such men as by suffering know the human, and by obedience the divine heart! *George Macdonald*

(3) He should not be remarried after his wife's death. Paul permitted remarriage for the widows (see 5:14). He also refers to this in Romans 7:2-3 and 1 Corinthians 7:39.

(4) He should be faithful, not having mistresses or affairs. This view takes Paul's phrase to mean that the leader should be a one-woman man. This seems to be the best choice because the leader was to go against the immoral standards present in the pagan culture at Ephesus. The Bible rejects marriage as convenience and demands faithfulness and participation in the one flesh created by husband and wife (see Genesis 2:24; Ephesians 5:22-33).

DESIRE PLUS
Do you hold a position of spiritual leadership, or would you like to be a leader some day? Your desire may not match God's plans for you, but aspiring to leadership can be a healthy incentive to promote spiritual growth. Check yourself against Paul's standard of excellence. Those with great responsibility must meet high expectations.

A church leader must also be *temperate,* meaning that his life should be marked by moderation, limits, not extreme or excessive, with an absence of extravagance. "Temperance" was sometimes used as an antonym for drunkenness, but, because Paul addresses the abuse of alcohol specifically in verse 3, the meaning here is broader. We might use the term *balanced* to indicate that this leader possesses the appropriate emphasis on each of the priorities in his life. Paul actually summarized this balance in Ephesians 5:18: "Do not get drunk on wine, which leads to debauchery. Instead, be filled with the Spirit" (NIV). The filling presence of God's Spirit brings healthy temperance to a believer's life.

That he be *self-controlled* was another way of saying a leader ought to possess sound and balanced judgment, or even common sense. Each of these qualities may be required for leaders, but they ought to be the goal of all believers. In his letter to Titus, Paul mentioned self-control as necessary for older men (Titus 2:2), older and younger women (Titus 2:4-5), and young men (Titus 2:6). Practical wisdom should mark the lives of believers. This quality combines the traits Jesus instructed his disciples to exercise: "I am sending you out like sheep among wolves. Therefore be as shrewd as snakes and as innocent as doves" (Matthew 10:16 NIV).

The term *respectable* (*kosmion*) refers to basic social graces—ordinary dignified behavior. The Greek word is derived from *kosmos*, "the world or universe," and pictures a person who lives in harmony with the way God created the world to function. The Pharisees described Jesus' behavior as less than "respectable" at times. But Jesus' behavior shocked and jarred at the very points where Jewish religious society no longer followed God's plans. Jesus expelled the money changers from the temple because he believed that God designed the place for one purpose, but people had treated his Father's house with disrespect (see Luke 19:45-48).

Hospitality was widely emphasized in Middle Eastern cultures and in the Old Testament (see Exodus 22:21). Believers are commanded to be hospitable (Hebrews 5:10; 13:2; 1 Peter 4:9; 3 John 5), so the leaders should also be *hospitable*.

OPEN HOUSE
Since Paul wrote to Timothy, our life has become considerably more privatized. Homes often act as sealed compartments, isolating believers from each other and from unbelievers. Instead we should use every opportunity to reach people. Hebrews adds a curious twist to the instruction about hospitality: "Do not forget to entertain strangers, for by so doing some people have entertained angels without knowing it" (Hebrews 13:2 NIV). We will certainly never entertain an angel if we never welcome strangers in our home.

Christian leaders must be *able to teach*. One of the most important tasks of any church leader is to teach the Scriptures to those in the congregation. The leader must understand and be able to communicate the profound truths of Scripture, as well as deal with those false teachers who mishandle them.

Among the qualities for leadership, the ability to teach comes closest to being part of a job description rather than a distinct character trait. However, the emphasis remains on ability, for the leader must have a proven record that he is able to teach (Romans 12:6).

For us, teaching tends to happen in structured settings, often in buildings set aside for that purpose. But schools in biblical times were not buildings. Students were apprentices or disciples of teachers. The relational priorities in teaching probably improved the process, but if the teachers were false, as in the case of several in Ephesus, the outcomes could be disastrous. Paul wanted able teachers whose teaching could be trusted.

PASSED ON
Some people are effectively "able to teach" who never take charge of a classroom. Their lessons are passed on to one or two others. They become mentors of spiritual truth. Paul described this intimate kind of teaching in 2 Timothy 2:2: "And the things you have heard me say in the presence of many witnesses entrust to reliable men who will also be qualified to teach others" (NIV).

More is learned through living than through lectures. If you have been able to communicate your faith clearly to another person, you have demonstrated teaching at its best. In measuring your ability to teach, don't consider how many students you have had; instead, ask how much truth you have passed on to even one student that God has brought your way.

To be a church leader is a heavy responsibility because the church belongs to the living God. Church leaders should not be elected because they are popular, nor should they be allowed to push their way to the top. Instead, they should be chosen by the church because of their respect for the truth, both in what they believe and in how they live.

3:3 Not a drunkard, not violent but gentle, not quarrelsome, and not a lover of money.NRSV Paul listed four characteristics the overseer must *not* have. The overseer's temperance (3:2) extended to his desires and his anger. He must not be addicted to drink (a *drunkard*) nor to *money*. Many of these qualities may have characterized the false teachers who caused quarrels in the church (see 6:3-4) and often were "in the business" of teaching in order to enrich themselves (see 6:5). True overseers, those who were placed in charge of the congregations (see Acts 14:23), exemplified the opposite—they taught only the truth (by its nature, truth does not lead to worthless discussion and quarrels), and they served out of love, not out of a desire for money.

A Christian leader should be free from the love of money (see 6:5-10). Leaders must have a proper attitude for handling finances in the church. This affects the ethical use of church funds and the administration of proper programs for raising money. It also implies that making money should not be a prime motive for a candidate seeking a church leadership position.

Many would-be leaders combine love of money with a quarrelsome nature and end up quarreling in the church over money matters. Such a person should not be selected to lead.

A potential leader must not be *violent* or *quarrelsome*. A violent person is an abusive individual. Abuse may take many forms (verbal, physical, sexual, even spiritual), but it rises from a deep disrespect for others. Mental illness may also be involved. The church should examine all areas of a leader's past and not be selective in that process.

A *quarrelsome* person exhibits an argumentative personality. Such a person tends to be defensive, insecure, and insensitive. This type of leader may undermine the legitimate gifts of others because he or she feels threatened by someone else's abilities, even though these abilities may be complementary to their own. A person with a history of verbal battles may find it difficult to lead effectively. Again, such a person should not be selected to lead.

In contrast to the danger of violence, Paul notes the value of gentleness. A *gentle* person is free from harshness, sternness, or violence. The Greek word for gentle (*epieike*) is used elsewhere in the New Testament. Paul exhorted the Philippian believers to "let [their] gentleness be known to everyone" (Philippians 4:5 NRSV). James explained that "the wisdom from above is first pure, then peaceable, gentle, willing to yield, full of mercy and good fruits" (James 3:17 NRSV). Clearly gentleness is an important quality for all believers.

3:4 He must manage his own family well and see that his children obey him with proper respect.NIV The qualifications for both elders and deacons hinge on the man's ability to manage his own household (see also 3:12). It is not absolutely required that an elder be married or have children. If he does, however, he must have a well-managed family. The word *manage* is not "rule" as in KJV. It means compassionate governing, leading, and directing (see 1 Thessalonians 5:12; 1 Timothy 5:17), not stern, cruel, tyrannical, and authoritarian dominance. This type of family leadership reflects the parallel between church and home seen in Ephesians 5:28–6:9.

It makes sense that Paul would use this requirement, for no one can run a household effectively without love and firmness, mercy and guidelines. And if parents don't model what they teach, children rarely follow except under pressure. There are two thoughts in this phrase: on one hand, while it is true that children should show respect, respect is a by-product of responsible leadership in the home. Children who show respect indicate that parents are doing their job correctly. The second thought is that the candidate should be pursuing his family management with all seriousness (proper respect), meaning that he fully devotes himself to that task.

The children must respect their father enough to submit to him, and his leadership must be exercised with firm but gentle authority (3:3). Paul explains the reason in the next verse.

3:5 For if someone does not know how to manage his own household, how can he take care of God's church?^{NRSV} The best way to see a person's ability to handle a large responsibility is to see how he or she performs a small one. The ability to handle his family forms a training ground for a man's ability to handle the family of God in a local congregation. The same love, compassion, firmness, and mercy are needed for both duties.

HOME FRONT
These words need to be applied before people become church leaders. Christian workers and volunteers sometimes make the mistake of thinking their work is so important that they are justified in ignoring their family. Spiritual leadership, however, must begin at home. If a man is not willing to care for, discipline, and teach his children, he is not qualified to lead the church. Don't allow your volunteer activities to detract from your family responsibilities.

3:6 He must not be a recent convert, or he may become conceited and fall under the same judgment as the devil.^{NIV} New believers should become secure and strong in the faith before taking leadership roles in the church. Too often, when desperate for workers, the church places new believers in positions of responsibility prematurely. Often newly saved sport stars and famous people have been put up front

> A proud faith is as much a contradiction as a humble devil.
> *Stephen Charnock*

to give a testimony before they have the maturity to handle the praise they might receive. New faith needs time to mature. New believers should have a part in God's service, but they should not be put into leadership positions until they are firmly grounded in their faith, with a solid Christian life-style and a knowledge of the Word of God. (Paul omitted this requirement in his instructions to Titus, perhaps because the church in Crete was much younger.)

This will be a corrective for conceit. The word *conceited* literally means "wrapped in smoke." A person can be so inflated with pride that he can't get a true picture of himself (6:4; 2 Timothy 3:4). Pride means more than self-esteem or satisfaction in a job well done; it means comparing oneself to others and setting oneself up as superior. It demeans another person's status or contributions, if only in one's thoughts.

The same judgment as the devil has two possible meanings. "Judgment" meant a trap or snare; so this could mean: (1) the same sentence passed on the devil because his sin was pride. Those who follow his example will get the same judgment; or (2) the devil will carry out his trap for Christians who fall into pride. In this verse, the sin of pride seems likely, since verse 7 talks more of Satan's trap.

> "O!" says one person, "if we had another minister. O! if we had another kind of worship. O! if we had a different sort of preaching." You do not need new ways or new people, you need life in what you have. If you want to move a train, you don't need a new engine, or even ten engines—you need to light a fire and get the steam up in the engine you now have!
> *Charles Spurgeon*

The reference to the devil teaches that in the same way Satan fell because of pride, there waits the danger of pride to new believers who are given responsibility before they are ready. New believers who are too quickly promoted can be easy targets for the devil's powerful temptation: pride. Pride can seduce emotions and cloud our reason. It can make those who are immature susceptible to the influence of unscrupulous people. Pride and conceit were the devil's downfall, and he uses pride to trap others. For more on Satan's downfall, see 1 Samuel 14:12-15; John 12:31; 16:11; 2 Peter 2:4; Jude 6.

TOO SOON, TOO MUCH
Addressing another volatile situation, Paul warned the Corinthians, "So be careful. If you are thinking, 'Oh, I would never behave like that'—let this be a warning to you. For you too may fall into sin" (1 Corinthians 10:12 TLB). The benefits of spiritual growth can be destroyed if our confidence leads to pride.

We must never let our pride get out of control. Vanity insists on being our constant traveling companion. As long as we recognize pride's dangerous trap, we will be less likely to heed its suggestions and fall into it. We must treat pride as an unwelcome guest so that it never takes us over.

3:7 He must also have a good reputation with outsiders, so that he will not fall into disgrace and into the devil's trap.^{NIV}

HISTORY OF CHURCH LEADERSHIP
FROM THE NEW TESTAMENT

Acts 6:1-6	Seven men were appointed to help the church by "waiting on tables," thereby relieving the disciples of this duty so they could concentrate on preaching the gospel. Many believe this was the beginning of the office of deacon.
Acts 14:23	As Paul and Barnabas prepared to return home to Antioch at the close of their first missionary journey, they appointed elders in each church to care for and continue to teach the newly formed congregations.
Acts 20:17	At the end of Paul's third missionary journey, as he headed toward Jerusalem, he sent for the elders of the church at Ephesus. Clearly this was a recognized group, and to this group Paul gave special instruction (Acts 20:18-35).
Acts 20:28	Paul instructed the overseers to remember their commission by the Holy Spirit and their primary duties—to keep watch over themselves and over their congregations.
1 Thessalonians 5:12-13	Paul gave instructions to the believers in Thessalonica to respect those who labored among them and who had God-given responsibility for them.
Philippians 1:1	Paul greeted the leaders in the church—overseers and deacons.
1 Timothy 5:17	Paul instructed the congregations to recognize the honor due to their leaders.

Requiring the leaders to have a *good reputation* with people outside the church (that is, nonbelievers in the community) gave the church at large a good reputation (and good advertising) in the community. Church leaders, being the most visible people in the church to the secular world, would do well to maintain the highest of standards and the best reputation. Seeing several church leaders make headlines in recent years for tax evasion, wrongful use of solicited funds, and sexual escapades certainly damages the credibility of the church. Church leaders who follow Paul's advice keep their church from facing unnecessary abuse. Otherwise, they fall into *disgrace* with both believers and nonbelievers, and into *the devil's trap*. This trap may either be the moral failure and resultant judgment that a man chosen as leader will fall into, or it could mean the trap of temptation leading to pride

as mentioned in verse 6. When Christian leaders have a bad reputation, it keeps nonbelievers from coming to Christ.

Christians must remember that we want to bring those *outsiders* into the church. The message of the gospel never changes, but
a good reputation does wonders to bring curious nonbelievers
into the church, where they can hear the gospel truth (see Colossians 4:5; 1 Thessalonians 4:12).

BRIDGES
The good reputation with outsiders that Paul required is realized when Christians act as dependable friends and good
neighbors. How we carry out our duties as citizens, neighbors,
and friends facilitates or frustrates our ability to communicate
the gospel. Do you have friends who are not believers? Does
your conduct help or hinder the cause of Christ? As the church
carries out its mission in an increasingly secular world, the
church needs those who build bridges with unbelievers in order
to bring them the gospel.

**3:8 Deacons, likewise, are to be men worthy of respect, sincere,
not indulging in much wine, and not pursuing dishonest
gain.**NIV *Deacon* means "one who serves." This position was possibly begun by the apostles in the Jerusalem church (Acts 6:1-6)
to care for the physical needs of the congregation, especially the
needs of the Greek-speaking widows (though some dispute this
because they were not called deacons but were assistants to the
elders). Deacons were leaders in the church, and their qualifications resemble those of the overseers; yet their roles were probably somewhat different as they carried out some of the more
practical tasks of running and maintaining a church.

We must remember, however, that Paul was probably describing a role or function, more than defining an office or position.
The original terms *overseers* and *servants* still generally applied
to the class of slaves. Paul's explanation of these roles within the
church emphasized the point that the name or title was to be
given to someone who was already living out these character
qualities. While Paul did not mention teaching requirements for
deacons, their lives would have still been models of Christian discipleship.

Deacons, as recognized leaders in the church, also had a high
profile and thus were required to be *worthy of respect* (*semnous*).
This is not the same term for respectability applied to the overseers (3:2). Here the term can mean "serious" or "honorable."

Deacons were to take their responsibilities seriously and conscientiously. They should be men of dignity.

The *sincere* quality of deacons referred to honesty without hypocrisy. Sometimes translated, "not double-tongued," this could refer to not gossiping, or to not saying one thing to one person and another to someone else.

Finally, like overseers, deacons ought not be addicted to wine or to money (see 3:3). They must be, in fact, uninterested in such pursuits.

In some churches today, the office of deacon has lost its importance. New Christians are often asked to serve in this position, but that is not the New Testament pattern. Paul said that potential deacons should be tested before they are asked to serve (3:10).

3:9 They must keep hold of the deep truths of the faith with a clear conscience.NIV Deacons must be men with spiritual depth.

The seven men chosen to help the apostles in the early church were "known to be full of the Spirit and wisdom" (Acts 6:3 NIV). While Luke never called Stephen and his companions "deacons," they have traditionally been held up as early models of the service orientation of that role. They were men whose outward actions demonstrated that the gospel had taken deep root in their lives. The *deep truths* (*musterion*) or mysteries refer to the plan of salvation now

> I have come to the conviction that if you cannot translate your thoughts into uneducated language, then your thoughts were confused. Power to translate is the test of having really understood one's own meaning. *C. S. Lewis*

fully known in Christ (Romans 16:26; 1 Corinthians 2:7; 4:1; Ephesians 3:3-9; Colossians 1:26). Originally unknown to humanity, this plan became crystal clear when Jesus rose from the dead. God's plan is still hidden to unbelievers because they refuse to accept it, choose to ignore it, or simply haven't heard about it. God kept his plan hidden, not because he wanted to keep something back from his people, but because he wanted to reveal it to everyone in his perfect timing.

The *faith* refers to sound doctrine and teaching (see 4:1, 6; 5:8; 6:10). In this "holding of the truth," deacons would do their most effective teaching.

The role of the deacon, then, was not to invent or teach "new truth" but to provide a stable example of the unchanging truth of the gospel.

Deacons must not only know God's truth, they must live it, resulting in *a clear conscience* (see note on 1:5). Their life-styles must be consistent with their beliefs. This must necessarily be

true for all Christians, and any man chosen for the office of deacon will have shown these qualities beforehand.

HOLD ON
Earlier (see 2:4) Paul explained that by the word *truth* he meant
the deepest components of the faith (see 2:5-6). These were:
(1) the oneness of God, (2) the uniqueness of Christ Jesus and
his ministry, and (3) the ransom that Jesus paid for all people.
All other Christian teaching flows from this foundation of truth.
   Like those early deacons, we need to have a firm grasp of
the basic message of God's Word. Putting what we believe into
words and actions helps us grow. Peter described this process:
"But in your hearts set apart Christ as Lord. Always be prepared to give an answer to everyone who asks you to give the
reason for the hope that you have" (1 Peter 3:15 NIV).

**3:10 And let them first be tested; then, if they prove themselves
blameless, let them serve as deacons.**[NRSV] This refers not to
some formal testing but rather to observation by those who
appoint deacons. The candidate will have shown the required
moral characteristics and approved doctrine (3:9) consistently in
the ordinary activities of church membership. A man who has
proven his quality over time can then serve as a deacon. Testing
deacons is needed today. They should not be appointed without
consideration of their doctrine and their Christian life.

**3:11 Women likewise must be serious, not slanderers, but temper-
ate, faithful in all things.**[NRSV] In Greek, the same word, *gune,* is
used for "woman" and for "wife." So three possible interpretations have been given for the identity of these servants:
   (1) These women were the deacons' wives. However, in the
Greek no *their* is present, and there is no article before *women* as
would be usual if this meant "wives."
   (2) These are women in general. However, the context of
church leadership speaks against this interpretation.
   (3) These women are female deacons or "deaconesses," such
as Phoebe in Romans 16:1. This interpretation is based on the use
of "likewise" or "in the same way" to show the parallel to verse 8.
   Whatever the case, Paul expected the behavior of prominent
women in the church to be just as responsible and blameless as
that of prominent men.
   Serious women are dignified, worthy of respect (see 3:8 for
Paul's use of the same term regarding men). They must not be
slanderers; that is, they must not have a problem with gossiping.
   Like the overseers, women are called to be *temperate* (3:2)—

marked by moderation and limits, not extreme or excessive, with an absence of extravagance. Being *faithful in all things* is an important requirement for anyone who would fulfill many duties on behalf of the congregation. A helper who constantly forgets to fulfill her duties or only does them halfway is not suitable for service in the church.

Although the women in the church at Ephesus were not (at least in the present circumstances) allowed to teach in the formal sense, they were still expected to model all the character qualities of mature believers.

Women have rarely found "the right to teach" easily granted to them in or out of the church. But history has also demonstrated repeatedly (recently with Mother Teresa of Calcutta and others) that a woman faithfully exhibiting the

> St. Jerome and St. Augustine not only exhorted excellent matrons and most noble virgins to study, but also, in order to assist them, diligently explained the abstruse meanings of Holy Scripture and wrote for tender girls letters replete with so much erudition that nowadays old men who call themselves professors of sacred science can scarcely read them correctly, much less understand them.
>
> *Thomas More*

character qualities of a believer will find that she has been teaching. Unfortunately, the church has often shown little wisdom in the treatment of females, who constitute more than half of the body of Christ. The church has often missed the benefits of recognizing women in the teaching roles that they, in fact, have already been performing.

3:12 A deacon must be the husband of but one wife and must manage his children and his household well.NIV This requirement matches the requirement for overseers spelled out in verses 2, 4-5, and is included for deacons for the same reasons.

3:13 For those who have served well as deacons obtain for themselves a good standing and great boldness in the faith which is in Christ Jesus.NKJV Deacons are required to have the same high standards as overseers for a position that, to many, might seem very unattractive and menial. But God doesn't see it that way. Those who fulfill their servant roles faithfully gain *a good standing* with fellow believers who recognize and appreciate their service, and *great boldness in the faith. Boldness* has also been translated "assurance." The faithful servant is able to speak boldly of the faith and serve confidently, assured that what he or she does is appreciated and valued by the Lord Jesus Christ.

Humble service may lack earthly rewards, but heavenly rewards are promised.

The range of qualifications for leadership roles within the church covered life itself. The standards were demanding. Paul confronted the status and position being pursued by the false teachers by minimizing the formal role of teaching in his list. Paul's instructions imply that the church in Ephesus was experiencing a glut of teaching but a drought of truth. There was too much meaningless talk (1:6) and too little purposeful living. Doubtless the apostle would have endorsed James's plea, "Not many of you should presume to be teachers, my brothers, because you know that we who teach will be judged more strictly" (James 3:1 NIV). Paul knew that a future supply of faithful teachers would only be available with a present renewal of faithful believers.

3:14-15 **I hope to come to you soon, but I am writing these instructions to you so that, if I am delayed, you may know how one ought to behave in the household of God.**^{NRSV} Paul hoped to arrive in Ephesus and see Timothy within a short time of this letter's arrival. In case Paul arrived later than planned, he wrote these instructions to Timothy and the Ephesian church. This letter most likely confirmed instructions about governing the church already given to Timothy by Paul. This letter's arrival, prior to Paul's appearance, would have bolstered Timothy's authority in the church to continue to guide the church according to these instructions and to counteract the false teachers.

Again, in opposition to the false teachers who were full of false beliefs, Paul aimed at truthful behavior within the church. Actions speak louder than words, and in harmony they create an attractive song. Paul also knew that if he got the Ephesian Christians behaving as God wanted them to live, the noise of the false teachers would be drowned out.

Which is the church of the living God, the pillar and foundation of the truth.^{NIV} Lest there be any doubt, Paul identified the "household of God" as *the church of the living God* (see also 1 Corinthians 3:16-17; 2 Corinthians 6:16; Ephesians 2:20-22). This "church" does not refer to any particular physical building; rather, the "church" is the collection of all believers in Ephesus and, by extension, across the world. These believers, each serving and worshiping in their individual churches, are the *pillar and foundation,* that is, the earthly support, of God's truth. The church is not the *source* of this truth; rather, it functions as the custodian of and the witness to the truth. Therefore, the church is not more important than the truth. God's truth rests upon and within the church. His truth would still exist if there were no churches; the truth would still exist whether anyone believed it or not. Those who *do* believe God's truth have the power to change the world. That truth is outlined in the hymn Paul quoted from in the following verses.

3:16 And without controversy great is the mystery of godliness.^{NKJV} In this short paragraph, probably an excerpt from an early hymn of the church, Paul affirmed the humanity and divinity of Christ. (For other examples of hymns, see Ephesians 5:19; Colossians 3:6; and Philippians 2:5.) By so doing, Paul revealed the heart of the gospel, *the mystery of godliness*. The secret of being "godly," of pleasing God by our lives, was hidden but is now revealed. To the godly, Christ is the mystery revealed (1 Corinthians 2:7-14; Colossians 1:27). This is a *great* mystery—that is, profoundly significant, overwhelmingly important. We can't please God on our own; we must depend on Christ. As a man, Jesus lived a perfect life, and so he is a perfect example of how to live. As God, Jesus gives us the power to do what is right. It is possible to live a godly life—through following Christ.

Every phrase of the hymn is a "mystery" beyond our comprehension yet available for us to believe. We accept the truth as it has been revealed to us. And the results of our belief are life changing.

He was revealed in flesh.^{NRSV} The oldest Greek manuscripts read, "[he] who was manifest in the flesh." Later scribes changed the text to read, "God who was manifest in the flesh." They did this by changing *hos* (he who) to *theos* (God) in their manuscripts. The King James Version reads, "God was manifest in the flesh." (The King James Bible based its translation on an edition of the Greek text—popularly known as the Textus Receptus—that included the change.) In the earliest Greek manuscripts, the subject is "who," which most translators render as "he"; most commentators clearly identify this "he" as Christ.

Jesus was a man; Jesus' incarnation provides the basis for our being right with God. "[Jesus] made himself nothing, taking the very nature of a servant, being made in human likeness. And being found in appearance as a man, he humbled himself and became obedient to death" (Philippians 2:7-8 NIV; see also Romans 1:3).

Justified in the Spirit.^{NKJV} Jesus' resurrection showed that the Holy Spirit's power was in him: "This Jesus God raised up, and of that all of us are witnesses. Being therefore exalted at the right hand of God, and having received from the Father the promise of the Holy Spirit, he has poured out this that you both see and hear" (Acts 2:32-33 NRSV). Not everyone agrees that *Spirit* should be capitalized, referring to the Holy Spirit. Part of the answer depends on whether the Greek preposition *en* should be understood as "in" or "by." Both choices allow us to arrive at some allusion to the Resurrection while emphasizing the contrast between spirit and body. A paraphrase might be: "He proved himself human in the body; he was proved God in his spiritual nature by the Spirit's testimony."

Seen by angels . . . received up in glory.^{NKJV} Jesus is divine and exalted. "Therefore God exalted him to the highest place and gave him the name that is above every name" (Philippians 2:9 NIV; see also Colossians 2:15; Hebrews 1:6). Presumably, the entire drama of the Incarnation was a spectacle for the angels. They were witnesses and heralds of his coming. But within this poetic expression, the role of the angels and their exposure to Christ exceeds his time on earth. The angels participate in the glorification of Jesus.

Preached among the Gentiles.^{NKJV} *Gentiles* (*ethnesin*) can also be translated "nations," pointing to the worldwide proclamation of the gospel. "This is the gospel that you heard and that has been proclaimed to every creature under heaven, and of which I, Paul, have become a servant" (Colossians 1:23 NIV).

Believed on in the world.^{NKJV} Christ is not only preached among all nations, but he also is believed on across the world. This points to a continual fulfillment today as Christ is still preached in nations that have not heard of him, and he is still being *believed on in the world.*

Received up in glory.^{NKJV} This refers to the Ascension: "He who descended is also the One who ascended far above all the heavens, that He might fill all things" (Ephesians 4:10 NKJV).

1 Timothy 4

Paul ended chapter 3 explaining that "the church of the living God [is] the pillar and ground of the truth" (3:15 NKJV). Paul's original letter, of course, had no chapter divisions, so the thought beginning chapter 4 continued Paul's line of thinking. His mind turned from the exalted role of the church in the plan of God to the obstacles that were preventing the Ephesian believers from being totally effective.

Paul warned the church of the tactics and teachings of its enemies. False teachers were (and still can be) a threat to the church. Paul knew that their teachings, if left unchecked, would greatly distort Christian truth. This critical danger would come from within the church.

The false teaching that Timothy faced in Ephesus may have been a form of Gnosticism (which became a major problem in the Colossian church). Gnostics believed that the physical world was evil and that only the soul mattered. Thus they refused to believe that a God who created the world could be good, because any contact with the physical world would have soiled him. Though these Greek-influenced church members honored Jesus, they could not believe he was truly human. Paul wanted Timothy to be well armed in his opposition to the false teachers that plagued the Ephesian church with this dangerous heresy.

> By entertaining of strange persons, men sometimes entertain angels unawares: but by entertaining of strange doctrines, many have entertained devils unaware. *John Flavel*

4:1 Now the Spirit expressly says that in later times some will renounce the faith by paying attention to deceitful spirits and teachings of demons.^{NRSV} Having expressed his vision of the timeless truth of the incarnation of Jesus, Paul turned to the immediate problems at hand. The false teaching in Ephesus was no surprise. The betrayal of the gospel had been foreseen. Paul's phrase, *the Spirit expressly says,* most likely refers to warnings repeatedly given by Jesus and the apostles against the dangers of false teaching (see the chart on page 74). But Paul's direct con-

BEWARE OF FALSE TEACHERS!

Speaker/Writer	Quote (from NRSV)	Section of Warning
Jesus	"False messiahs and false prophets will appear and produce signs and omens, to lead astray, if possible, the elect." (Mark 13:22)	Mark 13:21-23
Paul	"I know that after I have gone, savage wolves will come in among you, not sparing the flock. Some even from your own group will come distorting the truth in order to entice the disciples to follow them." (Acts 20:29-30)	Acts 20:28-31
Paul	"We beg you, brothers and sisters, not to be quickly shaken in mind or alarmed. . . . Let no one deceive you in any way." (2 Thessalonians 2:1-3)	2 Thessalonians 2:1-12
Peter	"First of all you must understand this, that in the last days scoffers will come, scoffing and indulging their own lusts. . . . You therefore, beloved, since you are forewarned, beware that you are not carried away with the error of the lawless and lose your own stability." (2 Peter 3:3, 17)	2 Peter 3:1-18
Jude	"In the last time there will be scoffers. . . . It is these worldly people, devoid of the Spirit, who are causing divisions." (Jude 18-19)	Jude 17-19

cern here was not just about the teachers themselves as much as for those who would be deceived by them. The teachers are referred to as "liars" in verse 2.

The *later times* began with Christ's resurrection and will continue until his return, when he will set up his kingdom and judge all humanity. Jesus and the apostles forewarned us that during that interim, including the time period we live in, false teachers will abound—loving money and attention, distorting the truth, dividing believers, and causing many to go astray as they follow *deceitful spirits and teachings of demons* (see Matthew 24:5; Romans 16:18; James 3:15; 2 Peter 2:1; 1 John 3:7-9). These participants in the church will *renounce the faith,* even though they may appear to still be faithful believers.

BETRAYED!
People who have been deceived or abused within the church have been made double victims. Not only have they been hurt, but they have also been cut off from spiritual help. The seeds of error yield a harvest of bitterness and disillusionment. Believers ought to respond swiftly when they sense false teaching being promoted. The truth does not mind honest questions. Sometimes the source may prove to be ignorant of the error and appreciate the correction. But a firm warning may at least keep potential victims from the disastrous results of apostasy that Paul described.

Paul had no patience for false teaching and no soft words for false teachers. He never said that the false teachers misunderstood the gospel or that they simply taught in error. Rather, Paul knew that false teaching comes from Satan himself through his *deceitful spirits* (demons). False teaching is one of Satan's many tactics to lead believers astray and to divide the church. Satan's influence leads people to apostasy. Teachers who resisted the Holy Spirit's conviction and rejected his control became tools of Satan and promoted the wrong doctrine. Paul wrote to the believers in this church in Ephesus: "For our struggle is not against flesh and blood, but against the rulers, against the authorities, against the powers of this dark world and against the spiritual forces of evil in the heavenly realms" (Ephesians 6:12 NIV).

A CURIOUS TRAP
Although he clearly pointed out the source of false teaching in Ephesus, Paul did not speculate on the nature or the tactics of Satan. Curiosity about the tactics of evil can become a trap for those who are not careful. Instead, Paul pointed out the results of Satan's work. He was confident that a clear understanding of demonic "fruit" would be a more effective inoculation against evil than curiosity about it.

Fascination with evil has been the downfall of many who otherwise might have been considered strong in the faith. We will have more success resisting evil by keeping as far from it and as close to Christ as possible.

4:2 Such teachings come through hypocritical liars.NIV After pointing out the tragedy of deception, Paul began to identify the means by which the subversion was achieved. The "deceitful spirits" and "demons" mentioned in verse 1 find particularly willing human agents in people who are *hypocritical liars* because such people do not sense the

> It is not controversy we have to dread as much as the spirit of controversy.
> *Richard Treffey, Jr.*

evil of their actions. They are bent on appearing to be teachers of the truth while they are, in fact, serving the evil purposes of Satan.

LIARS' TACTICS
Paul revealed several tactics of the "liars" who were false teachers:

- They corrupt the simplicity of the gospel with "meaningless talk" (1:6).
- They pervert preaching from its purpose to instruct others in the truth to gathering influence for themselves (1:7).
- They burden believers with needless controversies and endless rules (1:4; 3:3-5).
- They reject God and twist the evidence of his character by naming as evil what God has called good (3:3-5).

Whose consciences have been seared as with a hot iron.NIV These false teachers' consciences are past feeling—*seared* . (Greek *kausteriazo,* see below)—so they are willing to follow Satan's bidding (see also Ephesians 4:19). They have also

SIN-SEARED
Scholars have explained Paul's idea of the "seared conscience" in three ways:

1. Seared consciences have lost their sensitivity to moral issues. The distinction between right and wrong has been repeatedly violated. They can no longer tell the difference (see Ephesians 4:19). However, this interpretation is not strong enough for the word *seared.*

2. Seared consciences have received Satan's mark or brand of ownership. Their behavior indicates that they have come under the slavery of Satan, and they are in his service rather than God's. This interpretation fits well with verse 1, but if the Greek word means "cauterize," this wouldn't work.

3. Seared consciences have the scar tissue that the Bible elsewhere describes as a hardened heart (see Hebrews 3:12-19). In this view, the "hot iron" might be the judgment of God, wherein God "gives a person over" to his or her own persistent sin (see Romans 1:24; 1 Timothy 1:20).

become insensitive to the truth. The false teachers have themselves been so thoroughly deceived that they can no longer recognize how far they have gone from God's ways.

Satan is very crafty in his tactics: "For such boasters are false apostles, deceitful workers, disguising themselves as apostles of Christ. And no wonder! Even Satan disguises himself as an angel of light. So it is not strange if his ministers also disguise themselves as ministers of righteousness. Their end will match their deeds" (2 Corinthians 11:13-15 NRSV).

FALSE FRONTS
It is not enough that a teacher appears to know what he is talking about. He may be disciplined and moral, and even claim that he speaks for God. But if his words contradict the Bible, his teaching is false.

Like Timothy, we must guard against any teaching that causes believers to dilute or reject any aspect of their faith. Such false teaching can be very direct or extremely subtle. We must not be unduly impressed by a teacher's style or credentials; we must look to his teaching about Jesus Christ. His conclusions about Christ show the source of his message.

4:3 They forbid marriage and demand abstinence from foods.NRSV
Satan deceives people by offering a clever imitation of the real thing. The false teachers, perhaps under Jewish influence, gave stringent rules forbidding marriage and demanding abstinence from certain foods. Later, these teachings became part of what we know as Gnosticism—a belief that spirit is good, but the physical world is evil. Thus anything done for the body's pleasure or to fulfill its needs (such as sex or eating) was evil. To be "good" and to achieve a higher spiritual state, a person must deny all evil, including natural physical desires.

SCAR TISSUE
How do you react when someone questions or contradicts what you have said? Our natural tendency runs toward self-defense. We do not easily agree to being wrong. But as hard as we find it to accept our errors, we would experience greater tragedy if we lost the ability to recognize a mistake.

Paul's warning to the false teachers extends to us. Persistent refusal to admit we are wrong will make us insensitive to God's correction. One way to check yourself would be to ask three friends to tell you how well you respond to correction. Their answers may convince you to ask God for a resensitized heart and conscience.

At this point, Paul was responding to ideas and tactics that had not yet hardened into religious systems. Both the false teachers and their teaching were parasites upon the church in Ephesus, draining its life away.

Their demands made the false teachers appear self-disciplined and righteous. They established clear standards for their followers. But their rules violated God's principles and disturbed God's patterns for relationships and diet. Their strict disciplines for the body could not remove sin:

> *If with Christ you died to the elemental spirits of the universe, why do you live as if you still belonged to the world? Why do you submit to regulations, "Do not handle, Do not taste, Do not touch"? All these regulations refer to things that perish with use; they are simply human commands and teachings. These have indeed an appearance of wisdom in promoting self-imposed piety, humility, and severe treatment of the body, but they are of no value in checking self-indulgence.* (Colossians 2:20-23 NRSV)

Paul had explained the Christian understanding of marriage in 1 Corinthians 7 and Ephesians 5:21-33. Although Paul advised against marriage in some situations, he always upheld marriage as ordained by God and as an illustration of Christ's relationship to his church. But he denied the false teaching that marriage (and the sexual relationship between a man and wife) is evil and must be avoided in order for a person to be "good."

In the same way, a certain amount of abstinence from all food some of the time and from some kinds of food all the time is basic to good health. Abstinence from food for the sake of prayer (fasting) has a history of service in spiritual training. But abstaining from food does not make a person better than anyone else or bring him or her closer to God. Error can be taught under the guise of devotion.

The false teaching was wrong in its conclusions: the physical world is *not* inherently evil. The physical world **which God created**NRSV should **be received with thanksgiving by those who believe and know the truth.**NRSV All foods are acceptable by those who regard God as their Provider and thank him for them (Romans 14:6; 1 Corinthians 10:30). The Lord pronounced all foods clean (Mark 7:19; Acts 10:15). The instruction of thanksgiving applies to God's creation of marriage as well as his creation of food. Those who impugn either are offensive to God.

Instead of abiding by strict rules that deny the goodness of any pleasures, Christians are to thankfully receive all that God has given. Those *who believe and know the truth* need not refuse pleasure in order to gain special knowledge about God—they already know God! Because they know the Creator personally, they can enjoy his creation all the more.

4:4 **For everything created by God is good, and nothing is to be rejected, provided it is received with thanksgiving.**[NRSV] In opposition to the false teachers, Paul affirmed that everything God created is good, as God himself had said (see Genesis 1). The Greek word for *rejected* (*apobletos*) means "to be thrown away" or even "to regard as taboo." This doesn't mean that we are allowed to abuse what God has made and given for our pleasure or to disregard discipline regarding those pleasures. For example, food can be eaten and enjoyed, but gluttony abuses God's

> It is the biblical view of nature that gives nature a value *in itself;* not to be used merely as a weapon or argument in apologetics, but of value in itself because God made it. *Francis A. Schaeffer*

gift. Sex can be enjoyed within God's guidelines of marriage, but lust and adultery abuse God's gift. Some believers may need to practice self-discipline in order to keep from abusing God's gifts to them. We should enjoy God's creation by using his gifts to us to serve and honor him, remembering to receive *with thanksgiving.*

Acts 10:9-16 recounts a vision Peter saw in Joppa. While waiting for food to be prepared, he fell into a trance. In the dream, God directed him to eat foods that Jews regarded as nonkosher or unclean (Leviticus 11). God used the vision to impress upon Peter the importance of taking the gospel to the Gentiles. The voice during the trance said, "What God has made clean, you must not call profane" (Acts 10:15 NRSV; see also Mark 7:19).

RECEPTION AREAS
Paul provided us with three ways to respond to God's good creation:
1. Rather than taking life and its components for granted, or treating them as worthless, we should thank God for them.
2. Rather than measuring the value of any part of creation by its usefulness to us, we should regard their inherent goodness.
3. Rather than using the creation thoughtlessly or for our careless entertainment, we must use God's creation in ways that enhance our prayer life.
We should thank God and treat his gifts with respect.

In Ephesus the false teachers were known for their meddling in marriages and creating arbitrary diet restrictions. Paul responded from the perspective of God's goodness. His answer can be summed up by this statement: Given the declaration by hypocritical liars that marriage and food are bad, alongside God's affirmation that these are beneficial, who are you going to believe?

CONSUMERS OR STEWARDS
Perhaps we have drifted into the role of being merely "consumers," using and abusing more and more for our own pleasure. In contrast we find the biblical description of our role as stewards in creation. Genesis 2:15-16 describes God's purpose in placing Adam and Eve in the Garden. He gave them three responsibilities and one privilege. They were to (1) tend the Garden; (2) care for it; and (3) refrain from eating the fruit of one tree, the tree of the knowledge of good and evil. While carrying out these responsibilities, Adam and Eve were "free to eat from any tree in the garden" (Genesis 2:16 NIV). Unfortunately, too often we make decisions from day to day as if the original responsibilities had been rescinded and our only reason for being on earth was to consume what God has made. Paul's emphasis on "receiving" rather than consuming points us in the right direction. We are only stewards of what belongs to God.

4:5 For it is sanctified by the word of God and prayer.^{NKJV} As we recognize God's hand in all the pleasures of his creation and as we offer him thanks, we take what is ordinary and make it extraordinary. In short, we sanctify it, or "set it apart for special use," by making it a reason to praise and honor God.

The phrase *word of God* (*logos theou*) has drawn several interpretations:

■ Some identify Paul's expression with one of the commonly used Old Testament prayers of thanksgiving, though it seems a little redundant to refer to both formal prayers and (presumably extemporaneous) prayer as the means for sanctifying marriage and food.

■ Others point to the use of the phrase "word of God" in the Pastoral Epistles as Paul's term for the gospel itself (see 2 Timothy 2:9; Titus 1:3; 2:5). This phrase would refer to the freedom from dietary laws that the gospel brings. Food and marriage previously forbidden are set apart for special use because of Jesus' work and our response.

■ Still others see a parallel between "everything created by God is good" (4:4) and "word of God." Both phrases can allude to the Genesis account. There, God pronounced his creation good.

Therefore, we are in agreement with God's declaration when we see all creation as suitable for special use.

Taking this last possibility as the best, we could paraphrase the verse: "Everything . . . is set aside for special service because of God's declaration, to which we add our declaration of thankful prayer."

GRACE NOTES

When we prepare to eat a meal, how important is it to pause for prayer? Some may think of table grace as an irritating delay before eating. Others may think of it as a quaint but outmoded religious tradition. Many don't even think about it, having concluded that prayer before meals is unnecessary and probably meaningless. However, praying before meals is neither a formality, nor a drudgery, but a brief moment of genuine thanksgiving.

Christians who give God thanks before their meals do so for very good reasons:

- Praying before a meal reinforces a simple, clear, practical habit of acting, at least in one way, just like Jesus (see Mark 6:41; 8:6; Luke 24:30).
- Mealtime prayers are one way to obey God's family life commands (see Deuteronomy 6:4-9).
- When we offer grace at the table, we continue an unbroken tradition among believers. Paul wrote of it as an established pattern (see Romans 14:6; 1 Corinthians 10:30).
- A mealtime prayer reminds us and our children who is the real provider of our food.

4:6 If you put these instructions before the brothers and sisters, you will be a good servant of Christ Jesus, nourished on the words of the faith and of the sound teaching that you have followed.[NRSV] Here Paul directed some personal instructions for Timothy to take to the Ephesian church. His words establish a pattern of individual disciplines that would be helpful for any person taking on spiritual responsibilities. The aging apostle desired for his disciple both an effective ministry and a healthy personal life.

A *good servant* or "good minister" faithfully teaches the truth (as opposed to false teachings) to those in his care. The *instructions* are the teachings in this letter as a whole and, in particular, the opposition to false teaching described in verses 1-3. In his final letter to Timothy, Paul wrote, "And what you have heard from me through many witnesses entrust to faithful people who will be able to teach others as well" (2 Timothy 2:2 NRSV). If he would faithfully do this, Timothy himself would be *nourished* in the process. To "nourish" means to "maintain or support." In this context, nourishing involves spiritual feeding. Proper spiritual nourishment promotes spiritual growth. Proper nourishment for Timothy included constant meditation on *the words of the faith* (the gospel message) and *sound teaching* (Paul's instructions that Timothy was to communicate).

Timothy had been sent into a setting where there were conflicts over eating habits. Minor matters were being inflated into major issues. Paul was echoing the dietary concerns of the false teachers by emphasizing to Timothy that what really mattered was the feeding of the soul.

4:7 Have nothing to do with godless myths and old wives' tales.[NIV] The opposite of "words of faith" and "sound teaching" is false teaching. Paul emphasized the absurdity of the false teachings by calling them *godless myths and old wives' tales* (see also 1:3-4). *Have nothing to do with* translates one Greek word (*paraitou*—"reject, refuse, refute"). Timothy needed to understand the false teaching in order to fight it effectively

> Trying to live the Christian life implies and leads to failure; *training* to live the Christian life puts even failures to good use. *Neil Wilson*

with the truth, but then he was to completely reject it. There can be no compromise between the truth and false teaching. Timothy may well have remembered the counsel that he and Paul had given to the Christians in Colosse: "Let your conversation be always full of grace, seasoned with salt, so that you may know how to answer everyone" (Colossians 4:6 NIV).

SIDETRACKED
Christians who are convinced that they must answer every question and be familiar with every controversy will wear themselves out running down Satan's rabbit trails. Learning Scripture and understanding spiritual principles to give better answers to others provides more benefit than mentally cataloging issues and viewpoints. This is demonstrated by cults who use Scripture out of context to prove their point. Note, for example, how Satan tried to use Scripture in his tempting of Jesus. Jesus answered Satan's misuse of Scripture with properly applied Scripture.

We must not be ignorant of what others are teaching, but we must emphasize a thorough grasp of biblical truth and a central commitment to Christ.

Train yourself in godliness.[NRSV] Paul often borrowed athletic words to emphasize the need for spiritual training (see 1 Corinthians 9:24; Galatians 2:2; 5:7; 2 Timothy 4:7). "Training" emphasizes the point that spiritual development does not happen by chance. An athlete is focused and committed, constantly training, refusing to let up, always striving. Believers must have the same focus and commitment, refusing to be sidetracked by wrong teaching.

Godliness means correct behavior and genuine Christian faith, first in the heart but also in visible expression according to the standard of God's Word (3:16). It takes self-control, continual work, and commitment day by day as we strive to please God despite our sinfulness and weaknesses. But as we can train our bodies for physical feats, we can approach the various aspect of our spiritual life as training in godliness.

Paul was urging Timothy to model an alternative training program in Ephesus. The false teachers were promoting their system, which included controversy, heresy, legalism, and general rebellion against God. The freedom that we have through Jesus Christ does not give us license to live any way we want. Rather, it frees us from futile attempts to earn God's favor and challenges us to pursue a life of obedience based on love. In too many cases today, Christians have resisted training by calling spiritual disciplines legalism or asceticism. This has resulted, however, in ill-informed, spiritually malnourished, and unprepared believers. To use Paul's imagery, Christians want to be on Christ's Olympic team, but they don't want to live as athletes in training. We must never shift our primary focus from all that Christ has done for us, but we must not neglect the kind of living he expects of us.

TRAINING PLAN
Throughout much of Christian history, people have practiced the classic disciplines. Some of these, like study, meditation, prayer, and fasting, can be used for internal and private spiritual training. Others, such as solitude, silence, service, and submission, are external and visible experiences. Some, like worship and confession, require participation by other believers. All of them have been subject to misuse, but they have also proven to be effective "training exercises." They are worth exploring. Even though initially they may seem ineffective (remember what it was like to run around the track the first time when you were out of shape?), they can bring about beneficial change in your Christian life.

How would you describe your present spiritual training plan? How many "exercises" are you practicing, and how often do you do them? Compared to a year ago, how is your spiritual training progressing?

4:8 **For bodily exercise profits a little, but godliness is profitable for all things, having promise of the life that now is and of that which is to come.**^{NKJV} Physical exercise, while benefiting the body, has no eternal benefit. Some interpreters have drawn a distinction here between *bodily exercise* and bodily discipline. But since exercise serves as the most obvious form of physical discipline, it is not likely that this is what Paul had in mind. A body discipline such as fasting would not properly be called an exercise, though it may benefit the body in a dietary way. But it is not as common an experience as regular physical exercise. Being in good physical shape positively affects health and perhaps mental outlook; yet godliness affects everything. It benefits its practitioner both for this life and for eternity.

Paul is not devaluing physical exercise. He believed his readers would agree with the importance of physical training, so he could use it as an illustration. The key issue is how we use our time. Some people spend ten to fifteen hours a week in physical activity, but spend little time in Bible study, prayer, and service. Paul was not urging Timothy toward a life of asceticism or stiff and narrow godliness. His practical instructions (see 4:12-16) were to be carried out in relationship with others. Paul did not mean by "godliness" only personal piety, personal holiness, or deeper devotion to Christ; he implied service and ministry to others.

SHAPE UP
Are you in shape both physically and spiritually? While physical fitness offers benefits, spiritual health (godliness) is even more important. Like bodily exercise, spiritual exercise requires discipline, daily effort, and ongoing commitment. As an athlete performs daily exercises to strengthen muscles for better performance, so "spiritual athletes" must regularly train their "spiritual muscles." The following general disciplines ought to be part of every Christian's life:
- Reading God's Word
- Applying God's Word
- Attending public worship
- Praying
- Giving time, money, and abilities to God's service

4:9 **The saying is sure and worthy of full acceptance.**^{NRSV} Questions have been raised about whether the *saying* to which Paul referred is in the preceding or following passages. While the next verse does not easily fit the description of a "saying," Paul had twice before used this formula (1:15; 3:1), each time with the saying coming right after the introduction. Here, however, it seems reasonable to assume that Paul changed the order. He underscored the importance of the saying by following it with his approving statement.

That "godliness is profitable for all things, having promise of the life that now is and of that which is to come" (4:8 NKJV) is a true saying. Believers who train themselves for godliness really do have the best of both worlds—they receive immediate and eternal benefits, and they benefit others as they instruct and model the Christian life.

COMPASS POINTS
Paul reminded Timothy of key truths that they held in common. Believers can benefit by knowing important biblical teachings by heart. Jesus' statement of the great commandment (Mark 12:29-31), the brief gospel (John 3:16), the Lord's Prayer (Matthew 6:9-13), along with sayings like those Paul included to Timothy, are like compass points for Christians. Having these words readily in mind helps keep believers on course. How many trustworthy sayings can you recite? How many do you live?

4:10 **For to this end we toil and struggle.**^{NRSV} The *toil and struggle* in the daily spiritual exercise of godliness has a goal, an *end*— eternity with God. The "toil and struggle" do not assure us of eternity, rather we are already assured of eternity **because we have our hope set on the living God, who is the Savior of all people, especially of those who believe.**^{NRSV} We toil and struggle, not *for* eternity, but *because of* eternity. Eternity with God is not just hope for a possible occurrence, it is hope set on a certainty. Why? Because it is hope set on *the living God*—not on a philosophy, a human being, a material possession, or a standard of behavior (see Colossians 1:29).

Hope grows as we remember the promise of the resurrection. Because Christ came back to life, so will all believers. All Christians, including those living when Christ returns, will live with Christ forever. Therefore, we need not despair about tragedy and death. God will change defeat to victory. Paul comforted the Thessalonians with the hope of eternal life (1 Thessalonians 4:13-18).

As elsewhere (1:1; 2:3; Titus 1:3; 2:10; 3:4), Paul attached the role of Savior to God. God in his fullness—Father, Son, and Holy Spirit—was active in carrying out the plan of salvation. Christ is the *Savior of all people* in the sense that his work on the cross was sufficient to provide salvation for everyone (see 2:6). God desires that all people be saved (1:15); but people still may reject him. Some have interpreted "Savior of all" to mean that God does good to all people and will eventually save everyone. More likely, Paul was referring to God's offer of salvation to everyone.

The phrase *especially of those who believe* stresses that God's salvation actually becomes effective only for those who trust him. Universalism is not taught in this passage. The offer of salvation has a universal range but does not impose itself on those unwilling to respond. This argument was aimed at the false teachers who attempted to restrict salvation to an elite few and put many more requirements on it than believing in God.

THE RACE
Christian ministry and leadership require hard work. Jesus himself assured us we would have troubles (John 16:33). But the training on Paul's mind included resistance, difficulty, and hardship. Toil and struggle in spiritual matters parallel the effort and agony experienced by the athlete in training and competition.

Few athletes enjoy the drudgery of training, the pains that accompany and follow exertion, or the loneliness of preparation that the cheering crowds seldom see. But the thrill of competing, of doing one's best, of winning the race, somehow make the rest endurable. Again, Jesus is our example: "Let us fix our eyes on Jesus, the author and perfecter of our faith, who for the joy set before him endured the cross, scorning its shame, and sat down at the right hand of the throne of God" (Hebrews 12:2 NIV).

None of us deserve or earn the privilege of running the race (Hebrews 12:1); membership in Christ is a free gift. Once on the team, though, we are challenged to train and run our race!

4:11 Command and teach these things.[NIV] Timothy may have been somewhat shy, certainly less assertive than the fiery Paul (see also 1 Corinthians 16:10-11). Paul encouraged Timothy to take charge as he told Timothy to *command and teach.* The first word referred to the role of confrontation; the second, to the role of instruction. Timothy should teach *these things,* probably referring to all the matters in this letter. To people like the false teachers and their disciples, Timothy would have to issue commands. It was also his responsibility to continually train the believers in Ephesus.

4:12 Don't let anyone look down on you because you are young.[NIV] The Greek word *neotes* (translated "young") could refer to anyone up to the age of forty. By this time, Timothy was probably in his thirties. Although he was not a youth, he may have been considerably younger than some believers in his congregation. After serving under Paul, they may have looked down on this younger man who was put in charge of their church. Timothy could not control anyone's prejudice about his age, but he was not to be intimidated. He must not give anyone ammunition to use his youthfulness against him.

An implication of Paul's instructions applies to those in the church who were older. While youth were expected to persevere even in the face of belittling, elders were expected to avoid looking down on those with less experience.

But set an example for the believers in speech, in life, in love, in faith and in purity.[NIV] This is wise advice from a wise church planter and leader. Paul knew firsthand the potential for problems in any church where people of a variety of religious backgrounds, cultures, and ages come together. Timothy's character, and not his age, would determine his authority to lead. Paul called Timothy's specific role *an example*—meaning he was to be a pattern or model. Whatever his age, Timothy was not to allow anyone to minimize his role but was to persist in being a good example.

SET AN EXAMPLE
Throughout Scripture, setting an example is stressed as an important element of discipleship.

■ *Matthew 11:29—"Take my yoke upon you and learn from me."*
Jesus told his followers to learn from his example of gentleness and humility.

■ *Philippians 3:17—"Join with others in following my example."*
Paul urged believers to follow his example of enthusiasm, perseverance, and maturity.

■ *1 Thessalonians 1:6-7—"You became imitators of us and of the Lord. . . . And so you became a model to all the believers."*
The new Christians at Thessalonica received training in discipleship from Paul, and even in suffering they modeled before others what they had learned.

■ *1 Timothy 1:16—"In me . . . Christ Jesus might display his unlimited patience as an example for those who would believe on him."*
Paul used his unworthiness to receive Christ as an example of grace so that no one would hold back from coming to Christ.

■ *1 Peter 5:3—"Not lording it over those entrusted to you, but being examples to the flock."*
Peter taught Christian leaders to lead by example, not by commands.

As the body of Christ, believers must show Christ to the world by being examples. Nonbelievers should be able to see Christ in believers and be so drawn to what they see that they seek Christ and his salvation. What kind of example are you?

AGE *AND* BEAUTY
Timothy was young in comparison to many under his care in the Ephesian church. It would have been easy for older Christians to look down on him because of his youth. He had to earn the respect of his elders by setting an example in his speech, life, love, faith, and purity. Regardless of your age, God can use you. Whether you are young or old, don't think of your age as a handicap. Live so others can see Christ in you.

Timothy was not left to ponder how Paul expected him to be an example. Rather than offering general motivation to be an example, the old apostle issued a checklist:

- *Speech*—Our words create impressions that either facilitate or complicate all other communication. Timothy was to speak with gentle authority while avoiding useless or argumentative conversation (see 4:11; 5:1; 6:3-4, 20). Hopefully what we desire to say will be so important that we find the best way to say it. Otherwise, our tongue may ruin our best intentions (see James 3:1-12; Colossians 4:5-6).
- *Life*—Our life-style as well as our specific behaviors must be consistent with the gospel. Timothy was to conduct himself as a representative of Jesus Christ even in the details of daily living (see 6:6-10). Unfortunately, when actions loudly contradict words, the truth can hardly be heard (see Ephesians 4:22-28; 1 Peter 2:12).
- *Love*—When we say the right words and live the right way but lack love, we are demonstrating a legalistic view of God's expectations (see 1 Corinthians 13:1-7). After words and actions have had their say, love makes the message ring true or false.
- *Faith*—Sooner or later, people around us will need to understand what motivates our speech, life, and love. A genuine combination of the above will present to others a way of life filled with hope. They may attempt to deflect God's overtures through us by saying, "That stuff works for you; it could never work for me." We will have to remind them of our (all too obvious) humanity and point out that what they are sensing has much more to do with God's work in us than with our meager efforts (see Ephesians 2:8-10; 1 Peter 3:15-16). Faith finally speaks clearly when speech, life, and love have created a hearing.
- *Purity*—Paul ended this list with a rarely used term for virtue and chastity. As used here, the word implies integrity and consistency and reinforces the entire list. Perhaps Paul even had

the idea of transparency in mind. The above qualities were to
be developed, not just for public display, but as the uniform
texture of Timothy's life.

4:13 Until I arrive.^{NRSV} Paul hoped to visit Timothy and the believers
in Ephesus soon (see also 3:14-15). Besides carefully observing
his private life to keep it above reproach, Timothy was also to
give attention and preparation to his public ministry in three main
areas, which are then described.

**Devote yourself to the public reading of Scripture, to preach-
ing and to teaching.**^{NIV} The *Scripture* that Paul mentioned is the
Old Testament (although as Gospels and letters were written and
circulated, these were also read in the congregation). Timothy
was to regularly do *public reading of Scripture* in his congregation, a practice begun in Old Testament times (see Exodus 24:7;
Deuteronomy 31:11; Joshua 8:35; 2 Kings 23:2-3; Nehemiah 8:1-
18) and continued in the synagogues (Luke 4:16; Acts 15:21;
Colossians 4:16; 1 Thessalonians 5:27).

EXPOSED TO THE TRUTH
In ancient times, reading was done out loud. Furthermore, most
people did not own copies of the Scriptures. Therefore, the
Scriptures were read out loud in public meetings. Paul's letters,
for example, were written to be read aloud to people who were
good listeners. Moreover, Paul insisted that once the Scriptures
were read aloud, they were to be applied and taught. In your
personal life as well as in your church, is the Bible regularly
read and studied?

Teaching refers to training in Christian doctrine. The people
needed to know, understand, and constantly be reminded of the
great truths of the Christian faith.
    Preaching could also be translated "exhortation." In addition
to reading the Scripture, Timothy was to exhort, that is, to warn,
advise, and urge his listeners regarding the words of Scripture,
helping them apply those words to their daily lives.

WHAT TO LOOK FOR IN A CHURCH OR MINISTER
Paul's instructions to Timothy provide helpful criteria in choos-
ing a church or calling a minister:
■ How does the church or pastor exemplify the Christian life?
   (4:12)
■ How does the church or minister regard the reading of God's
   Word? (4:13)

- How are various gifts used in the overall ministry of the church? What are the pastor's gifts? (4:14)
- What evidence can be seen that the church or pastor is making spiritual progress? (4:15)
- In what ways does the church or pastor practice honest self-examination? (4:16)
- How does the church or pastor demonstrate a genuine concern for the salvation of others? (4:16)

4:14 Do not neglect your gift.^{NIV} Others should not look down on Timothy (4:12), and neither should he look down on himself. Paul reminded Timothy that he had the necessary requisites to do the difficult work in Ephesus. Among them was a spiritual *gift* from God. Though Paul did not define the gift specifically, he was concerned that Timothy might hesitate or fail to use it. When we see abilities of all kinds (spiritual, relational, technical) as gifts from God, we will be in a better position to see his hand at work through people's efforts.

Which was given to you through prophecy with the laying on of hands by the council of elders.^{NRSV} Timothy's commission as a church leader was confirmed by prophecy (see also 1:18) and by the laying on of hands by the elders of the church. Timothy's gift had been publicly recognized. This should help Timothy's wavering confidence. Timothy could do the task because God had called him to do it, had equipped him to do it, and would be with him through it.

Paul had been through the experience he was recalling for Timothy. He had been set apart for ministry through prophecy by the elders in Antioch. Acts 13:1-3 describes the process. In the context of worship, God's Spirit impressed on the gathered believers that Paul and Barnabas were to be sent out as representatives of Christ. Timothy may have been identified in this way before he

---

RESPONSE-ABILITY
As a young leader in a church that had a lot of problems, Timothy may have felt intimidated. But the elders and prophets encouraged him and charged him to use his spiritual gift responsibly. Highly skilled and talented athletes lose their abilities if their muscles aren't toned by constant use, and our spiritual gifts become ineffective if we don't put them to work. Our talents are improved by exercise, but failing to use them causes them to waste away from lack of practice and nourishment. What gifts and abilities has God given you? Use them regularly in serving God and others. (See Romans 12:1-8; 2 Timothy 1:6-8 for more on using our God-given abilities.)

left Lystra with Paul (Acts 16:1-5), or the laying on of hands may have occurred in Ephesus itself before Paul left him there.

The *laying on of hands* usually signified a passing on of leadership (see also Numbers 27:18-23; Deuteronomy 34:9; Acts 6:6; 13:1-3; 8:18; Hebrews 6:2). It was a physical gesture of empowerment. In the early history of Christianity, the "laying on of hands" made prayer and encouragement visible. Though this became a traditional gesture of ordination, it probably still had a more immediate spiritual impact here—the elders acting as vehicles for the Spirit to reveal and confirm his plans for someone's life.

4:15 Be diligent in these matters; give yourself wholly to them, so that everyone may see your progress.[NIV] Paul called Timothy to be *diligent* in carrying out the instructions included in this letter. *Wholly* means to give yourself completely over to the task, to make it your number one priority. As Timothy applied himself *wholly* to Paul's instructions, progress would be seen both in his personal life and in the church, and this would end any questioning about Timothy's maturity or credibility.

PERFECTION OR PROGRESS
Paul's expectations for Timothy may have been as intimidating as the circumstances facing the young leader. His character standards were high and difficult. Here Paul added a ray of hope. He wanted Timothy to make *progress*. The yardstick of perfection measures discouragement; but progress keeps a person going even beyond failures.

When we claim or aim at perfection, we invite others to focus on our all-too-obvious shortfalls. When we give ourselves to making progress as we train ourselves in godliness, progress will be noticed. If we think we have "arrived," others will point out how little we have changed. But if we demonstrate we are "in motion," they will note how far we have come. They may even be tempted to come along!

Paul began this chapter pointing out that the Spirit had predicted the falling away of believers into error. The false teachers were promoting progress, but it was progress in the wrong direction! Some were renouncing the faith and pursuing training in godlessness. Timothy's task was to correct those who had gone astray and to provide an example for all the believers of what it means to make progress in the right direction.

4:16 Pay close attention to yourself and to your teaching.[NRSV] In conclusion, Paul advised Timothy to *pay close attention* to his private life and his public ministry to the church according to Paul's instructions. His conduct in both areas must be above reproach.

A CHECKLIST FOR PROGRESS
The following questions, focused on your past year, may help you measure your personal spiritual progress:
- What are the three significant spiritual lessons you have learned?
- What relationships have you begun or strengthened?
- What special projects have you completed?
- What causes have you advanced?
- In what areas of your personal character have you progressed toward maturity?
- How have you utilized your resources and gifts?

Continue in these things, for in doing this you will save both yourself and your hearers.NRSV Timothy was not only supposed to watch his steps, he also was to *continue* in motion. *Continue* means "to persevere, to make progress." *Save yourself* refers to perseverance. We cannot save ourselves by good works (Titus 3:5); we cannot earn our salvation. Paul was talking about being an example, leading, and teaching the value of being faithful to the end. All believers must apply this. Those who had been believers for a while

> The minister must be concerned with his own spiritual discipline. In the development of his spiritual life, he cannot lead others any farther than he is willing to go himself. *Holmes Rolston*

should be examples to the recent converts. And the recent converts should persevere so as to realize the full benefits of their salvation.

Timothy's progress would benefit others. His example would facilitate the salvation of his *hearers.* Of course, God alone can save, but Paul's words focus on the responsibility of spiritual leaders. By paying attention to his personal spiritual life, Timothy would work out his own salvation (in the sense described in Philippians 2:12), and by paying attention to his public ministry, he would help others do the same.

ON GUARD!
We know the importance of watching our life closely. We must be on constant guard against falling into sin that can so easily destroy us. Yet we must watch what we believe and teach just as closely. Wrong beliefs can quickly lead us into sin and heresy. We should be on guard against those who would persuade us that how we live is more important than what we believe.

1 Timothy 5:1–6:2

Beginning with 4:6, Paul focused on Timothy's personal life. He included wide-ranging instructions designed to keep his youthful appointee on track. Paul assured Timothy that his efforts would ensure the salvation of his "hearers" (4:16).

Paul thought of Timothy's audience in Ephesus. There, men and women of all ages were under Timothy's care. Paul thought of the groups within the congregation needing special attention. He wanted Timothy to practice good general principles of personal care and also to deal with some specific people-needs. Paul chose the treatment of widows and elders as prime examples. He also had some instructions concerning slaves who were believers.

IT'S RELATIVE
Paul did not see the church as a replacement for the family. People need to take their family responsibilities seriously. But the church must respond to special opportunities for service. The following principles govern how the church should respond to special needs:

- There are appropriate ways to treat others of different sex or age, and they must be painstakingly followed (5:1-2).
- In the absence of other resources, the church should meet the needs of those who are destitute (5:3, 5, 16).
- Families must carry the primary responsibility for their own needs (5:4, 8, 16).
- If at all possible, those being helped should help others even while they themselves are in need (5:10).
- Churches should not encourage overdependence from those who can still make significant contributions (5:11-15).

These relational principles can benefit most churches today. Our helping tends to be too sporadic, too crisis-oriented, and lacking in either consistency or the courage to call family members to care for their relatives or believers to really care for one another.

5:1 Do not speak harshly to an older man, but speak to him as to a father, to younger men as brothers.^{NRSV} Paul had instructed Timo-

thy to "set an example for the believers in speech, in life, in love, in
faith and in purity" (4:12 NIV). The wise apostle knew that for this
young minister to remain above reproach in dealing with the variety of people in his church, he would have to treat them as family.
Speak harshly refers to "verbal pounding," or disrespectful treatment. If correction became necessary, Timothy should not speak
harshly; instead, he should appeal to the older men with kind exhor-
tation, as if he were speaking to his father. Even correction or
rebuke was to be phrased in encouraging terms.

In the same way, Timothy was to speak kindly to younger men,
as if they were his brothers. He was to lead them gently. Without
using the specific term, Paul was speaking about submission.
Timothy was to practice submissive gentleness in correcting his
seniors. He was to do the same in treating his juniors.

PECKING ORDER
Most human systems quickly establish a pecking order. The
purposes of the system are often lost in the scramble for
power. Many leaders spend more time scheming to remain
leaders than they do leading. Conversely, Paul's directions to
Timothy would only be effective for someone who desires effectiveness rather than prestige.

Paul directed Timothy into a leadership style described by
Jesus himself: "Whoever wants to become great among you
must be your servant, and whoever wants to be first must be
the slave of all" (Mark 10:43-44 NIV). The same directions hold
true today. In whatever systems we find ourselves (family,
social, work, church), we should not seek leverage over others.
Instead, we should treat others as we want to be treated. We
should serve instead of insisting on being served.

**5:2 Older women as mothers, younger women as sisters, with all
purity.**^NKJV Jesus recognized the personhood of women. They
were no longer to be treated as property and, therefore, no longer
to be demeaned. Paul affirmed this principle as he explained to
Timothy how to treat his sisters in the faith. The most effective
method for remaining above reproach would be to treat church
members as family members. Evidence from elsewhere in the
Pastoral Epistles suggests that there may have been some sexual
exploitation occurring within the church, perhaps by the false
teachers (see 2 Timothy 3:6-7).

Paul perceived even within pagan cultures an awareness of the
respect required for families to survive. Healthy relationships between sons, fathers, daughters, and mothers were appropriate
analogies for how to treat others.

Today, men in the ministry can avoid improper attitudes toward women by following Paul's advice. Men who see women as fellow members in God's family will treat them *with all purity*—respecting, protecting, and helping them grow spiritually. Purity refers to the same quality that Paul mentioned in 4:12. It covers moral behavior and transparent attitudes without hidden intentions.

ALL IN THE FAMILY
The same guidelines that guard families from immorality and impropriety can guard our relationships within the body of Christ:

- There should be no sex outside of marriage, and even lustful thoughts are prohibited.
- Believers are to guard one another against sexual exploitation in the same way that we would protect a family member. Depending on the culture, certain members may require special protection. In our own culture, women and children have been subjects of mistreatment.
- We are to pursue each other's best interests and development as people. Inappropriate sexual conduct would surely hinder a person's spiritual growth.
- Sexual humor, overfamiliarity, and inappropriate or unwelcomed touching are unacceptable behaviors for believers.
- Pursuing uncomfortable verbal intimacies or suggestive conversations, even if not accompanied by physical contact, can be harmful to another believer, hindering his or her spiritual growth and blocking further ministry.
- Brotherly attitudes demand a respect for privacy and an active effort to relate to women with emphasis on their personhood rather than their sexuality.
- Even "innocent" behavior at inappropriate times or places should be avoided. Counseling or visitation one-on-one with members of the opposite sex should be done with another person present. "Abstain from every form of evil" (1 Thessalonians 5:22 NRSV).

5:3 Honor widows who are really widows.NRSV The helpless, especially widows and orphans, always have received God's special care and concern. Paul's insistence rested on the numerous Old Testament passages where God had made known his will in these specific matters. Note the following verses from God's law (quoted from NRSV):

- *"The LORD your God is God of gods and Lord of lords . . . who executes justice for the orphan and the widow."* (Deuteronomy 10:17-18)
- *"Every third year you shall bring out the full tithe of your produce for that year, and store it within your towns; . . . the*

> orphans, and the widows in your towns, may come and eat
> their fill so that the LORD your God may bless you in all the
> work that you undertake." (Deuteronomy 14:28-29)
> ■ "You shall not take a widow's garment in pledge. . . . When
> you reap your harvest in your field and forget a sheaf in the
> field, you shall not go back to get it; it shall be left for the
> alien, the orphan, and the widow. . . . When you beat your
> olive trees, do not strip what is left; it shall be for the alien,
> the orphan, and the widow. When you gather the grapes of
> your vineyard, do not glean what is left; it shall be for the
> alien, the orphan, and the widow. . . . I am commanding you
> to do this." (Deuteronomy 24:17, 19-22)

(See also Exodus 22:22-24; Proverbs 15:25; Isaiah 1:17; Jeremiah 7:6; Zechariah 7:8-10; Malachi 3:5; James 1:27.)

The believers in the early church pooled their resources to help those in need (Acts 2:44-47); they gave generously to help disaster-ridden churches (1 Corinthians 16:1-4); they took care of a large number of widows (Acts 6:1-6). These widows, in turn, gave valuable service to the church. Paul mentioned some of these acts of service in verse 10.

Because there were no pensions, no Social Security, no life insurance, and few honorable jobs for women, widows were usually unable to support themselves. But the care of widows was apparently becoming a major burden to the congregation in Ephesus and called for clarification as to who was really a widow qualifying for support. Paul advised Timothy to identify those widows who were *really widows* and help them. The responsibility for caring for the helpless naturally falls first on their families, the people whose lives are most closely linked with theirs. Paul stressed the importance of families caring for the needs of wid-

---

A HELPING HAND
We should support those who have no families and should also help the elderly, young, disabled, ill, or poverty-stricken with their emotional and spiritual needs. Often families who are caring for their own helpless members have heavy burdens. They may need extra money, a listening ear, a helping hand, or a word of encouragement. Interestingly, people who are helped often turn around and help others, turning the church into more of a caring community. Don't wait for people to ask. Take the initiative and look for ways to serve them.

---

ows and not leaving it for the church to do, so that the church can

care for widows "who are really in need"—those who have no
families. A widow who had no children or other family members
to support her was doomed to poverty. The church should *honor*
such widows ("give [them] proper recognition," NIV), meaning
both respectful care and material support. Their worth to the
body of Christ was to be demonstrated in every way possible.

**5:4 But if a widow has children or grandchildren, these should
learn first of all to put their religion into practice by caring
for their own family and so repaying their parents and grandparents.**[NIV] A widow who had children or grandchildren should
be able to look to them for support. By caring for their widowed
mother or grandmother, these children would be putting *their religion into practice.* Paul pointed to the cycle of life as an opportunity to practice obedience to God and show appreciation to our
parents for earlier care. Our parents watched over us when we
were helpless. We ought to do no less when the roles are
reversed. Family members should look after their parents and
grandparents. Paul affirmed this as basic common sense understood even by those who were unbelievers (see 5:8).

PRACTICE FACILITY
Young people hear from society about the importance of caring
for the elderly, but they should see that value demonstrated
within the church. Local congregations are ideal settings for
youth to practice caring skills that the Bible teaches. They can
also gain confidence in those skills by practice and repetition. A
local church may team them up with "adopted parents and
grandparents" so they can practice elder care.
     In this way, children can return love and care that was shown
to them when they were young and unable to support themselves. God has never withdrawn the fifth commandment,
"Honor your father and your mother" (Exodus 20:12 NKJV). He
intends it to be a pattern for all generations (see also Jesus'
teaching in Matthew 15:4-6).

What then transforms a commonsense awareness into putting
"religion into practice"? One way of defining common sense
describes it as a collection of actions that most people agree
ought to be done. Belief in action, or piety, points to a greater
consistency between what we say and what we do. Putting religion into practice, or "religious duty" (NRSV), implies that believers are busy doing what most people agree are important and
worthwhile things to do, like caring for one's parents in their old
age. Applying what we understand to be true involves (1) willful

decisions, (2) learned behavior, and (3) God's help. When a local church is functioning by biblical standards, believers have a God-designed environment to learn what it means to put their faith into action.

PRACTICAL SPIRITUALITY
The church (at least in North America) will face the needs of the elderly in greater numbers. People are living longer. As a result of family mobility and broken relationships, more and more isolated persons may seek out local churches for help and companionship. In addition to teaching that believers should care for their parents and grandparents, churches will have to respond to the needs of those who are alone.

How does your church presently address the needs of the elderly? What plans have you made to care for your parents or grandparents? Paul's warning in verse 8 provides a haunting rebuke to any believer who would treat lightly his or her family responsibilities.

Paul wanted Christian families to be as mutually supporting as possible. He insisted that children and grandchildren take care of the widows in their families; he suggested that younger widows remarry and start new families (5:14); he ordered the church not to support lazy members who refused to work (2 Thessalonians 3:10). The church has always had limited resources and has always had to balance financial responsibility with generosity. It only makes sense for members to work as hard as they can and to be as independent as possible, so they can adequately care for themselves and for less fortunate members. When church members are both responsible and generous, everyone's needs will be met.

HELP FROM HOME
It is a great scandal for Christian families to let their parents languish in loneliness in nursing homes. Aging parents need more than economic attention. But churches often realize that certain families, who are able, refuse to care for their own. What principles should be considered by a church fulfilling its duty to the aged poor?
- The church must challenge those who are shirking their family duties.
- Because relatives refuse to provide care does not exempt the church from responsibility.
- The church should move cautiously in making judgments about family care. Sometimes those who seem to have resources may be deficient in ways not immediately apparent to outsiders. Family history and emotional problems may affect the ability of relatives to assist.

■ Care should also be taken for the care-givers. While some relatives abandon family members, others end up carrying a
crushing burden in caring for a loved one. Sometimes, the
real ministry of the church means giving support for the ones
who faithfully fulfill their family duties.

 HELPING WIDOWS
Churches can offer very practical help to those without a mate.
Help usually comes when people are informed. Church leaders
should ask about the specific needs of members of the congregation who are living alone.
■ Churches should help grieving members when they lose a
loved one immediately and with long-term recovery.
■ Churches can encourage and assist in the writing of wills.
■ Churches can help widows plan and manage their money so
that it goes further by offering counseling or classes on financial planning. Widows should be protected from being
exploited by unscrupulous investment and insurance sales-
people.
■ Churches can offer training, support, and prayer to family
members who care for the aged. Many people are uninformed of the steps and costs involved in various phases of
care. Information on nursing homes, in-home nursing or hos-
pice care, estate settling, etc., can all be offered through the
church.
■ Churches should develop tactful ways to call on and encourage the children of Christian widows to share in their responsibilities. Distant relatives may need to be contacted.
Coordination and objectivity can sometimes be offered by
church members who care but are not directly involved in the
family situation.
■ Teaching on the care and the usefulness of the elderly should
be a regular part of the ministry of the church.

For this is good and acceptable before God.^{NKJV} God is pleased
when we care for our family members' needs. God underscores
the importance of fulfilling these duties by connecting them with
the promise of personal benefits in the fifth commandment:
"Honor your father and your mother, so that you may live long in
the land the LORD your God is giving you" (Exodus 20:12 NIV).
Honor certainly involves more than providing care in old age, but
the caring treatment of our seniors is part of God's plan.

**5:5 The real widow, left alone, has set her hope on God and con-
tinues in supplications and prayers night and day.**^{NRSV} The
real widow (see also 5:3) is *left alone,* that is, destitute, with no
one to turn to for help. However, a Christian widow could turn to
the church, setting her hope on God. The widows that the church

should support are described as women who, since their husbands' deaths, dedicated themselves to God, with a constant attitude of *supplications and prayers* in service to the Lord. Anna, the prophetess, fit this description: "This woman was a widow of about eighty-four years, who did not depart from the temple, but served God with fastings and prayers night and day" (Luke 2:37 NKJV).

This verse sets up a spiritual contrast regarding the lives of two kinds of widows. The "real widow" lives trusting God and ministering to others. She is not wrapped up in self-pity, but finds a place of effective service, beginning with prayer for others. Meanwhile, the other widow is lost to a self-centered life-style that Paul described as death.

5:6 But the widow who lives for pleasure is dead even while she lives.NRSV Unlike their duties to the dedicated widows described in verse 5, the church was *not* to support widows who used their widowhood to live for pleasure or resorted to immoral means of supporting themselves (possibly a reference to prostitution—practically the only "job" a woman could find in New Testament times). A widow who used her life chasing after pleasure was *dead even while she lived* (see also Matthew 8:22; John 11:25; and Ephesians 5:14). Indeed, those who choose to live for pleasure alone will inevitably experience such profound spiritual emptiness that they are actually dead even as they live (see Ecclesiastes 2:1-11, 24-26 for more on the emptiness of living for pleasure). Obviously, such widows should not be supported by the church.

Paul's instructions establish a strong case for wise assistance. In pointing out the error of widows who waste their lives, Paul did not excuse the church to refuse ministry to those deserving. Rather, the widow's choices define the ministry the church can have in her life. Honoring and assisting a widow who lives for pleasure would enable her to do wrong. But correcting her and offering forgiveness through repentance could still be an effective ministry by the church.

5:7 Give the people these instructions, too, so that no one may be open to blame.NIV Repeating his command from 4:11 to "command and teach these things," Paul told Timothy to also give *these instructions* (regarding the church's responsibility to widows, family members' responsibility to widows, and the widows' life-style) to the people. If all the instructions would be followed, no one would be open to reproach.

PLAN, DON'T FAIL
In caring for widows, the church that fails to plan actually plans to fail. The biblical instructions regarding these responsibilities should be common knowledge among the members of a church. In many cases, the church should have specific programs to prepare people for the needs created by the aging and the death of spouses. When a church does not prepare for the inevitable, it loses opportunities for effective ministry.

How does your church respond to the immediate needs of families when a loved one dies? What specific programs or plans are in place to respond to long-term needs of widows and others left without support? How specific are your own family plans regarding the care of parents and grandparents?

5:8 **Whoever does not provide for relatives, and especially for family members, has denied the faith and is worse than an unbeliever.**NRSV To default on the basic care and support of a family member is the same as denying the faith, for no one can claim love and allegiance to God and at the same time neglect his or her family (see Matthew 5:46-47). To do so makes a person *worse than an unbeliever,* for even unbelieving idol-worshipers understood the responsibility of caring for family needs. There are some obligations to those who have given us life that simply must be honored. Our families provide an arena in which we can demonstrate the quality of our love for God. John provided a scathing rebuke to any believer who would dare to claim affection for God while blatantly ignoring the needs of others: "If anyone has material possessions and sees his brother in need but has no pity on him, how can the love of God be in him?" (1 John 3:17 NIV). For an illustration from the Old Testament, John referred to the failure of Cain to care for his brother Abel (1 John 3:11-20; Genesis 4:1-12). Believers who neglect the most basic human responsibilities have, for all practical purposes, *denied the faith.*

5:9 **No widow may be put on the list of widows unless she is over sixty, [and] has been faithful to her husband.**NIV Paul spelled out the "proper recognition" (5:3) that the "real" widows should receive. The *list of widows* may have been a particular group or order of widows who had taken a pledge committing themselves to work for the church in exchange for financial support. Part of this pledge was a commitment not to remarry so that these women could serve the Lord without distraction (see 5:12). Most importantly, however, the existence of a list indicates that the church identified those in need. The believers combined their resources to meet the needs of a known group.

FAMILY TIES
Frequent mobility and family fragmentation weakens or destroys the capability of family members to care for one another. Dependence on government programs may replace personal accountability for the welfare of loved ones. How can grandchildren care for grandparents they barely recognize?

The home remains the best possible training environment for healthy people. Parents teach their children unforgettable lessons. Children take most of their cues about honoring their parents by watching how Mom and Dad honor the grandparents. If our children see the way we, as parents, care for our parents, they will understand the importance of providing for our care in the future. Healthy, practical honor becomes a priceless gift that one generation gives to another. Disrespect and lack of care provide harmful guidance to those who must next fill the role of parents.

In order to be included on this list, a widow had to meet three qualifications:

First, she had to be at least sixty years old. (Paul's reasons for keeping younger widows off the list for the church's support are explained in verses 11-15.) This was probably not so much a strictly observed age as it was a generally accepted stage beyond which a person's prospects for remarriage were doubtful. Second, she must have been faithful to her husband. This phrase is also translated, "married only once" (NRSV). This qualification is the same as that given for church leaders and deacons (3:2, 12) for the same reason. Obviously a widow who remarried should not be receiving assistance from the church. The third qualification is described in the next verse.

5:10 Well reported for good works: if she has brought up children, if she has lodged strangers, if she has washed the saints' feet, if she has relieved the afflicted, if she has diligently followed every good work.^{NKJV} The third qualification required that these widows be well known for their kind deeds. The examples that Paul cited span her good reputation in the home, the community, and the church. To *wash the saints' feet* means to help and serve other believers with humility, following the example of Jesus who washed the feet of his disciples at the Last Supper (John 13:1-17; see also 1 Samuel 25:41). A woman who has raised children (orphans perhaps), practiced hospitality, helped those in need, established a good reputation for her kindness, and rendered service to the church would be qualified to be on the list of widows.

Paul listed character qualities that were to be evident about these widows. Many of the actions described would have been done while their mates were still alive. They are not "things widows do," but rather, good works for which a worthy widow is already well known.

SERVICE AVENUES
Three out of four wives today eventually are widowed, and many of the older women in our churches have lost their husbands. In what ways does your church provide an avenue of service for these women? Could you help match their gifts and abilities with your church's needs? The church should identify and facilitate roles of service for these women. Caring for each other, praying for others, or volunteering for the many activities in the church can provide a sense of purpose for women at this place in life. Often their maturity and wisdom can be of great service in the church.

5:11 But refuse to put younger widows on the list; for when their sensual desires alienate them from Christ, they want to marry.[NRSV] While at first sounding harsh, Paul actually was showing great compassion in this instruction. Widows younger than sixty should not be put on the list of widows (described in 5:9). Most likely, this did not mean that

> Virtue is nothing but well-directed love.
>
> *Augustine of Hippo*

younger widows were refused assistance by the church; rather, younger widows were not to take a pledge of service to the church, which probably included not remarrying. Paul understood that younger women might face normal *sensual desires* and might want to remarry. For instance, according to verse 4, a young widow would not even be a candidate for the list if she had children, because until a certain age she would be busy caring for them, and later, they would be caring for her. So, the "sensual desires" may well include the idea of wanting to bear children. While this was perfectly acceptable in most instances, it would be unacceptable if the woman had taken a pledge to the church. To remarry would then necessitate breaking that pledge. Breaking a pledge was serious business, leading to judgment; it would *alienate them from Christ* because they would be breaking a vow made to him. Vows of this kind were not required nor demanded, but when made, they were considered as binding as marriage itself.

Because verses 11 and 12 appear to be an overly harsh indictment of widows who remarry, four explanations have been put forward to alleviate the tension:

(1) Paul was concerned about widows who broke their commitment to remain widows for the sake of ministry and service.

(2) Paul was concerned about widows who rejected the ideal of being married only once (5:9).

(3) Paul was concerned about widows who might even marry nonbelievers and turn away from Christ.

(4) Paul was addressing a particular problem at Ephesus; therefore, his dictum for widows' remarrying should not necessarily be applied to all churches.

The context of this passage reveals two certain concerns of Paul: (1) Some young widows did not qualify for inclusion among the widows under long-term care by the church (5:9-11), and (2) those young widows not under the care of the church should marry and raise a family in a manner honoring to Christ (5:14).

Paul was concerned that these young widows would become victims of undisciplined desires. To whatever degree these two points express an aspect of Paul's thinking, the fact that he would condone or even encourage the remarriage of some supports the idea that his fears revolved around the *kind* of marriage these young widows might choose. There was a distinct possibility that they might deny Christ in favor of an unbelieving husband. Paul revealed these same concerns in 1 Corinthians 7:8ff.: chaste singleness is the ideal if a person is called to be single; otherwise, people should marry within the faith.

5:12 **Thus they bring judgment on themselves, because they have broken their first pledge.**NIV A broken pledge must incur judgment (see Numbers 30:2; Deuteronomy 23:21; Acts 5:1-10). Paul preferred that a young widow not put herself in the position of trying to meet an ideal of chaste widowhood and then wishing she hadn't; instead, she should be free to remarry (see discussion above). In fact, as Paul goes on to point out, a young widow needed to have direction, since merely submitting to her own desires might well lead to a denial of the faith through marriage with an unbeliever or to a life-style dishonoring to Christ.

5:13 **Besides, they get into the habit of being idle and going about from house to house. And not only do they become idlers, but also gossips and busybodies, saying things they ought not to.**NIV Another reason for not allowing younger widows to be put on the list and receive full support from the church was that these younger energetic women, with too much time on their hands, were more susceptible to distractions. With no family to care for and the full support of the church, their lack of wisdom that comes with age might lead them to be *idlers,* doing visitation for purposes of catching up on and sharing gossip and generally being nothing but *busybodies.* The picture here describes women

WORTHY WIDOWS

Widows in Ministry (vv. 3-10)	*Widows in Misery (vv. 11-13)*
Good works	Idle
Hospitality	Going house to house
Active prayer life	Active gossips, busybodies
Helping the afflicted	Saying hurtful things
Hope set on God	Hope set on own desires

busy accomplishing little good and much that is destructive. While this may sound like an extremely negative comment about these women, we ought to note the context and take into account that *anyone* with too much free time can often get into trouble. Paul's answer was adamant: If they will not give themselves to ministry, then the next best choice is marriage.

STEWARDSHIP OF AGE

A wise church makes use of the wisdom of its elders. What they lack in energy (although some have plenty of energy!), they may well make up for in knowing what way to go. Besides, the main reason older people feel worthless comes from their being treated that way. Inability and uselessness have little to do with age. Many older people would just as soon not get quite so much rest. The church ought to lead in defining retirement not as a state of permanent idleness but as a transition when a wise person chooses some other endeavor. The Bible does not picture older people winding down as they serve God; rather, it depicts them gloriously winding up!

What areas of ministry and service are open to older people in your church? Who might assist the leadership within the church to find the best places for older people to serve? What do you see yourself doing for Christ when you reach seventy?

5:14 So I would have younger widows marry, bear children, and manage their households.NRSV Paul's advice to younger widows was to remarry (if that became an option), raise their families, and run their homes. As any mother knows, that is enough to keep her busy and out of trouble!

Paul had much more in mind here than merely providing a way to keep young widows off the streets. He placed before them a high calling. Note the two specific roles that he envisioned for these women within marriage. They were to *bear* children (giving them life and then bearing with them along their road to adulthood). But they were also to *manage their households* (*oikodespotein,* a single word in Greek that means "rule their homes"). This passage agrees with 2:11-15 in giving women distinct authority within their homes. In Christ women have worth and worthwhile roles. The immeasurable importance of training the next generation presents a demanding challenge. The outside community would judge Christianity based on how these young widows conducted themselves.

So as to give the adversary no occasion to revile us.^{NRSV} The *adversary* probably refers to Satan and/or those he uses to tear Christians down. Obviously, young women supported by the church who became local busybodies would not give the church a good reputation in the community and would give nonbelievers *occasion to revile* (speak contemptuously of) the church and Christians. Satan and his followers would give the believers enough trouble without them bringing it on themselves.

5:15 **For some have already turned aside after Satan.**^{NKJV} *Turned aside after Satan* explains much of the intensity in Paul's expressions throughout this passage. Some women from the church had already broken their commitment to Christ. Though they might still be superficially affiliated with the believers, their lives were representing Satan's power. These women were not living up to their commitment. Turning aside after Satan was probably not total apostasy, but rather the pursuit of a sensually oriented life-style leading to idleness, gossip, and at times even false teaching. Their loss bothered Paul. He was determined to help Timothy prevent further losses.

> Until we sin, Satan is a parasite; but when once we are in the devil's hands he turns tyrant.
>
> *Thomas Manton*

5:16 **If any believing woman has relatives who are really widows, let her assist them; let the church not be burdened, so that it can assist those who are real widows.**^{NRSV} The "whoever" of verse 8 included women as well as men. A *believing* woman bore the same responsibility of care for widows in her family as any man would. Presumably, this role was part of effective household management (5:14) that was expected of married women. In this way, those in need received assistance from their families; those without families could then receive assistance from the church, and the church, in turn, could help and *not be burdened* in the process.

This epistle has been attacked frequently as uncharitable toward women. Paul's limitation on the teaching ministry of women recorded in 2:11-15 has often been taken to summarize all that Paul thought and wrote about women in the church. But given the compromised condition of the church in Ephesus, with Timothy and Paul struggling to stem the tide of false teaching, the specific roles, responsibilities, and value given to women are rather remarkable. Male believers were to exemplify the best treatment of women, especially widows. Women themselves were challenged to live full lives, raising children, managing households, caring for others, and being deeply involved in serving ministries. Those who chafe under Paul's seeming failure to give women "up front exposure" ought to remember that Jesus defined that kind of leadership as the most insignificant by kingdom standards. Hunger for visibility betrays an all too human tendency for personal glory. Women, though often not by choice, have historically taken the different, and better way: "Jesus said to them, 'The kings of the Gentiles lord it over them; and those who exercise authority over them call themselves Benefactors. But you are not to be like that. Instead, the greatest among you should be like the youngest, and the one who rules like the one who serves. For who is greater, the one who is at the table or the one who serves? Is it not the one who is at the table? But I am among you as one who serves'" (Luke 22:25-27 NIV).

5:17 Let the elders who rule well be considered worthy of double honor, especially those who labor in preaching and teaching.NRSV The *elders* (*presbuteroi,* see 5:1) were the older men. Several from this group occupied official leadership positions in the church (see 3:1-6 for their qualifications; also Acts 20:17-18; Titus 1:5-7). Their elder status in age and experience was a factor in their eligibility for leadership, but the term was not as ecclesiastically technical as it has come to be. Elders not in specific leadership roles were still to be respected. The exception to this rule were the false teachers, who were probably also elders who had fallen away from the faith. Even with them, however, the tone of rebuke was to be considerate (5:1). Here, Paul lifted up the servant role of those who lead truthfully and effectively.

These particular leader-elders carried significant responsibilities in overseeing the congregation. Those who excelled should receive *double honor.* The Greek word for honor is the same word used in verse 3, where it refers to respect and material support (other passages where the word means "pay" include Matthew 27:6; Acts 4:34; 7:16; 1 Corinthians 6:20). Both their age and their abilities were worthy of deference. Paul singled out those elders who carried the twin responsibilities of *preaching and teaching* as particularly worthy of "double honor" (for related passages, see Matthew 10:5-16; Luke 10:1-12; 1 Corinthians 9:3-14). Double honor does not mean twice the pay, but both respect and remuneration.

TARGETS OF CARE OR CRITICISM?
Faithful church leaders should be supported and appreciated. Too often they are targets for criticism because the congregation has unrealistic expectations. How do you treat your church leaders? Do you enjoy finding fault, or do you show your appreciation? Do they receive enough financial support to allow them to live without worry and to provide for the needs of their families? Unfortunately, we often take church leaders for granted by not providing adequately for their needs or by subjecting them to heavy criticism. Think of ways you can "honor" your preachers and teachers.

Preaching and teaching are closely related. Preaching (literally, "laboring in the word") involves proclaiming the Word of God, explaining its truth, helping learners understand difficult passages, and helping them apply God's Word to daily life. Teaching refers more to the extended training of others in Christian doctrine and the gospel message. These roles carried added importance because the New Testament was not yet available in written form. Elders who worked hard for the believers by adding to their responsibilities both preaching and teaching should be paid a stipend.

5:18 **For the Scripture says, "Do not muzzle the ox while it is treading out the grain," and "The worker deserves his wages."**[NIV] Paul supported his instruction that the elders should be paid by quoting first the Old Testament (Deuteronomy 25:4) and then the words of Jesus himself (Matthew 10:10; Luke 10:7). This double reference shows that both the Old Testament and the Gospels were considered "the Scripture" by Paul.

While seeming odd at first, the reference to the ox is very appropriate. Often oxen were used to tread out the grain on a threshing floor. The animal was attached by poles to a large millstone. As it walked around the millstone, its hooves trampled the grain, separating the kernels from the chaff. At the same time, the millstone ground the grain into flour. Muzzling the ox would prevent it from eating while it was working. Paul used this illustration to argue that productive Christian workers should receive financial support. The fact that a person is in Christian ministry doesn't mean that he or she should be poorly paid.

At the same time, Paul's instruction does not free a minister from financial accountability. Whereas the ox could dip into the corn, the minister may not dip into the church's funds. The Scriptures Paul quoted cannot be used to argue against the need for integrity and openness in the handling of finances or reporting expenses. Wise churches and ministers create systems that avoid both the temptation and the appearance of impropriety in financial matters.

While those who devote time and energy to serving the congregation are not to be doing so for the money (like the false teachers may have been doing), they ought to receive fair payment for their services. Although Paul made it a point not to receive a stipend from any of the churches he served (see 1 Corinthians 9:15-23; 1 Thessalonians 2:9), he clearly believed that each congregation should offer adequate support to its leaders (see also 1 Corinthians 9:4-10; Galatians 6:6).

STRONG SUPPORT
Ministers of the gospel deserve to be supported, and it is our responsibility to make sure they have what they need. There are several ways to encourage those who serve God in his church. First, see that they have an adequate salary. Second, see that they are supported emotionally; plan a time to express appreciation for something they have done. Third, lift their spirits with special surprises from time to time. Our ministers deserve to know we are giving to them cheerfully and generously.

5:19 **Never accept any accusation against an elder except on the evidence of two or three witnesses.**[NRSV] Wherever a group of people work together, conflicts occur. The church and its leaders are not exempt from sin, faults, and mistakes. But criticism may arise for wrong reasons or impure motives—minor imperfections, failure to meet someone's expectations, personality clashes. Thus Paul called upon the Old Testament stipulation that accusations should not even be heard unless two or three witnesses confirmed them (see Deuteronomy 17:6; 19:15; Matthew 18:16; John 8:17; 2 Corinthians 13:1). But just because there were two or three witnesses doesn't mean the accused was automatically guilty. A thorough investigation of charges was still required. Elders needed to have the respect and confidence of their congregation, but by their very presence and accessibility at the head of a church they would be the first targets for malicious accusations. Paul wisely instructed that accusations should not be considered proven until they were confirmed by *two or three witnesses.*

When Paul instructed Timothy to *never accept any accusation against an elder,* he was not advocating ignoring individual charges. The expression "never accept" conveys more the sense of caution rather than rejection. But an *accusation* should be treated seriously. Corroboration or contradiction should be pursued. Failure to correctly handle these matters has led to great harm to clergy and by clergy.

ACCUSED!
There are few patterns more shameful in church history than the incidences in which victims have been silenced or ignored when their charges against ministers were valid. For the protections of both clergy and congregation members, every church ought to have a well-thought-through and thoroughly discussed system for handling grievances and accusations against the ministerial staff. The preservation of anonymity, the required verifications, and the ways in which such matters will be settled should be spelled out for all to understand. What are your church's guidelines for handling accusations?

5:20 As for those who persist in sin, rebuke them in the presence of all, so that the rest also may stand in fear.NRSV If an accusation was confirmed, however, discipline was in order. Then if the church leader persisted in that sin, Timothy was to publicly expose his sins and rebuke him. (*In the presence of all* could mean the entire church or all the elders.) The rebuke must be administered fairly and lovingly for the purpose of restoration, but it should cause all who see it to *stand in fear* of receiving any such discipline. Timothy could not be lax in dealing with elders who persisted in sin. The witness and reputation of the church to the outside world, as well as its own inner purity, depended on fair but consistent discipline.

5:21 I charge you, in the sight of God and Christ Jesus and the elect angels, to keep these instructions without partiality, and to do nothing out of favoritism.NIV As difficult as it might be, Timothy was not to waver on any of these instructions (and perhaps particularly the instructions about rebuking elders when needed). Perhaps Timothy had avoided difficult confrontations in the past or had shown partiality or favoritism in dealing with sin. Whatever the case, Paul gave Timothy this charge in the sight of God, Christ Jesus, and the elect angels (i.e., the angels who did not rebel against God)—all of whom judge sinners (see Matthew 25:31-46; Luke 15:10; 1 Corinthians 4:9; 2 Peter 2:4; Revelation 14:7; 20:1-3). Any needed discipline or rebuke must be administered without regard to Timothy's personal inclinations, as if Timothy were pronouncing judgment before God, Christ, and the elect angels. For the sake of the church, Timothy needed to be impartial and not show favoritism.

PLAYING FAVORITES
We must be constantly on guard against favoritism, against giving preferential treatment to some and ignoring others. We live in a society that plays favorites. It's easy to give special treatment to those who are gifted, intelligent, rich, or beautiful without realizing what we are doing. We can also fall into the trap of deliberately working against people we happen not to like. The impartiality that Paul insisted on goes both ways: for example, we are neither to undermine those with whom we have a superficial disagreement, nor are we to overlook false teaching or sexual improprieties of a pastor who happens to be a dynamic speaker. Make sure that you honor people for who they are in Christ, not for who they are in the world.

5:22 Do not ordain anyone hastily.^{NRSV} One way to avoid the sticky problem of disciplining an elder is to be very careful about *who* is placed in that important position. *Ordain* translates the expression "laying hands on," which described one public way to identify and authorize a leader. Paul was saying that Timothy should never be hasty in choosing leaders in the church because he might overlook major problems or sins. Choosing church leaders today is a serious responsibility. They must have strong faith and be morally upright, having the qualities described in 3:1-13 and Titus 1:5-9. While some commentators have suggested that Paul was giving directions here about how soon to receive back the elders who had been censured in verse 20, there is little in the context to commend this view. Prevention would have most likely been a higher priority to the apostle.

Not everyone who wants to be a church leader is ready or capable. Timothy needed to be certain of an applicant's qualifications before asking him to take a leadership position. The reason is explained in the next phrase.

Do not participate in the sins of others.^{NRSV} In 3:6, Paul had instructed that an elder should not be a recent convert, but that he should have time to grow in the faith and prove his ability to handle responsibilities in the church. Anyone who took part in ordaining an elder who later proved to be unfit for the position shared in the blame for negative effects on the church. If Timothy ordained a man who became a liability because of his persistent sinning, and if Timothy allowed that man to remain in the office despite those sins, Timothy would actually *participate in* those sins by compromising himself.

Keep yourself pure. By staying pure, Timothy would be able to more clearly judge those capable of serving the church as elders. In addition, by dealing immediately with sin among the elders, Timothy would show his convictions, his unwillingness to compromise with sin, which would also help him to remain pure.

ACCESSORIES
If we know about and yet enable the sins of others, those actions make us to some degree accessories in their wrongdoing. Our endorsement of the ministry of others must always be truthful. What we know carries with it heavy responsibilities. If we treat the damaging of truth lightly, we may end up indirectly participating in harm done to other people.

5:23 **Stop drinking only water, and use a little wine because of your stomach and your frequent illnesses.**[NIV] The very mention of wine has given rise to questions about why Paul gave this advice to Timothy. Perhaps Paul feared that his previous advice, "Keep yourself pure" (5:22), could be interpreted too rigidly by Timothy, and Paul wanted Timothy to understand that purity and asceticism were not necessarily related. Perhaps Timothy was avoiding any connection to drunkenness so as to keep the qualifications for an elder (3:3). There is evidence that the expression *drinking only water* was a term used by prohibitionists within extreme ascetic groups.

Perhaps drinking water of poor quality (water did not come clear and clean from the tap in those days) had led to Timothy's stomach problem and frequent illnesses, so he should stop drinking only water. Paul's counsel here was to make use of alcohol for its medicinal value.

Those who come to this text for either open permission to use alcohol or for prohibition against the use of alcohol will be forced to meet on a middle ground. Paul has in fact stated a limited application for alcohol. Within this letter, he has already expressed the other extreme by insisting that those in leadership positions not be "drunkards" (3:3). The distance is great between "a little wine for the stomach" and drunkenness, but some know all too well how quickly that ground can be covered and what destructive results there can be. The validity of the case for either total abstention from or some degree of consumption of alcohol must be constructed from other principles (such as freedom, self-control, moderation, discipline, etc.), and may well have to rely more honestly on personal, situational, and cultural factors.

Whatever the extent of Paul's advice here, it gives us insight into Timothy. Paul's kind words to his dear friend show his concern for Timothy's physical well-being. It also demonstrates his awareness that people in ministry function as whole beings, and that dysfunctions in mental, emotional, spiritual, and physical areas take their toll on effectiveness.

5:24 The sins of some people are conspicuous and precede them to judgment, while the sins of others follow them there.^{NRSV} Picking up directly from verse 22, Paul revealed the key difficulty in the task of choosing good leaders in the church. All people are headed toward *judgment.* Along that path, some people's sins are *conspicuous* (easy to spot), while others pass by us before their sins become apparent, if they become apparent at all. A person must be known well before deciding whether he is qualified to serve the church in a leadership position. The "judgment" Paul referred to included both the judgment of God and the judgment required by Timothy in authorizing leaders. Paul was warning Timothy and us about the importance of not judging by immediate appearances. Sometimes problems are easy to see, but other times they remain hidden for quite a while.

OPEN AND HIDDEN SINS
At times, the desire to have a great speaker or a growing church has caused people to overlook warning signs in ministerial candidates. Or, when improprieties occur, people avoid taking action because they want to "keep the peace." Churches that have too quickly overlooked the possibility of wrongdoing in leaders who appeared so acceptable have had to endure shocking and shaming humiliation when extramarital relations, wife and child abuse, alcoholism, and mismanagement have been uncovered. But Paul also mentioned inward qualities in 6:3-10 that can be equally devastating to a ministry in the long run.
What questions must be answered by those taking leadership in your church? How are they held accountable? How are moral and ethical failures by leaders handled? Who would be the best person to initiate the development of such procedures?

5:25 So also good works are conspicuous; and even when they are not, they cannot remain hidden.^{NRSV} In the same way, some people's good works may be *conspicuous,* while others' good works, though perhaps done behind the scenes, *cannot remain hidden* and will eventually reveal the true character of the doer. Many of the leadership qualities that Paul listed in 3:2-7 fit in this category. Some, like hospitality and gentleness, create immediate and visible results, while others, like household management and guilelessness, only become apparent over a period of time.

Both verses 24 and 25 explain why Paul instructed Timothy to choose church leaders carefully. Hasty assessment of men for leadership positions could mean overlooking sins or good qualities; then unqualified men might be chosen and qualified men set aside. The hard fact is that in time, a man's true personality is revealed, for better or for worse. It is far better for the church when leaders are carefully and prayerfully selected.

6:1 All who are under the yoke of slavery should consider their masters worthy of full respect, so that God's name and our teaching may not be slandered.^{NIV} In the Roman culture of Paul's day, slavery was a deeply rooted institution. It was also widespread, since estimates place the number of slaves at 60 million, or half the population of the empire.

Slaves conducted most of the functions of society, from the most menial tasks to work as tutors for children and estate managers. They were used as we use tools, machinery, and technology today. Slavery was economic rather than racially motivated. People usually became slaves as a result of war or poverty.

A great social and legal gulf separated masters and slaves. Paul's word choice, *under the yoke,* captures the essence of slavery—most slaves were treated no better than cattle, than mere property. But when a master and his slave became Christians, they became spiritual equals, brothers (and sisters) in Christ Jesus (Galatians 3:28). In some instances, a slave who had been a Christian for some years might even be an elder in a church and thus "over" a newly converted master. Equality in the church but inviolable separation at home obviously made for interesting interpersonal relations in and out of the church. This issue often caused concern in the early church. Both Paul and Peter gave instructions about master/slave relations (see 1 Corinthians 7:20-24; Galatians 3:28; Ephesians 6:5-9; Colossians 3:22-25; Titus 2:9-10; the book of Philemon; 1 Peter 2:13-25). The abolition of slavery was not on the horizon for masters and slaves in the Roman Empire, so instructions about this touchy topic became extremely valuable. While not speaking against the institution of slavery, they gave guidelines for Christian slaves and Christian masters.

Paul wrote specifically to slaves here, explaining that their attitude toward even their unbelieving masters should be *full respect*—the same word used for "honor" in 5:3, 17. This appeared to be an obvious instruction if the master were a Christian. Yet that itself caused some problems, as noted in verse 2. However, Paul instructed that even if the master were an unbeliever, the Christian slave should still treat him or her with full respect. By so doing they would maintain a good reputation among nonbelievers so *God's name and [the leaders'] teaching may not be slandered.*

Paul's counsel for the master/slave relationship can be applied to the employer/employee relationship today. The attitude and behavior of believers on the job will help or hurt others' openness to the gospel they share. Employees should work hard, showing respect for their employers. In turn, employers should be fair (Ephesians 6:5-9; Colossians 3:22-25). Our work should reflect our faithfulness to and love for Christ. In that way, Christian employees will be a positive witness for Christ to an unbelieving employer.

WHY DIDN'T CHRISTIANS OPPOSE SLAVERY?
Looking back over almost twenty centuries, many people have wondered why biblical writers did not speak more directly against human slavery. Here are some of the reasons:

- Slavery was widespread and an integral part of the very fabric of society. Some slaves lived in wretched conditions and were treated terribly. But many functioned as though they were free. Anarchy would have resulted if Christians had led a slave revolt, and believers stood for peace.
- Christians were, for a long time, such a small minority that they would have been wiped out. Their allegiance to Christ was already highly suspicious, and many believers lost their lives for love of Christ alone. The Romans would have crushed such a seditious response to their power.
- Christians also believed that this world was on the verge of passing away. Given the impending end, freeing people from sin seemed a higher priority than freeing them from slavery.
- The actual accommodation of slavery by Christian slaves and masters gutted the power of slavery from within. As a satanic device, slavery is only as effective as its ability to destroy humans physically, morally, and spiritually. Having declared slave and master brothers and sisters, a deeper freedom was achieved in Christ.

6:2 **Those who have believing masters must not be disrespectful to them on the ground that they are members of the church.**NRSV It might be easy for a slave to justify slacking off in his or her work, thinking that a believing master would understand or would not be able to reprimand him since they both belonged to the church.

Instead, they are to serve them even better, because those who benefit from their service are believers, and dear to them.NIV

Those slaves fortunate enough to have believing masters should not reduce but double their efforts to serve well. The reason is obvious—the person benefiting from the slave's service is a brother or sister in Christ.

Teach and exhort these things.^{NKJV} Once again Paul repeated the command for Timothy to teach what Paul had instructed. Some Bible versions separate this sentence from verse 2 and add it to the beginning of verse 3, believing that the command to *teach and exhort* belongs with Paul's words about false teachers in verses 3-5. Whatever the case, it is obvious that what Paul wrote was meant to be taught to the believers.

GODLY RELATIONSHIPS
God's Word has established guidelines for how to live in all kinds of relationships. Whenever two or more are in a relationship, God has directions for each person involved. Each party must obey God, even if one does not listen or obey. Thus, both husbands and wives, parents and children, slaves and masters each have duties and commands to carry out.

Good relationships require more than one person doing his or her share at the right time to contribute to that relationship. At times it is a wife's patience that saves the day. Other times a husband's leadership prompts a wise decision. Sometimes a child's need overcomes parental selfishness. A wife's integrity may change her husband's mind. Obedience to God makes relationships the best they can be.

Yet some partners in a relationship have so hardened their hearts toward God or have such a dysfunctional past that they lash out with immoral or destructive behavior. God does not require submission to unjust, immoral, or hurtful behavior.

---

1 Timothy 6:3-21

In this closing section of his instructional letter, Paul returned to discussing how Timothy should handle the false teachers in Ephesus (see 1:3-11). After all, they were one of the causes for this letter. Repeatedly, Paul has used forceful language to encourage Timothy's bold response. Words like *urge* (1:3; 2:1; 6:2), *command* (1:3, 5; 4:11; 6:14, 17-18), *teach* (4:6, 11, 13; 6:2-3), and *instructions* (1:18; 3:14; 5:7, 21; 6:3) all reinforce Paul's determination to intervene for the good of the church in Ephesus.

Paul told Timothy to stay away from those who just want to make money from preaching, and from those in the church who stray from the sound teachings of the gospel into controversial arguments. Paul revealed the greedy motives behind the efforts of the false teachers. They were pursuing prestige and power to satisfy their intense desire for money. Paul wanted these men stopped in their tracks, and he wanted to make sure that Timothy was not also deceived.

As noted above, some Bible versions separate the last sentence of verse 2 and add it to the beginning of verse 3, believing that the command to "teach and exhort" belongs with Paul's words about false teachers in verses 3-5. Whatever the case, Paul wanted these words to be taught to the believers. Furthermore, "these things" most likely refers to all of Paul's instructions in this letter, not just the immediate ones.

6:3 If anyone teaches false doctrines and does not agree to the sound instruction of our Lord Jesus Christ and to godly teaching.^{NIV} The older apostle could hardly review his instructions to his younger representative without thinking of those undermining the church he had planted in Ephesus. He wanted to make sure Timothy understood that *anyone* was capable of leading others astray. Paul identified three characteristics of false teachers by the content of their teaching:

First, they "taught false doctrines" (*heterodidaskalein*). In 1:3-4, Paul had written, "Instruct certain people not to teach any different doctrine, and not to occupy themselves with myths and endless genealogies" (NRSV). The Greek word is the same for "false" and "different" in these verses. Any teaching different from the Christian doctrine, based upon God's Word, was suspect as false teaching. The following two explanations enlarge Paul's idea of false doctrine.

Second, they did not *agree to the sound instruction of our Lord Jesus Christ.* In 1:10-11, Paul described such teaching as "contrary to the sound doctrine that conforms to the glorious gospel of the blessed God" (NIV). Any teaching different from the sound instruction of the gospel of Christ is false teaching. The Greek word for "sound" could be translated "healthy." Such instruction is life-giving. Some commentators believe that at least one of the Gospels (perhaps Luke) may have already been in circulation, allowing believers access to that "sound instruction" in written form. In any case, those teachings had been preserved orally and constantly taught to believers.

However, Paul's concern here was not about the form of the instruction, but that the false teachers disagreed with what Jesus Christ had taught and demonstrated. They erred in contradicting and discounting Jesus.

> Which is more the possessor of the world—he who has a thousand houses, or he who, without one house to call his own, has ten in which his knock at the door would rouse instant jubilation? Which is richer—the man who, his large money spent, would have no refuge; or he for whose necessity a hundred would sacrifice comfort? Which of the two possessed the earth—King Agrippa or tentmaker Paul?
> *George Macdonald*

Third, the false teachers did not agree to *godly teaching.* False teaching is ungodly teaching; it cannot result in righteous living. Whereas *sound instruction* (literally, "healthy words") can refer to the transmission of knowledge and understanding, *godly teaching* points to practical actions. Godly teaching exposes believers to timely applications of the timeless truths of sound instruction. The false teachers broke with orthodoxy and therefore had no basis for effective orthopraxy (right conduct). Our applications of God's Word will always depend on how accurately we have understood the teaching of God's Word (note the same kind of contrast in 4:7-10).

But these false teachers were not merely mistaken in their doctrine; their evil went deeper. Or rather, it originated in deeper problems. They were not well-intentioned teachers who had made unfortunate mistakes. Their basic motivations were evil.

6:4 Conceited, understanding nothing, and has a morbid craving for controversy and for disputes about words.^{NRSV} Paul revealed the real character of the false teachers behind their veneer of prestige. These are not very flattering words for a group of teachers who apparently thought very highly of themselves! Note the contrast with Paul's outline for Timothy's teaching as "love from a pure heart, from a good conscience, and from sincere faith" (1:5 NKJV).

"Conceit" describes the trait of a person having an excessively favorable opinion of his own ability or importance. The false teachers showed all that and more, yet Paul confronted that conceit by explaining that they actually understood *nothing*. In 1:7, Paul had explained that these men wanted "to be teachers of the law," but were "without understanding," either in "what they are saying or the things about which they make assertions" (NRSV). The utter falsehood of both the content and the conclusions of their teaching was worthy, not of pride, but shame.

They do not agree with "sound" (or "healthy") instruction (6:3), but instead have a *morbid craving* (literally, are "diseased with") *controversy and . . . disputes.* Again, Paul repeated his assertions from chapter 1 that the false teachers were caught up in "myths and endless genealogies" (1:4 NRSV) and "meaningless talk" (1:6 NRSV) that promoted speculation and led to arguments about ideas that came, not from Scripture, but from the minds of the false teachers. The controversial ideas and the disputes about words (Greek *logomaxias,* "word wars") fed the "morbid craving" of the false teachers, but they had a devastating effect in the church.

WORD WARS
Do you know anyone who loves to "split hairs" over theological issues, insisting on having the last word in any disagreement over meaning—someone who constantly wages word wars with others?

In fairness, a passion for truth can lead to controversy. An honest desire for knowledge and understanding may bring arguments or disagreements. When arrogance, lack of direction, anger, and defensiveness mark a discussion, little good can come from it. Those who engage in these arguments are driven by their own elevated egos; they delight in winning arguments. If arguments never lead to practical action, they may come from evil motives.

Jesus warned about those who major on the minors and miss what is truly important (see Matthew 23:24). Those who strain life too finely often discover that they have swallowed a camel instead of a gnat!

That result in envy, strife, malicious talk, evil suspicions.^{NIV}
When the truth and application of God's Word is replaced by
meaningless and false drivel, believers may lose their moral
foundation and incredible evil can result. With the believers
embroiled in arguments over meaningless theories and false doctrine, relationships began to deteriorate. *Envy* is followed by
strife; strife means competition and/or violent and bitter conflict.
Malicious talk and *evil suspicions* surely follow.

Jesus warned his followers about false teachers: "Beware of
false prophets, who come to you in sheep's clothing, but inwardly
they are ravenous wolves. You will know them by their fruits"
(Matthew 7:15-16 NKJV). The seeds of false teaching in Ephesus
were yielding a harvest of bitterness.

**6:5 And constant friction between men of corrupt mind, who have
been robbed of the truth and who think that godliness is a
means to financial gain.**^{NIV} Here are more characteristics of false
teachers: even among themselves there was *constant friction*
because they all had *corrupt* (debased, depraved, tainted) minds.
Not only did they understand nothing (6:4), but their minds were so
corrupt that *the truth* (God's truth) was completely absent. They
were motivated by money. Their ultimate goal was to enrich themselves! How completely opposite this is from Old Testament teaching, from the teaching of the Lord Jesus and from the apostles, and
from the generous and caring attitude of the early church:

■ *Old Testament*
"He humbled you, causing you to hunger and then feeding
you with manna, which neither you nor your fathers had
known, to teach you that man does not live on bread alone
but on every word that comes from the mouth of the
LORD." (Deuteronomy 8:3 NIV)
"This is what the LORD says: 'Let not the wise man boast of
his wisdom or the strong man boast of his strength or the
rich man boast of his riches, but let him who boasts boast
about this: that he understands and knows me, that I am the
LORD, who exercises kindness, justice and righteousness
on earth, for in these I delight,' declares the LORD." (Jeremiah 9:23-24 NIV)

■ *Jesus*
"Still others, like seed sown among thorns, hear the word; but
the worries of this life, the deceitfulness of wealth and the
desires for other things come in and choke the word, making it unfruitful." (Mark 4:18-19 NIV)

"One thing you lack: Go your way, sell whatever you have
and give to the poor, and you will have treasure in heaven;
and come, take up the cross, and follow Me." (Mark 10:21
NKJV)
"Foxes have holes and birds of the air have nests, but the Son
of Man has nowhere to lay His head." (Luke 9:58 NKJV)

■ *The apostles*
"Silver and gold I do not have, but what I do have I give you:
In the name of Jesus Christ of Nazareth, rise up and walk."
(Acts 3:6 NKJV)
"Look! The wages you failed to pay the workmen who
mowed your fields are crying out against you. The cries of
the harvesters have reached the ears of the Lord Almighty.
You have lived on earth in luxury and self-indulgence. You
have fattened yourselves in the day of slaughter." (James
5:4-5 NIV)

■ *The early church*
"Now the multitude of those who believed were of one heart
and one soul; neither did anyone say that any of the things
he possessed was his own, but they had all things in common. . . . Nor was there anyone among them who lacked;
for all who were possessors of lands or houses sold them,
and brought the proceeds of the things that were sold, and
laid them at the apostles' feet; and they distributed to each
as anyone had need." (Acts 4:32, 34-35 NKJV)

THE GIVING FLOW
Clearly, selfish gain was never meant to be the Christian's goal.
The heart of the gospel pulses with giving. God himself gave
the greatest example: "For God so loved the world that He
gave His only begotten Son . . ." (John 3:16 NKJV). Conse-
quently, those who have been filled with the Spirit of God naturally demonstrate his presence by their giving. In a believer's
life, the emphasis should be on what flows out to others rather
than on what flows in from others.
　　Once a person has Christ, nothing else is too costly to give
up, even life itself. The giving flow can take many forms, from
the sharing of material possessions to the compassionate care
given to the poor, defenseless, and hurt.

While Paul instructed the church about the Christian leaders'
right to be paid for their services, he made it clear that they
should not be "greedy for money" (3:3, 8) and should not consider their ministry as a way to get rich. Those who did clearly

could not be serving the Lord Christ with pure motives, but instead were serving their selfish desires.

MONEY MATTERS
The New Testament church gathered resources to support widows and others in need. At times the leaders handled large sums of money. Even in a poorer area, the combined finances of a local church can be rather remarkable when believers give generously. The lure of those funds was as powerful then as it is today. Some people, even ministers, have misused these funds, destroying their integrity and deeply harming their church's ability to minister to people in need. Wise churches structure themselves in such a way that no individual has sole authority to deal with the finances of the church.

6:6 Now godliness with contentment is great gain.[NKJV] Picking up the words *godliness* and *gain* from verse 5, Paul here presents the truth about both. The false teachers thought godliness was a means to financial gain; instead, godliness *is great gain* in itself when accompanied by contentment. Godliness does not come and go with the uncertainties of material wealth; godliness, with contentment, *is* the wealth, independent of one's bankbook and possessions. The false teachers had it backward.

> He is no fool who gives what he cannot keep to gain what he cannot lose.
> *Jim Elliot*

CASHING IN
Even Christians whose teaching meets orthodox standards can become false teachers if they become motivated by financial rewards. If we lose our sense of mission, our desire to serve God and the people in our sphere of influence, we can become entirely self-serving.
   Take an intentional inventory of your deepest desires and your record of carrying out responsibilities. Is your faithfulness determined by obedience to God or by the size of the financial incentives?

Each of these three components contribute to understanding the abundant life Jesus offers (see John 10:10):

- *Godliness*—Throughout chapter 4 of this letter, Paul contrasted the characteristics and consequences of godliness and godlessness. Godliness requires training (4:7) and develops inner spiritual qualities, while at the same time being apparent in the way we relate to others (4:12). Godliness exhibits true character exemplified in the way we serve others.

■ *Contentment*—Like godliness, contentment grows from our attitude toward living God's way. "Contentment" was one of the highest Greek ethical qualities, meaning "sufficiency in self." Christians turned it around to mean sufficiency in Christ. Paul revealed that he had discovered the secret to contentment to be complete reliance on Christ: "I can do everything through him who gives me strength" (Philippians 4:13 NIV).

To have *contentment* in Christ requires four decisions about the events and possessions of our life:

(1) We must focus on what God has already allowed us to have.
(2) We must disregard what we do not have.
(3) We must refuse to covet what others may have.
(4) We must give thanks to God for each and all of his gifts (4:3-4).

If we fail to make these decisions, our contentment will diminish.

■ *Gain*—The benefits or profit that motivated the false teachers were neither lasting nor capable of bringing contentment. Their earthly profits would be left behind, as Paul explained. What brings *great gain* has to do with eternal values. When material treasures become our focus, we quit contributing to our eternal accounts. Whatever gains we may experience in this life mean nothing if they cause us eternal bankruptcy (see Matthew 6:19-24).

This statement provides the key to spiritual growth and personal fulfillment. We should honor God and center our desires on him ("godliness," see Matthew 6:33), and we should be content with what God is doing in our lives (see Philippians 4:11-13).

6:7 For we brought nothing into this world, and it is certain we can carry nothing out.NKJV Paul followed up his statement about the true source of contentment by discounting any hope of ultimate contentment based merely on this life. The correct perspective on material possessions—money, houses, clothing, vehicles, jewels, land, etc.—remains eternally the same. They cannot last forever. We can lose, break, or ruin them in this life, and we cannot take them with us when we die.

MONEY AND CONTENTMENT

Everything comes from God	1 Chronicles 29:11-14; Colossians 1:15-17; 1 Timothy 4:4
Money cannot buy salvation	Proverbs 11:4; Ezekiel 7:19; Matthew 16:26; Luke 16:19-31; 18:18-25
Riches do not last	Jeremiah 17:11; 1 Timothy 6:17; James 1:10-11; Revelation 18:11-19
Money never satisfies	Ecclesiastes 5:10-11; Luke 12:15
Don't show favoritism to the rich	James 2:1-9
Money carries responsibility	1 Timothy 6:17-19
Obey God rather than chasing after money	Psalms 17:15; 119:36; Proverbs 19:1; 1 Timothy 6:17
Be content	Philippians 4:11-13; 1 Timothy 6:8; Hebrews 13:5

There should be no doubt about the matter, for Scripture repeats this theme:

- "Naked I came from my mother's womb, and naked shall I return there. The LORD gave, and the LORD has taken away; blessed be the name of the LORD." (Job 1:21 NKJV)
- "As they came from their mother's womb, so they shall go again, naked as they came; they shall take nothing for their toil, which they may carry away with their hands." (Ecclesiastes 5:15 NRSV)
- "But God said [to the rich man], 'You fool! This very night your life is being demanded of you. And the things you have prepared, whose will they be?' So it is with those who store up treasures for themselves but are not rich toward God." (Luke 12:20-21 NRSV)

6:8 But if we have food and clothing, we will be content with these.NRSV Human beings have basic needs. Believers and unbelievers alike require food and clothing (also implying shelter) for survival. The difference should be that when believers' basic needs are met, they ought to be satisfied and content, requiring nothing more. In contrast, unbelievers are driven by society's standards and desires; they cannot be content with only basic needs being met because they must always strive for more.

> So we ask that every day we may be given our daily bread (that is, Christ) so that we who live in him may be strengthened and made holy. *Cyprian*

One helpful discipline in contentment involves distinguishing between *needs* and *wants*. We may have all we need to live but let ourselves become anxious and discontented over what we merely want. Much of the advertising industry attempts to change our perception so that more and more of what we want becomes what we think we need. Paul lived what he preached: "I have learned in whatever state I am, to be content: I know how to be abased, and I know how to abound. Everywhere and in all things I have learned both to be full and to be hungry, both to abound and to suffer need" (Philippians 4:11-12 NKJV). Like Paul, we can learn to be content without having all that we want. Otherwise we will become slaves to our desires. The writer of Hebrews offered this advice: "Keep your lives free from the love of money, and be content with what you have; for [God] has said, 'I will never leave you or forsake you'" (Hebrews 13:5 NRSV).

FLAT BROKE
There is no money to pay bills. . . . The church is in the red. . . . The ministry is behind in paying its staff. . . . What should we do? God works in infinitely varied and creative ways to supply our needs. Our work has a place in God's plan. We should always look for God's hand at work in all of life. The following steps will focus your attention on God:
- Ask God to clarify your desires and remove those that are inappropriate.
- Thank God for all that he has already provided.
- Claim God's promises of provision and help.
- Ask him for wisdom to undertake the tasks he wants you to do.
- Determine what other spiritual needs God might be meeting in your life by *not* meeting the physical need that seems so pressing.
- Look each day for opportunities to rely on Christ's power and love.
- Remind yourself out loud that God is in complete control.

Paul's words do not guarantee that every Christian in the world will always have adequate food and clothing. He was very familiar with deprivation (see Philippians 4:11-12 above). Nor should we make this statement an excuse for selfishness. Paul's insistence that families and the church provide for their widows surely implies that God provides abundance to some so they might share with others. Paul would have endorsed James's warning to believers: "Suppose a brother or sister is without clothes and daily food. If one of you says to him, 'Go, I wish you well; keep warm and well fed,' but does nothing about his physical needs, what good is it?" (James 2:15-16 NIV). If we are distressed at unmet needs in someone else's life when God has supplied to us the resources to help, but we do nothing to help, we are being both unloving and disobedient.

6:9 But those who want to be rich fall into temptation and are trapped by many senseless and harmful desires that plunge people into ruin and destruction.NRSV After stating the simple plan for living faithfully, Paul challenged the world's view by showing the outcome of trying to gain contentment through the pursuit of wealth. The desire to be rich is, by its very nature, a desire that cannot be satiated. *Those who want to be rich* cannot understand contentment because they can never have enough money. The *temptation* of money eventually traps people into doing anything to get money—illegal or immoral—even being willing to hurt others. Verses 9-10 show the results of refusing God's plan for contentment. By refusing to be content, people's desire for money feeds their greed. Soon their passion makes "wanting more" the only value.

> Some day we shall live without money, so we should prepare ourselves now by accepting the discipline of putting God's commandments first, and ensuring that integrity is our watchword whenever money is concerned. *Polycarp*

GOLDEN ADDICTION
Despite overwhelming evidence to the contrary, most people still believe that money brings happiness. Rich people who allow their resources to serve God may be happy, but only because they do not let money and possessions control them. But people who constantly crave *more* wealth and *more* possessions are caught in an endless cycle that only ends in disillusionment, ruin, and destruction. How can you keep away from the love of money? God, through Paul, provides guidelines:
- Realize that one day riches will all be gone (6:7, 17).
- Be content with what you have (6:8).
- Monitor what you are willing to do to get more money (6:9-10).
- Love people more than money (6:11).
- Love God's work more than money (6:11).
- Freely share what you have with others (6:18).
See Proverbs 30:7-9 for more on avoiding the love of money.

6:10 For the love of money is a root of all kinds of evil.^{NKJV} People often misquote this verse, saying, "Money is the root of all evil." But it is the love of money that Paul speaks against. Money itself is not evil; in fact, money can do much good for the furthering of God's kingdom.

> Every spending decision is a spiritual decision.
> *Ron Blue*

Money supports missionaries around the globe; money helps organizations fight for Christian causes in government; money supports churches and church leaders; money helps feed the hungry and clothe the poor. Obviously, while God doesn't *need* money (in fact, all the money in the world belongs to him), he can use money given by generous people to help those in need. These people can give because they control their money. The problem happens when money controls people.

People who *love* money are controlled by a ruthless, insatiable master, for the love of money can never be satisfied. Greed is a root of *all kinds of evil* (literally, "all the evils"): marriage problems, illegal acts, blowups in partnerships, envy, immorality, lying, ruthlessness, stealing, and a willingness to even hurt others if it makes money. To master money instead of becoming its slave,

> Having, first, gained all you can, and secondly, saved all you can, then give all you can.
> *John Wesley*

we must get rid of the desire to be rich. Admittedly, this is extremely difficult in a materialistic society; but instead of rationalizing our love for money, we need to seek God's help to overcome these desires.

CHECKBOOK
Have you ever thought of your checkbook as a diary? Like pictures, the checkbook entries speak a thousand words. If a stranger came into possession of your checkbook, what would he or she conclude about your values? About your stewardship? About how you honor God?

And in their eagerness to be rich some have wandered away from the faith and pierced themselves with many pains.^{NRSV} The worst scenario, of course, is that money would actually lead a person *away from the faith.* It's tragic when money replaces God in a person's life. Apparently this had happened in Ephesus; the *some* who had wandered away probably had faces and names known to Paul and Timothy. These greedy people found themselves *pierced . . . with many pains.* The picture is that they were being impaled by sharp objects that they continued to push against. Instead of God's way, they chose a path that was taking them deeper and deeper into a briar patch of trouble. Instead of the happiness they expected, money brought grief.

It would be a hazardous mistake to conclude that Paul is teaching that we should not be concerned about money. In fact, we should be respectfully asking God for funds with which to carry out our responsibilities and to help others. It is right to ask God for provision for daily life and to do his will (help children through college, pay off the church mortgage, etc.). Paul was concerned about greed more than he was about money.

HEALTHY AND WEALTHY AND WISE
Some have interpreted God's promises of provision and protection to mean that God wants all believers to be healthy and wealthy by worldly standards. Interestingly, those who have promoted this line of thinking have often accumulated considerable wealth through the donations of less well-off believers, making the donors even less wealthy.

Health and wealth are *among* the ways in which God can bring good into a person's life. They are certainly not the only means, nor are they necessarily the best. Suffering has made many people acutely sensitive to God. Christians can be wealthy (and those who are not should refrain from judging them)—but great wealth means great responsibility for using what God has given for furthering his kingdom. If you believe that health or wealth is the only thing standing between you and service or obedience, you need to reevaluate what God is actually doing in your life.

Twice in verses 9 and 10 Paul outlined the steps taken by those who had given in to the attraction of pursuing contentment through earthly gain. The outcome was inevitable. He described two parallel pathways with the same destination:

In verse 9:
■ Some want to be rich.
■ Some fall into temptation (immediate trouble).
■ These people are trapped by inappropriate desires.
■ Their lives are ruined and destroyed.

In verse 10:
■ Some are eager to be rich.
■ Some wander away (gradual trouble).
■ These people experience increasingly painful results of their greed.

Jesus understood the power of money, for he warned: "No one can serve two masters; for a slave will either hate the one and love the other, or be devoted to the one and despise the other. You cannot serve God and wealth" (Matthew 6:24 NRSV); and "How hard it will be for those who have wealth to enter the kingdom of God! . . . It is easier for a camel to go through the eye of a needle than for someone who is rich to enter the kingdom of God" (Mark 10:23, 25 NRSV).

PAUL'S FINAL INSTRUCTIONS / 6:11-21

As with many preachers, Paul had a difficult time concluding his message. He encouraged, challenged, warned, and instructed right up to the last sentence of his letter. In these final verses, he included personal words to Timothy, a final doxology to Jesus Christ, and parting words of instruction about those who were being false to the gospel by their lives and teaching.

6:11 **But you, O man of God, flee these things.**^{NKJV} **But you, O man of God, flee these things.**[NKJV] In contrast to the "some" of verse 10 who had wandered from the faith in their quest for riches, Paul addressed Timothy as a *man of God* who should run away from the temptation of money.

RUNNING IN PLACE
Why do we find it so hard to flee from the love of money?
    We are constantly bombarded by TV and the rest of the media to buy, buy, buy. We are not even required to pay . . . at least not right away. All the pleasures of having money are offered to us on credit! Even the typical vacation simply takes us to a new location to go shopping.
    Christians need times of solitude and isolation in order to quiet the urgent messages to live up to our identity as consumers. It is helpful to physically cut ourselves off for a while from the intrusions of materialism. Spending time alone in nature can have an amazing healing effect. It restores our closeness with God, restores our perspective, and enables us to cope with the financial pressure. When did you last go camping or fishing? Even a long, leisurely hike in the woods has anti-materialistic therapeutic value.

Pursue righteousness, godliness, faith, love, patience, gentleness.[NKJV] This list compares both with the fruit of the Spirit (see Galatians 5:22-23) and with the qualifications for church elders (see 3:1-3), although differences in these lists indicate that Paul was offering an assortment rather than a specific set of qualities. It would be impossible to pursue money and these spiritual traits—we cannot go opposite directions at the same time. Jesus made it very clear that the elimination of evil from our lives will last only if the vacuum is filled with good (see Matthew 12:43-45). We need a positive strategy of service and discipline.

Righteousness refers to actions that are morally upright and virtuous. Here Paul was not thinking of the foundational righteousness that God, through Christ, freely gives us. That righteousness we receive by faith. Rather, this righteousness involves our wholehearted efforts to grow into the kind of people God has already declared we will be in eternity. *Godliness* refers to actions in line with God's character. Paul used this term more than any other in the Pastoral Epistles (see 3:16; 4:7-8; 6:5-6) to indicate a person's interest in thinking and living to please God. Righteousness and godliness certainly overlap in meaning. But righteousness emphasizes obedience, while godliness emphasizes the God-centered motives for our obedience. Godliness always includes righteousness, but there are also many forms of worthless righteousness. Jesus was constantly at odds with those who were righteous in appearance only, while their motives were entirely self-centered (see, for example, Matthew 23:23-28). He described those who are only outwardly righteous as dazzling painted tombs inside of which everything is rotting.

Faith and *love* are fundamental to Christianity and basic to Paul's teaching (see 1 Corinthians 13:13). The qualities of faith and love are constantly under improvement by the work of God's Spirit. Our capacity to trust must grow and be renewed, and the development of our love for God and for others involves a life-long construction project. We are to pursue these in the sense that we practice what we already understand, while praying that we might understand and practice more.

Patience (Greek *hupomone,* "endurance") in persecution and trouble are vital for all believers; Timothy would need an extra dose of patience as he led a large congregation through difficult days ahead. Timothy had been with Paul when the apostle had written to the Romans to explain that patience was the first positive by-product of suffering (see Romans 5:3-5). In Timothy's present circumstances, pursuing patience would require a willingness to undergo suffering. People often desire patience, but few are willing to take the road that leads to that destination (see also James 1:2-4).

Gentleness seems an odd quality for Timothy to pursue; after all, he was already timid, and Paul had told him to deal firmly with false teaching. However, gentleness can reveal more power than roughness or harshness. Perhaps by mentioning this Paul was affirming a positive quality that was already a part of Timothy's character. The false teachers could have no power against a righteous, gentle leader with the truth on his side.

RUN FOR YOUR LIFE
Paul's counsel contradicts our human tendencies. We tend to try to get as close as possible to temptation without actually falling into sin. We want to know how far we can go toward sin rather than how to stay far away. Paul encourages us not to flirt with disaster and to flee from temptation and sin.

Paul pinpoints the solution. We are to replace our fascination with worldly values with a passion for godly ones. Fleeing evil becomes doubly useful if it puts us in hot pursuit of Christlikeness. The qualities that Paul urged Timothy to pursue ought also to be our passionate quest.

6:12 Fight the good fight of the faith.[NRSV] Using the same word he used in 1:18 to describe Timothy's work in Ephesus, Paul described furthering the gospel as a *fight*—but it is *the good fight of the faith.* The verb tense in Greek implies that this fight is an ongoing, continual process requiring diligence and discipline. Timothy would continue a "fight" already begun by others. Believers today continue the "fight" for which Timothy and Paul offered their lives. The Greek word for "fight," *agonizou,* has military overtones; it was also used to refer to athletic contests. It suggests agonizing and contesting.

THE AGONY OF COMPETITION
Paul used the word *agonizou* to describe the Christian fight. We hear about the "agony of defeat," but agony also describes the commitment required to participate in any challenge. Athletes know the agony of training, the strain of preparation, and the pain that comes from maximum performance. All this suffering must be endured as "beneficial agony" by those who want to do their best.

Christian service, like athletics, requires training and sacrifice. Our discipline and obedience largely define whether or not we will be contributors or merely spectators under Christ's guidance (see Hebrews 12:1-2). How would other believers rank your contributing role on Christ's team?

Take hold of the eternal life to which you were called when you made your good confession in the presence of many witnesses.[NIV] The prize motivates the fighter. Paul said "press on to take hold" when he wrote to the Philippians—"not that I have already obtained all this, or have already been made perfect, but I press on to take hold of that for which Christ Jesus took hold of me" (Philippians 3:12 NIV). How fitting that Paul should challenge his disciple with the same goal.

Those who fight the good fight of the faith can already *take hold* of their prize. An important part of effective athletic competition involves identifying the goal to be reached. Here, as in Philippians, the identified goal revolves around Jesus Christ: "Brothers, I do not consider myself yet to have taken hold of it. But one thing I do: Forgetting what is behind and straining toward what is ahead, I press on toward the goal to win the prize for which God has called me heavenward in Christ Jesus" (Philippians 3:13-14 NIV).

Eternal life began for Timothy (as for all believers) at the moment of conversion (see John 5:24; 1 John 3:14; 5:13). When a person confesses faith in Jesus Christ as Savior, eternal life begins. Their "goal" becomes clear. Timothy could hold on to that eternal life that became his when he confessed Christ as his Savior.

GET GOING!
Paul used active and forceful verbs from athletics to describe the Christian life: *flee, pursue, fight, take hold.* Some think Christianity is a passive religion that advocates waiting for God to act. But we must have an *active* faith, obeying God with courage and doing what we know is right. Is it time for action on your part? Don't wait—get going!

Reflecting the confidence Paul had in the outcome of Timothy's life, Paul reminded him of his *good confession in the presence of many witnesses.* The specific incident Paul had in mind has been identified in at least three different ways by scholars: (1) Some think Paul was referring to Timothy's baptism, since that occasion would have been a likely time for public confession. (2) A few think this occurred at some point during Paul and Timothy's ministry together when, during persecution, Timothy stood out by his faithfulness. (3) Others suggest Timothy's ordination, which is the most likely interpretation because Paul had already made reference to this earlier in the letter (1:18; 4:14). However, none of these positions can be definitely proven, but the fact of Paul and Timothy's long association would have given the elder any number of occasions to observe the younger's faith in action.

6:13 I urge you in the sight of God who gives life to all things.^{NKJV}
Several times in this letter, Paul has charged, commanded, and

urged Timothy toward various actions. Here again, Paul urged Timothy "to keep this command" (see 6:14) before several witnesses, including God, who, as the giver of earthly and eternal life, is an all-seeing and ever-present witness of Timothy's service. As important as the witnessing role of other believers might be, the key witnesses to faithfulness are God himself and Jesus Christ.

And before Christ Jesus who witnessed the good confession before Pontius Pilate.^{NKJV} Just as Timothy made a good confession before many witnesses, Christ had made the good confession before Pontius Pilate. Timothy's confession focused on his belief in Jesus as Savior and Lord. Jesus' confession focused on his *being* Savior and Lord. Thus, the *good confession* is understanding and telling who Jesus is. Jesus' trial before Pilate is recorded in the Gospels: Matthew 27:11; Mark 15:2; Luke 23:2-3; John 18:36-37. No matter how difficult circumstances might become, Timothy always would have the example of Jesus who remained faithful in the face of death. Paul was setting before Timothy the same example noted in Hebrews: "Let us fix our eyes on Jesus, the author and perfecter of our faith, who for the joy set before him endured the cross, scorning its shame, and sat down at the right hand of the throne of God" (Hebrews 12:2 NIV).

6:14 **To keep this command without spot or blame until the appearing of our Lord Jesus Christ.**^{NIV} Paul urged (6:13) Timothy to keep "this command." He might have been referring to the "sound instruction" and "godly teaching" explained in verse 3; perhaps he was referring to Timothy's commission as a leader in the early church, specifically in Ephesus. The third and most likely option is that Paul was referring to his previous instruction for Timothy to continue in his pursuit of godly character. Timothy's ministry could then also keep his congregation safe, *without spot or blame* until the return of Jesus Christ. The commands need only be followed *until* Jesus returns. At that time, the good fight will be over; the battle will be won.

The *appearing of our Lord Jesus.* "Appearing" (Greek *epiphaneia*) is one of the three terms in the New Testament referring to the return of Christ (see also 2 Timothy 1:10; 4:1, 8; Titus 2:11-13). Neither of the other two words ("revelation," *apocalupse*) or ("coming," *parousia*) are used in the Pastoral Epistles. Some scholars have suggested that the Greek influence indicated by this particular term points to a late date for the letter itself. In their view, this term and its context imply a dwindling hope that Christ's return would be soon approaching. However, Paul's explanatory phrase about God's timing clearly indicates a confi-

dence, not a doubt, that Christ's return will occur not one
moment sooner or later than God himself intends.

6:15 Which God will bring about in his own time.NIV The "appearing
of our Lord Jesus Christ," the Second Coming, will happen according to God's timetable. Jesus had told his disciples, "No one knows
about that day or hour, not even the angels in heaven, nor the Son,
but only the Father" (Matthew 24:36 NIV). Paul's early teachings
and writings show that he believed this return would occur very
soon. However, at the time of this letter to Timothy, Paul realized
that this return might not occur before his death. It would occur in
God's own time. As Paul contemplated the glorious display of love
and power that will be revealed when Christ returns, he acknow-
leged God's awesome and transcendent nature.

GOD'S TIMETABLE
It may be difficult to accept God's timing in world events, but we
must not forget that God has a sovereign right to exercise control. We have neither the wisdom nor the perspective to question his judgment. Being all-knowing and all-loving, God can be
trusted to control the lives of people and the destinies of
nations in order to accomplish his purposes. Eventually we will
see that all has been done for our best interests.
    Though we cannot change God's plans, our response to his
actions will deeply affect our destiny. We must be careful not to
resent or second-guess God's timetable; otherwise we will miss
out on many of the immediate benefits he has for us. Are you
trusting God with the timetable?

**He who is the blessed and only Sovereign, the King of kings
and Lord of lords.**NRSV Paul's doxology may be words from an
early Christian hymn or even a Jewish blessing. See Deuteronomy 10:17; Psalm 136:2-3; Revelation 17:14; 19:16 for similar
words of praise to God. In any case, Paul's reference to God's
plan immediately filled his mind with a word-vision of the one he
served with his life. Paul created a special parenthesis in this letter in order to describe God, and he used the most exalted language he had at his disposal.

    The word for *Sovereign* indicates chieftan or prince. Paul's
usage indicated that God was the independent, absolute, and
unique possessor of power. The phrases *King of kings* and *Lord of
lords* used together reveal that there is no other way to ascribe
more power and authority than to God alone. Paul used the common titles for human power, but enlarged them by investing in
God supreme power over those we consider most powerful. God
has no peer.

A PORTRAIT OF GOD

As before in this letter (1:17), Paul needed no excuse at all to launch into an exuberant doxology. In this case, he chose eight wide verbal brushstrokes to picture the awesome nature of God:

Name	What It Means	Other References
Blessed and only Sovereign (Most High)	Control and power are God's alone.	Acts 4:24; Revelation 6:10
King of kings	No king has more power or authority (first used of Babylonian and Persian emperors).	Daniel 4:34; Revelation 17:14; 19:16
Lord of lords	God possesses absolute superiority over all powers, human and divine.	Deuteronomy 10:17; Psalm 136:2-3; Revelation 17:14; 19:16
Immortal	God alone has inherent immortality; ours comes from him.	1 Corinthians 15:53-57
Unapproachable light	God's glory is blinding.	Exodus 24:15-17; Psalm 104:2
Unseen (Invisible)	God is so holy that no one can see him and live.	Exodus 33:17-23; 1 Samuel 6:1-5; John 1:18
Worthy of honor	God is to be honored for who he is and what he has done.	Psalm 96:6; John 5:23; Romans 2:7-10
Eternal dominion (Power)	God's power continues from eternity to eternity; it has no end.	1 Peter 4:11; Revelation 1:6

6:16 **It is he alone who has immortality and dwells in unapproachable light, whom no one has ever seen or can see; to him be honor and eternal dominion. Amen.**^{NRSV} Having established some idea of an appropriate title for God, Paul now lists several of the notable characteristics of our divine ruler. God alone is eternal (*has immortality*) from everlasting to everlasting. God is the only one having immortality in himself. He is not subject to death. Others may be given immortality, but only God has it inherent in his being.

Because he is eternal, he gives us eternal life. The bright glory of God's presence creates a barrier of light through which no

GOD'S ETERNAL AUDIT

Earthly treasures: Dangers of money	Forgetting God	Deuteronomy 6:10-13; 8:11-20; Proverbs 18:11; Luke 18:24; 1 Timothy 6:9-10
	Acting dishonestly, taking advantage of others	2 Kings 5:20-27; Proverbs 10:2; 22:16, 22-23; Isaiah 5:8-9; Amos 3:10; 5:11; 8:4-7; Micah 6:10-12; James 5:1-6
	Being greedy	Exodus 20:17; Luke 12:15-21; Ephesians 5:5
	Allowing it to take God's place	Proverbs 11:28; 18:11; Jeremiah 9:23-24; Matthew 6:24; Luke 6:24
Heavenly treasures: Good use of money	Give generously and cheerfully to help the poor	Proverbs 11:24-25; 19:17; 21:13; 22:9; 28:27; Luke 12:33-34; 2 Corinthians 9:7
	Give generously to those doing God's work	Deuteronomy 25:4; Nehemiah 13:10-11; 1 Timothy 5:17
	Tithe	Malachi 3:8-10; 1 Corinthians 16:2
	Pay your taxes	Romans 13:6-7
	Always be honest	Deuteronomy 25:14-16; Proverbs 20:10, 23; Luke 16:10-12
	Provide for your family	1 Timothy 5:8
	Plan wisely for the future	Proverbs 21:20; 22:3; 24:3-4, 27; 27:23-27

human can approach. Even if the light were removed, God remains invisible, unseen by human eyes (see Exodus 33:17-23; John 1:18). This does not mean God is unknowable, but that his holiness keeps us from seeing him.

God's legitimate power and position require two responses from us: *honor* and submission to his *eternal dominion.* When we approach God, we must not emphasize our own understanding or self-confidence; instead, we must submit to him and worship his awesome majesty. Any claim to equality with God simply widens the gulf between us. As Paul pointed out to the Romans (Romans 1:21-22), those who treat God lightly will not be able to bear the weight of his judgment.

6:17 Command those who are rich in this present age not to be haughty, nor to trust in uncertain riches.^{NKJV} After concluding his doxology with a decisive "Amen," Paul returned to the matters at hand. Those most in danger of having an incorrect attitude toward God were the wealthy. In verses 3-10, Paul had instructed those who did not have wealth, but deeply desired it. Here he focused on those who already possessed wealth. Ephesus was a thriving city, and the Ephesian church probably had at least some prosperous members. Perhaps some of the false teachers had already succeeded in amassing a degree of wealth for themselves.

Paul advised Timothy to deal with any potential problems by teaching that having riches carries great responsibility. The wealthy must not be *haughty* (high-minded or arrogant), as though they deserved their riches. Rather, they must be generous. Even then, they must avoid feeling proud that they had a lot to give. Their perspective on their riches should copy Paul's words in verse 7: "For we brought nothing into this world, and it is certain we can carry nothing out" (NKJV).

The rich were not to indulge in pride over their success nor to place their *trust in uncertain riches.* Pride was inappropriate because it indicated that the rich were basing their lives on what might appear to be valuable and dependable but which was, in fact, terribly uncertain. Clearly, Paul believed that as dangerous as it was to want to be wealthy, actually having riches was at least as risky for a person's well-being (see Proverbs 23:4-5).

PROBLEMS WITH MONEY
The possession and pursuit of money invariably creates certain dangerous difficulties:
- The desire for wealth is insatiable.
- The promises of wealth are illusory.
- The presence of wealth promotes anxiety.
- The potential of wealth tends to facilitate selfishness.
- The pursuit of wealth invites immoral suggestions to obtain more.
- The preoccupation with wealth tends to control a person's life. When a steward of wealth forgets the source of wealth, a soul lives in grave danger. Does your life demonstrate that you control whatever wealth God has placed under your authority?

The wealthy must trust not in their wealth **but rather on God who richly provides us with everything for our enjoyment.**^{NRSV} The rich must be careful to trust only in the living God for their security. The rich need not be ashamed of their riches;

A CHOICE OF TRUST

Since we cannot trust both God and wealth, we must choose one or the other. We can expect the following results:

Trust in God leads to:	Trust in riches leads to:
Peace	Anxiety
Service of others	Self-centeredness
Satisfaction	Dissatisfaction
Humility	Arrogance
Certainty	Uncertainty
Contentment	Restless greed

---

those riches are a gift from God, given to be enjoyed. There must always be a balance between avoiding a stale, ascetic life while at the same time keeping oneself from self-indulgence.

6:18 **Let them do good, that they be rich in good works, ready to give, willing to share.**^{NKJV} The rich are not to consume their riches on selfish pleasures; rather, they must share their bounty with those in need. The general goal to *do good* is broken down into three categories:

(1) As they do good to others they become *rich in good works,* practicing "hands-on" giving to others. People are sometimes more effectively helped by personal involvement than by the giving of material objects or money.

(2) Doing good improves our ability to respond quickly and effectively. Experience can help us become *ready to give* in a wholehearted way.

(3) Becoming *willing to share* will strike a blow against the self-centeredness of our times. We learn to do with less so that more may do with some.

For "share," Paul used a word related to "fellowship" (*koinonikous,* "those willing to share"). We can experience a deep fellowship when believers make their resources available to one another. Being rich in good works may not necessarily benefit our financial statement, but in the long run it will be a far more valuable asset in God's eyes.

6:19 **In this way they will lay up treasure for themselves as a firm foundation for the coming age, so that they may take hold of the life that is truly life.**^{NIV} Jesus talked about treasure in his Sermon on the Mount: "Do not lay up for yourselves treasures on earth, where moth and rust destroy and where thieves break in and steal; but lay up for yourselves treasures in heaven, where neither moth nor rust destroys and where thieves do not break in and steal. For where your treasure is, there your heart will be also" (Matthew 6:19-21 NKJV, see also Luke 12:33; 18:22). The rich must make certain to lay up treasures in heaven, investing their riches for eternity. This kind of investment includes tithing and giving offerings in church but is much broader. Any unselfish giving to meet the needs of others, especially the poor, creates a deposit in eternity. The person without God who selfishly pursues wealth will lay up a treasure of God's wrath (James 5:1-5).

In so doing, those who give are those who provide a *firm foundation* for the future and experience life as it is meant to be. In contrast to those seeking riches and ending in ruin and destruction (6:9), these generous rich people find true life, both on earth and in eternity. To again quote Jesus Christ: "And this is eternal life, that they may know You, the only true God, and Jesus Christ whom You have sent" (John 17:3 NKJV). The expression *life that is truly life* also reminds us of Jesus' stated purpose for his ministry: "The thief comes only to steal and kill and destroy; I have come that they may have life, and have it to the full" (John 10:10 NIV). Because God is the source of all life (6:13), all those who live his way experience real living!

6:20 **Timothy, guard what has been entrusted to you.**^{NRSV} One last time, Paul exhorted, encouraged, and urged Timothy to *guard* or "keep" (5:21) the teachings and instructions given him. No matter how influential the false teachers would become, Timothy would remain guardian of the truth, teaching it without wavering and without compromise. Paul's ministry on earth would eventually end with his death; Timothy was *entrusted* with the truth of the gospel so that he, in turn, would pass it along to others. The terms here come from the banking language and are consistent with the earlier instructions about being "rich in good works" and "storing up . . . treasure" (6:18-19). Paul considered all that Timothy had learned to be a priceless deposit that needed to be preserved or guarded by carefully investing it in the lives of others.

Paul would write in a later letter to Timothy: "And the things that you have heard from me among many witnesses, commit these to faithful men who will be able to teach others also" (2 Timothy 2:2 NKJV).

Turn away from godless chatter and the opposing ideas of what is falsely called knowledge.^{NIV} A guardian of the truth should not be involved in *godless chatter* or spend time talking about *opposing ideas of what is falsely called knowledge.* See 1:3-7 and comments for the makeup of this false teaching.

TALK SHOWS
What would Paul have to say about the endless round of media "talk shows" available today? They sometimes even get around to discussing religious topics, at least when there is a clergy sex scandal of some kind. His term "godless chatter" seems particularly appropriate. We have witnessed the replacement of truth with a constant appeal to opinion polls and shouted slogans. Our age has been called the age of information. Too bad there is so little truth. The more facts that are piled up, the less knowledge seems available. Paul's warning to Timothy can be applied practically without interpretation in our world today.

6:21 Which some have professed and in so doing have wandered from the faith.^{NIV} Those who followed the false teachers *wandered from the faith.* "Wandered" (literally "missed the mark") does not imply a permanent condition, but a dangerous and fruitless one. True believers would not lose their salvation, but if they followed the false teachers, they would waste valuable time in nonsense—time that could have been spent learning about and sharing the Good News.

Grace be with you. The closing benediction includes a plural *you* indicating that Paul expected this letter to be read to the congregation and to other churches. Paul began and ended with *grace.* For him, as it should be for us, grace was never a sociable courtesy but a costly gift from God. Having experienced the grace of God, Paul never tired of praying that others would also experience this grace.

The book of 1 Timothy provides guiding principles for local churches, including rules for public worship and qualifications for overseers (elders, pastors), deacons, and special church workers (widows). Paul told the church leaders to correct incorrect doctrine and to deal lovingly and fairly with all people in the church. The church is not organized simply for the sake of organization, but so that Christ can be honored and glorified. While studying these guidelines, don't lose sight of what is most important in the life of the church—knowing God, working together in harmony, and taking God's Good News to the world.

2 TIMOTHY

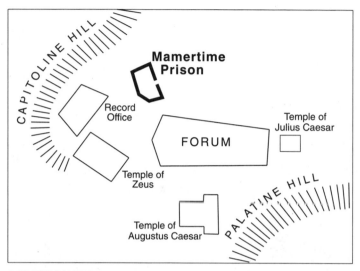

2 TIMOTHY MAP
Paul's second imprisonment in Rome was in the Mamertine dungeon. Interestingly, this damp dungeon was in the center of Rome near the Roman forum, which was like a huge town square. At the forum, processions, trials, victory ceremonies, political meetings, and elections took place. The Roman forum was the city's heartbeat. In this square, decisions about the future and fate of Rome were made. If only more of them had listened to the gospel, preached by a man who was imprisoned only blocks away.

INTRODUCTION TO 2 TIMOTHY

Paul, the great apostle and missionary of the church.

What thoughts and feelings must have filled Paul as he sat again in prison, knowing that he soon would face his executioner . . . and then his Lord. Reflecting on his ministry, Paul must have felt joy, remembering his conversion on the road to Damascus, his session with the Jerusalem elders, his trips throughout the world preaching the gospel and planting churches, the explosive spread of Christianity among Gentiles, and his faithful coworkers and close friends: Barnabas, Silas, Priscilla, Aquila, Luke, Peter, James, Mark, Lydia, and so many others. But Paul must have felt a twinge of sadness and regret as he recalled those who had harmed or deserted him or had left the faith: Demas, Alexander, Hymenaeus, and others. Undoubtedly Paul also experienced moments of intense loneliness. He had been deserted twice—first by those in Asia (1:15), and then by those in Rome at his arrest (4:16). Paul's emotions also must have included concern . . . for young believers, for the churches, and for those he had appointed to carry the ministry forward—young leaders such as Titus, Timothy, and Tychicus.

Paul knew that the new generation of church leaders was ready—trained, experienced, confident, articulate, courageous, and totally committed to Christ. In fact, already they had ministered in very difficult circumstances, confronting false teachers, organizing local churches, evangelizing the lost, and discipling believers. Titus had worked effectively with the infamous Cretans, and Timothy had led and nurtured the church at Ephesus.

As Paul lay in his cell, awaiting martyrdom at the command of the madman Nero, he was not alone with his feelings: Visitors had come, Luke was present (4:11), and God was there. And Paul did not spend his final days and hours wallowing in despair—he encouraged and taught others, read (4:13), and wrote.

Paul's final words were bundled in a letter to his beloved Timothy, his "true son in the faith" (1 Timothy 1:2). A much more personal and somber letter than the others, 2 Timothy contains no complex refutations of apostasy, detailed instructions for church leaders, profound theological treatises, extensive lessons for young believers, or exhilarating doxologies and benedictions. Instead, in this last letter, brimming with quiet emotion, Paul reflected on his life and encouraged, warned, instructed, and exhorted Timothy. It's as though Paul were saying, "I'm trusting you to carry on, Timothy. Stay faithful, stay strong, watch out, and take care!"

What last words would you write to your loved ones and friends? Paul's words flowed from his life of faith and reflected his deep commitment to his Lord. What could you say or write to encourage someone now? Remind that person of God's love and presence, and challenge him or her to live for Christ.

SETTING

Paul was confined to a Roman prison; Timothy probably was still in Ephesus.

Nero, the fifth Roman emperor, began to reign in A.D. 54, at sixteen years of age. The first few years of his rule were peaceful and gave promise of a bright future. During that time, Paul had appealed to Caesar at his trial in Caesarea (Acts 25:10-11) and thus had been brought to Rome to present his case (A.D. 61). When Paul eventually went to trial, he was cleared of all charges and freed to resume his ministry. For the next few years, Paul traveled extensively and wrote 1 Timothy and Titus (see the suggested itinerary under "Date" in the introduction to 1 Timothy). All this occurred during Nero's reign.

After marrying Poppaea, Nero became brutal and ruthless, killing his own mother, his chief advisers Seneca and Burrus, and many of the nobility to seize their fortunes. Nero's thirst for publicity pushed him into excessive acts of decadence, including chariot races, combat between gladiators, and the gory spectacle of prisoners thrown to wild beasts. In A.D. 64, fire destroyed a large part of Rome. Suspected of ordering the fire himself (to make room for a new palace), Nero deflected blame by accusing the Christians, a devout religious minority who refused to worship the emperor. Thus began the terrible persecution of the church, with torture, executions, and Coliseum entertainment. Tacitus wrote:

■ *Their death was made a matter of sport; they were covered in*
wild beasts' skins and torn to pieces by dogs; or were fastened
to crosses and set on fire in order to serve as torches by night
. . . Nero had offered his gardens for the spectacle and gave an
exhibition in his circus, mingling with the crowd in the guise of
a charioteer or mounted on his chariot. Hence, . . . there arose
a feeling of pity because it was felt that they were being sacri-
ficed not for the common good, but to gratify the savagery of
one man. (Tacitus, Annals 15.44)

During this reign of terror for Christians, Paul was taken prisoner again, apparently at Nicopolis where he had intended to
spend the winter (Titus 3:12). Paul was taken to Rome and
imprisoned in the Mamertine dungeon, in the center of Rome
near the forum (see the map).

Paul's first imprisonment (about A.D. 60–62) had been similar
to house arrest. He lived in a rented house, in relative comfort but
under Roman guard, and was able to welcome numerous visitors
(Acts 28:23-30). In contrast, Paul's second Roman prison was
dark, damp, dirty, and difficult to find (1:17). In the first, Paul
had awaited trial with the privilege of a Roman citizen. In the second, he waited for death as a condemned criminal. Paul still was
allowed to write and read, but he was lonely (he wanted to see
his friends—4:9-11) and he was cold (he wanted his cloak—
4:13).

A few months after writing this letter to Timothy, according to
tradition, Paul was beheaded on the Ostian Way outside Rome.
This occurred shortly before Nero's own death, by suicide, in
A.D. 68, just as the Roman senate was declaring Nero "an enemy
of the people" because of the atrocities he had committed. Peter
also was martyred during Nero's reign.

Timothy probably was still in Ephesus when he received
Paul's letter. Paul was lonely and wanted Timothy to come and
see him. He sent Tychicus to Ephesus with this letter, with the
probable understanding that Tychicus would relieve Timothy
of his duties there. Sent as the apostolic representative to that
city, Timothy had been charged in Paul's first letter (about A.D.
64) with the responsibility of organizing the churches there
and for rooting out the false teachers. While 2 Timothy contains pastoral counsel and instruction for the church, it is
essentially a personal letter—Paul revealing his heart and soul
to his dear friend.

For more on the church at Ephesus, see the comments under
"Setting" in the introduction to 1 Timothy.

AUDIENCE

Timothy and the church at large.

Timothy represented the new generation of leadership for the church. He, Titus, and others were expected to fill the shoes of Paul, Peter, and the other apostles and church leaders. Paul had left Timothy in Ephesus and had given him responsibility for refuting the false teachers and organizing the local congregations. Paul had written Timothy (1 Timothy) with specific instructions for choosing elders and deacons and with a challenge to sound doctrine and personal discipline.

It is not surprising that Paul's final words would be penned to Timothy. Paul was instrumental in Timothy's coming to faith, and he thought of Timothy as a son. They experienced a closeness in friendship and in the body of Christ. Paul knew he could count on his beloved friend and coworker. For more on Timothy, see the comments under "Audience" in the introduction to 1 Timothy.

Through the inspiration of the Holy Spirit, Paul also was writing to the church at large—believers everywhere, then and in the years to come. Because this letter is so specific and personal, its message applies directly to individual Christians, especially church leaders. Much also can be learned from the close relationship enjoyed by Paul and Timothy. Like father and son, siblings, or very close friends, these men had worked together, prayed for each other, and loved one another. In a world hostile to Christ and those who would claim his name, Paul and Timothy had learned the importance of teamwork and of caring for their brothers and sisters in Christ. In fact, in the last few sentences of this letter, Paul referred to at least nine other fellow servants of Christ. If you were writing your last letter, what coworkers in the ministry would you name? Who is your "Timothy"? We must learn to work closely with other believers—the need and our task is too great to try to minister alone.

OCCASION

Apostasy in Ephesus and Paul's loneliness during his final days in prison.

Paul felt deserted (1:15). The churches in Asia were discarding his teachings, and many had failed to support him while he languished in prison. Paul knew that his days remaining on earth were few, so he wanted to encourage Timothy to boldly confront the false teachers and lead the church back to the truth. Paul urged Timothy to remember his call, to be strong and have courage, to use his spiritual gifts, and to remain faithful to the gospel.

Paul felt lonely (4:11). Isolated and alone in a dark and damp Roman prison and awaiting death, Paul wanted to see Timothy again (4:9-13, 21). Paul asked him to come to Rome and to bring Mark, a cloak, and especially the scrolls and parchments with him.

Prisons come in many forms—abandonment, destructive relationships, obsessive habits, debilitating illnesses, dead-end jobs. Those trapped inside such prisons feel isolated and alone. Even Paul, who enjoyed an intimate relationship with God, experienced loneliness in prison; many had left, and he wanted Timothy to come to him. To whom can you be a Timothy? What prisoners do you know? Take them your love, another friend, a coat, and especially God's Word.

PURPOSE

To inspire, challenge, and motivate Timothy to carry on the gospel ministry.

This letter to his beloved Timothy is tinged with sadness because Paul realized that soon he would be executed. Reminiscences (1:1-5; 3:10-11), references to death (1:10; 2:11) and suffering (1:12; 2:9; 3:11-12), mention of prison life (1:15-16; 2:9), and hints of impending martyrdom (4:6-8, 18) reveal Paul's realistic understanding of his plight. But this letter is not depressing—Paul filled it with notes of triumph as he wrote of his lifelong commitment to Christ (1:12; 2:11-13; 4:7-8) and as he challenged Timothy to carry on with the work to which they had both been called (1:6-7, 13-14; 2:1-7, 15; 3:14-17; 4:1-2, 5).

Paul had prepared Timothy for this day, and he was sure that his protégé was ready. So he wrote to remind Timothy of his call and the task that lay ahead. Paul also was aware of Timothy's shortcomings; he virtually called Timothy's timidity (1:7) being "ashamed" of Christ and of Paul himself (1:8). Paul was challenging Timothy to get his act together.

Paul was amazing. Although deserted by former friends and facing death, he continued to fight the good fight (4:7) and to challenge and inspire others to greatness. Paul's primary focus was to be faithful to Christ and to his call as a minister of the gospel. Next on Paul's list of priorities, however, stood his deep concern for the church and its new leaders. What holds top billing in your life—personal comfort, financial security, pleasure? As with

Paul, if you focus on Christ, you will know how to live . . . and you will know how to die.

DATE

About A.D. 66 or 67, from Rome.

Paul had written letters to Timothy (1 Timothy) and Titus in approximately A.D. 64–65, during his time of freedom between Roman imprisonments. Just about two years later, he wrote to Timothy again, but this time from prison. Note that the last three of Paul's thirteen letters were written to men who would lead the church after his death. Paul knew the importance of entrusting the ministry to reliable men and women who would be able to teach others (2:2).

MESSAGE

Boldness; faithfulness; preaching and teaching; error.

Boldness (1:5-12; 4:1-5). Paul knew that Timothy soon would face opposition and persecution and might become disheartened by Paul's imprisonment and death (1:8-9). He also knew that Timothy had the tendency to be timid, so Paul reminded him that God gives a spirit of power, love, and self-discipline, not timidity (1:7). And Paul urged Timothy to carry out his ministry without fear or shame, to utilize boldly the gifts of preaching and teaching that the Holy Spirit had given him.

Importance for Today. We can easily become discouraged when we are persecuted for our faith. And we can be intimidated by the threats of those who oppose us. But the Holy Spirit helps us to be wise and strong, and God honors our confident testimony for him even when we suffer. To get over our fear of what people might say or do to us, we must take our eyes off people and look only to God, remembering that he has promised to be with us through everything (see Romans 8:38-39). In what situations are you afraid to speak up for what you believe? What can you do to strengthen your resolve to live more boldly for Christ?

Faithfulness (1:13-14; 2:1, 3-13; 3:14-15). Because of his difficult situation, Timothy may have been tempted to waver in his faith or even to desert the cause of Christ as others had done (4:10, 16). To resist this temptation, Timothy was to remember Christ's faithfulness in suffering and dying for our sins. In addition, Paul's own example was important, for he had been faithful through countless trials and was still serving Christ, even in prison. Paul urged Timothy to maintain sound doctrine, to be loyal and diligent, and to endure.

Importance for Today. We followers of Christ can count on being opposed and suffering because of what we believe and how we live. People don't like to be reminded that they are sinning and headed for hell. Even in our churches we may face rejection when we stand for the truth. But regardless of the cost, we are to be faithful to Christ and to faithfully proclaim his Word. As we trust Christ, he counts us worthy to suffer, and he will give us the strength we need to be strong and faithful to him. What can you do to prepare for times of discouragement?

Preaching and teaching (2:2, 22-26; 3:16-17; 4:1-5). Paul had spent most of his life spreading the Good News, winning people to Christ, teaching new Christians, and establishing new churches. Paul had trained Timothy to follow in his footsteps, to preach and teach the gospel. So facing the reality of his own death, Paul passed the leadership torch to Timothy and encouraged him to train others who would be able to carry on after Timothy was gone. Timothy should train these men and women in sound doctrine, in being totally committed to Christ, and in how to teach. In large measure we have heard the gospel and have believed because Paul and Timothy were faithful to teach others how to teach others.

Importance for Today. The two most important tasks of a Christian leader are evangelism (sharing the gospel with others and leading them to Christ) and discipleship (establishing new believers in the faith). A vital part of the discipleship process is preparing people to transmit God's Word to others so that they in turn might pass it on. Of course it is not enough just to teach—teaching must be of the highest quality, mining the depths of God's Word. Whom are you helping to disciple? What is your church doing to carefully train men and women to teach?

Error (2:14-21; 3:1-13; 4:9-18). Wherever there is truth, lies will arise. Human beings are sinful and will use anything, even religious causes, to meet their self-centered needs. Remember, too, that Satan is constantly twisting the truth and attempting to deceive, so we shouldn't be surprised that false teachers abound. Paul warned Timothy about heretics and spiritual dropouts. Timothy was not to be surprised, discouraged, or defeated by these false teachers and deserters. Instead, he should stay strong in his faith, confront and refute those who would lead the church astray, and continue to boldly preach and teach the truth. And Paul

reminded Timothy that God's Word, not theories and philoso-
phies, contains God's truth (see 2:15; 3:16-17).

Importance for Today. The Bible warns that in the final days
before Christ returns, false teachers will be prevalent. Thus spiritual error and heretics will be increasing through the years. The
antidote for false teaching is keeping our eyes on Christ and
studying God's Word. We must be disciplined and ready to reject
heresy. We must know the Word of God as our sure defense
against error and confusion. How much time each week do you
spend in Bible study? What new Christian friend can you help
get grounded more firmly in the Word?

VITAL STATISTICS

Purpose: To give final instructions and encouragement to Timothy, leader of the church at Ephesus

Author: Paul

To whom written: Timothy, and all Christians everywhere

Date written: About A.D. 66 or 67, from prison in Rome. After a year or two of freedom, Paul was arrested again and executed under the emperor Nero.

Setting: Paul was virtually alone in prison; only Luke was with him. Paul wrote this letter to pass the torch to the new generation of church leaders. He also asked for visits from his friends and for his scrolls (portions of the Old Testament) and especially the parchments (possibly portions of the New Testament).

Key verse: "Do your best to present yourself to God as one approved, a workman who does not need to be ashamed and who correctly handles the word of truth" (2:15 NIV).

OUTLINE

1. Foundations of Christian service (1:1–2:26)
2. Difficult times for Christian service (3:1–4:22)

2 Timothy 1

Paul's second letter to Timothy was written sometime between two and four years after his first letter. Penned in approximately A.D. 66 or 67, these are the last words we have from Paul. Timothy had been Paul's traveling companion on the second and third missionary journeys, and Paul had left him in Ephesus to help the church there (1 Timothy 1:3-4). As in his first letter, Paul encouraged Timothy in his ministry in Ephesus. Paul's first letter to Timothy had focused on silencing the false teachers and choosing effective leaders for the church. The ministry in Ephesus presented overwhelming challenges for the young minister, and Paul had expressed hope to visit Timothy in Ephesus at some point (1 Timothy 3:14).

As Paul wrote this second letter, the Christian church throughout the empire was facing severe persecution and hardship. Emperor Nero had begun a major persecution in A.D. 64 as part of his plan to pass the blame for the great fire of Rome from himself to the Christians. This persecution spread across the empire and included social ostracism, public torture, and murder.

> Although [this second message] was an intensely personal communication to his young friend Timothy, it was also—and consciously—his last will and testament to the church. *John Stott*

Thus, the tone of this letter is somber. Paul, imprisoned for the last time, knew he would soon die. Unlike Paul's first imprisonment in Rome, when he was in a house (Acts 28:16, 23, 30) where he continued to teach, this time he was probably confined to a cold dungeon, awaiting his death (4:6-8). As Paul awaited execution, he wrote this letter to his dear friend Timothy, a younger man who was like a son to him (1:2). How Timothy must have cherished this last letter from his beloved mentor and friend.

1:1 Paul, an apostle of Christ Jesus by the will of God.^{NRSV} As at the beginning of 1 Timothy, Paul had identified himself by name and also by his authority. Paul was an *apostle* (*apostolos*), mean-

PAUL'S TWO IMPRISONMENTS

	First Imprisonment A.D. 60–62	Second Imprisonment A.D. 66–67
Reason	Accused by Jews and appealed to Rome	Persecuted by the Roman government
Conditions	Relatively comfortable: in a rented house (Acts 28:30-31)	Cold, dark, lonely dungeon
Relationships	Visited by many friends	Almost totally alone
Freedom	Had many opportunities to witness for Christ—eventually was freed	Was totally confined to prison but was able to read and write
Outlook	Expected freedom (Philippians 1:24-26)	Expected to be executed (4:6), but looked forward to heaven (1:12, 2:8; 4:18)

ing "one who is sent." Paul was not one of the original twelve disciples (who were called apostles after Jesus' resurrection), yet Jesus appeared to Paul personally and commissioned him to be an apostle (Acts 9:1-6; 26:12-18).

God chose Paul for special work: "He is an instrument whom I have chosen to bring my name before Gentiles and kings and before the people of Israel . . ." (Acts 9:15 NRSV). Paul did not seek this apostleship; instead, he was chosen by God. Thus, Paul could truthfully say he was an apostle *by the will of God.* Here Paul used a different emphasis than in his first letter. In 1 Timothy, Paul said that his apostleship was by "command of God," emphasizing God's active role in sending him to carry the gospel. That command was still being carried out. As Paul neared the end of his life, he could resolutely claim that his ministry had been a product of God's plan. As the rest of this letter will show, Paul's thinking had shifted from the work that needed to be done (in his first letter to Timothy) to the work he had accomplished (see 4:6-7).

Obviously, this formal introduction

One evening I shall never forget, I invited him into my heart. What an entrance he made! It was not a spectacular emotional thing, but very real. It was at the very center of my life. He came into the darkness of my heart and turned on the light. He built a fire in the cold hearth and banished the chill. . . . I have never regretted opening the door to Christ and I never will—not into eternity!
Robert B. Munger

was unnecessary for Timothy; however, Paul knew that his letters and teachings ultimately would reach a much larger audience, so he included these credentials in the salutation.

According to the promise of life which is in Christ Jesus.^{NKJV} The Greek word translated "according to" (*kata*) could give two meanings for this phrase. One meaning implies cause (Paul became an apostle when he received the *promise of life* in the gospel of Jesus Christ). The other meaning implies goal or purpose. (The "promise of life" in the gospel became the message Paul had taken across the Roman Empire.) The promise of life is the promise of eternal life. Although fully realized at the return of Christ, this life begins at conversion (see Titus 1:2).

Among the twenty-nine Greek words that make up this greeting, Paul used the title *Christ Jesus* three times. In Paul's mind Christ Jesus defined his role as an apostle, guaranteed a powerful promise out of which flowed life itself, and was the source of "grace, mercy and peace."

Everything Paul was and hoped to be was wrapped up "in Christ Jesus."

THIS IS THE LIFE
When we are united with Christ, life takes on both immediate and eternal dimensions. Paul's use of the word *promise* can apply to the "life" that Jesus gives immediately to those who trust him, as well as to the "life" fully realized in eternity. On one hand, Paul said, "If anyone is in Christ, he is a new creation" (2 Corinthians 5:17 NKJV). So new life begins at conversion. Yet on the other hand, "We wait eagerly for our adoption as sons, the redemption of our bodies. For in this hope we were saved" (Romans 8:23-24 NIV). The present experience we enjoy provides a foretaste of our complete redemption at Christ's return. When we struggle with difficulties in this life, remember that the best is yet to come.

The phrase "in Christ Jesus" provides almost a summary statement of Paul's theology. He used the phrase in every one of his letters with the exception of 2 Thessalonians and Titus, each of which include a slightly different format (see 2 Thessalonians 1:12; Titus 3:4-6). (For defining usages see Romans 6:11; 8:1; 1 Corinthians 1:4; 15:22; 2 Corinthians 5:17, 19; Galatians 2:16-17; 3:28; Ephesians 2:10; 4:32; Philippians 3:8-9; Colossians 1:28; 2:9-10; 1 Thessalonians 4:16; 1 Timothy 1:14; 2 Timothy 2:1). In Paul's thought, the phrase "in Christ Jesus" refers to the mystical union between Christ and the believers. This means that the relationship that exists between Jesus and those who have received him (John 1:12) is unlike any other. In one place, Paul describes this as "Christ in you, the hope of glory" (Colossians 1:27 NIV), while in another he affirms, "If anyone is in Christ, he is a new creation; the old has gone, the new has come!" (2 Corinthians 5:17 NIV). To be "in Christ Jesus," then, involves trusting him, identifying with him, seeing ourselves under his protection and authority, and recognizing his presence in us.

1:2 To Timothy, a beloved son.NKJV Paul most likely met the young Timothy and his mother, Eunice, and grandmother Lois (1:5) when Paul and Barnabas visited Lystra, a city in the province of Galatia, on the first missionary journey (see Acts 14:8-21). On the second missionary journey, Paul and Silas traveled to several cities that Paul had already visited, including Lystra, "where there was a disciple named Timothy, the son of a Jewish woman who was a believer. . . . He was well spoken of by the believers in Lystra and Iconium. Paul wanted Timothy to accompany him" (Acts 16:1-3 NRSV). So the young disciple, Timothy, traveled the empire with Paul, preaching and teaching the Good News. He became Paul's assistant—traveling with, and sometimes for, the great apostle. (For an outline of Timothy's activities for Paul, see the comments on 1 Timothy 1:2.)

That Paul referred to Timothy as *a beloved son,* or "my beloved child" (NRSV) reveals the special relationship that had developed between them, like a father and son. Paul wrote of Timothy: "As a son with a father he has served with me in the work of the gospel" (Philippians 2:22 NIV). The term of endearment also indicates that this letter will be directed more toward Timothy himself.

Grace, mercy, and peace from God the Father and Christ Jesus our Lord. *Grace* and *peace* appear in the greeting of all of Paul's letters. In his letters to Timothy, however, he added *mercy* (see also 1 Timothy 1:2). "Mercy" pictures God's "loving-kindness" so often written about in the Old Testament. God's mercy helps us day by day. Paul loved Timothy dearly, so he added "mercy" to reassure Timothy of God's constant protection and guidance, especially important as Paul faced his own death.

Paul did not mention the Third Person of the Trinity, the Spirit, until verses 7 and 14, but here he wrote of both the *Father and Christ Jesus* as the sources of grace, mercy, and peace. The phrase not only mentions what we desperately need, it also conveys the fact of our abundant source. Therefore, as the writer of Hebrews encourages us, "Let us then approach the throne of grace with confidence, so that we may receive mercy and find grace to help us in our time of need" (Hebrews 4:16 NIV).

PAUL ENCOURAGES TIMOTHY TO BE FAITHFUL / 1:3-18

Even if we did not know of the ancient practice of beginning letters with prayers for the expected readers, we would conclude that it was certainly Paul's habit to do so. In most instances, his prayers took the form of thanksgiving. Paul's assurance to Timothy of his prayers has a familiar ring (see Romans 1:8; Philippians 1:3), but with an added note of intimacy found nowhere else.

Paul's gentle words provide a clearer picture of Timothy's character. After their years of working companionship, the separated ministries had been difficult for both men. The parting had been painful (1:4). When Paul thought of his young disciple's faithfulness, he was reminded of Lois and Eunice, who had made a contribution to Timothy's faith. With these examples in mind, Paul was encouraged, and he proceeded to offer encouragement to Timothy. He elaborated on their shared role as guardians, heralds, and teachers of the gospel.

1:3 **I am grateful to God—whom I worship with a clear conscience, as my ancestors did—when I remember you constantly in my prayers night and day.**NRSV Paul constantly prayed for the churches he founded and visited (see Romans 1:8; Philippians 1:3; Colossians 1:3); and Paul constantly prayed for Timothy, his friend, his fellow traveler, his son in the faith, and a strong leader in the Christian church. Although the two men were separated from each other, their prayers provided a source of mutual encouragement. Sitting in a damp Roman prison cell, the great missionary Paul could no longer preach and travel, but he could pray. Paul's dearest friend, Timothy, ministered with believers very dear to him, in Ephesus. Paul expressed his gratefulness to God for Timothy and his ministry, praying for him *night and day.* Paul knew he would die soon, but Timothy had been well prepared to carry on strong leadership in the Christian church. Paul would die; Christianity would not.

Paul's almost parenthetical statement, that he worshiped God *with a clear conscience,* mirrors his words in 1 Timothy 1:5 and their contrast in 1 Timothy 4:2. Earlier in his ministry, Paul had said, "I do my best always to have a clear conscience toward God and all people" (Acts 24:16 NRSV). Three possibilities have been proposed to explain Paul's "clear conscience":

1. Paul was thinking of his own present situation in prison and claiming innocence as he faced charges in Rome.

2. Paul was stating his own moral integrity in contrast to the guilt of the false teachers and other opponents he and Timothy faced.

3. Paul was describing his life of service to God as being whole-hearted and without regrets (see Romans 1:9).

The last of these possibilities seems to fit best in the context. As Paul looked back over his life (mainly his life since his call to apostleship and ministry), he could confidently say that he had accomplished what God had called him to do. He could worship with a clear conscience. Paul's word for "worship" (*latreou*), means "service," and makes the context broader than a religious ceremony.

Paul's *ancestors* were God-fearing Jews. The phrase "as my ancestors did" reveals Paul's understanding that the Christian faith was based on the Jewish faith.

QUITE A FOLLOWING
Just as Timothy had been influenced by Lois and Eunice, Paul recognized that he had been influenced by faithful and God-fearing ancestors, not only people of Old Testament times, but people in his own family line. Christians today have a key role, to be witnesses not just to our neighbors and friends, but to those in our family line who will come after us. Our faith builds a heritage and a legacy for all those who follow. Will the generations to come see the evidence of your love for God and faithfulness to his Word? As the psalmist knew: "A posterity shall serve Him. It will be recounted of the Lord to the next generation" (Psalm 22:30 NKJV); "I will make Your name to be remembered in all generations; therefore the people shall praise You forever and ever" (Psalm 45:17 NKJV).

1:4 Recalling your tears, I long to see you so that I may be filled with joy.^{NRSV} We don't know when Paul and Timothy had last parted, but it was probably when Paul was arrested and taken to Rome for his second imprisonment. The tears they had shed at parting had revealed the depth of their relationship. Timothy brought Paul great joy. Paul longed to see Timothy again, so twice more in this letter Paul requested that Timothy do his best to come to him soon (see 4:9, 21).

Although the first words of the sentence set us up to expect a statement of compassion for Timothy, instead Paul confesses his own longing to be reunited with the young man. Paul felt concern for Timothy, as well as intense loneliness in prison. Paul's description of his relationship with Timothy as a father-son bond accurately portrayed what they had come to mean to each other.

1:5 I have been reminded of your sincere faith, which first lived in your grandmother Lois and in your mother Eunice and, I am persuaded, now lives in you also.^{NIV}

1:5 I have been reminded of your sincere faith, which first lived in your grandmother Lois and in your mother Eunice and, I am persuaded, now lives in you also.[NIV] Timothy's mother and grandmother, Eunice and Lois, were early Christian converts, possibly through Paul's ministry in their home city, Lystra (Acts 16:1). They had communicated their strong Christian faith to Timothy, even though his Greek father (Acts 26:1) was probably not a believer. Paul mentioned Timothy's *sincere faith* probably because Timothy's genuine, unhypocritical faith stood in bold contrast to the insincerity of many who had deserted Paul (see 1:15; 2:17-18; 3:1-9, 13; 4:3-4, 10, 14, 16). Paul had no doubts concerning Timothy's faith.

AT GRANDMA'S KNEE
Perhaps God can use a grandmother to help mold a future minister. No greater meaning to life could be found than for a devout grandmother to pray for, encourage, and challenge grandchildren to keep the faith. She can begin by reading Bible stories and challenging grandchildren to read the Bible and memorize verses. Then she can encourage them to get involved in church summer activities or to attend Christian camps (maybe with her help). Grandparents need to be more than examples; they must encourage and teach whenever possible.

Sincere faith means our possessing heartfelt trust, not merely professing religious words. We must have genuine, authentic faith to face our work and challenges. Faith requires us to be steadfast and unwavering when we are under pressure or facing opposition. To trust God each day is a decision we must make, not an emotion that we feel. Is your faith half-hearted? Do you rely on how you feel to determine your faithfulness to God?

While "I am sure" (NRSV) accurately translates Paul's word *pepeismai,* the phrase strikes us in English as if it was wishful thinking. But the words mean *I am persuaded,* and Paul used them again in verse 12 ("I am convinced" NIV) to speak of his own confidence in Christ. Timothy had been "on the job" in Ephesus for a few years. Perhaps his outward success may have been in doubt, but Paul was certain of his faithfulness.

HOMEGROWN FAITH
Don't hide your light at home. Families are fertile fields for planting gospel seeds. Let your parents, children, spouse, brothers, and sisters know of your faith in Jesus, and be sure they see Christ's love, helpfulness, and joy in you. Being a faithful witness to one's own family is a Christian's biggest challenge, for it is a daily task. But along with it comes the incomparable joy of having part in the conversion of those closest to us.

1:6 **For this reason I remind you to fan into flame the gift of God, which is in you through the laying on of my hands.**[NIV] The *reason* was the fact that Timothy possessed sincere faith (1:5), a precious treasure in a church leader. In telling Timothy to *fan into flame the gift of God,* Paul was encouraging him to persevere. At the time of his ordination, Timothy had received a special gift of the Spirit to enable him to serve the church: "Do not neglect the gift that is in you, which was given to you through prophecy with the laying on of hands by the council of elders" (1 Timothy 4:14 NRSV). This gift was most likely the gift of ministry, the special grace from God to do Christian service. Verse 7 supports that concept. The phrase *the laying on of my hands* most likely means that Timothy's spiritual gift had been given to him, along with a prophecy, when Paul *and* the elders laid their hands on him and set him apart for ministry.

Rather than asking Timothy to restart a cold fire, Paul was encouraging him to fan a young fire to keep it at full flame. Timothy did not need new revelations or new gifts; he needed only to "fan" the gift of leadership he already had received, as well as to have courage and self-discipline for holding on to the truth in the days to come (see 1:13-14). "Fan into flame" does not suggest that Timothy had fallen away from the faith; instead, Paul was encouraging Timothy to continue to step out boldly in faith and proclaim the gospel. In 1 Timothy 4:12 and 1 Corinthians 16:10-11, Paul indicates that he was concerned for Timothy, who was younger and much less forceful and bold than Paul. Paul did not want the false teachers to get an upper hand. Timothy needed to take charge. When Timothy used his gift, the Holy Spirit would go with him and give him power. God never gives us a task to do without empowering us to carry it out.

The challenge to "fan into flame" (*anazopurein*) helps us understand how spiritual gifts work. Spiritual gifts are neither "gas jets" that can be turned on or off at our whim, nor "neatly packaged spiritual powers" with clear boundaries and qualities that the user fully understands. A "gift" requiring "fanning" implies that an ability for ministry may be neglected or ill-used. We cannot be sure if Paul thought Timothy had allowed his gift to die down to embers or whether he was encouraging the young pastor to keep stoking the fire to avoid having it burn low. In either case, the illustration shows that we must cooperate with God's work in our lives. We are not simply possessed by God's Spirit; we are indwelt. As Christians, we must actively host God's presence in us.

Paul taught that the Spirit's presence provides believers with gifts for ministry (see Romans 12:3-8; 1 Corinthians 12–14; Ephesians 4:7-13). Some of the gifts seem very specific (i.e., "tongues," "prophecy," "healing"), but the attention must always focus on the Spirit's work through those gifted rather than the gifts they have. Our focus ought to be on contributing to others rather than on identifying our gift.

LESSONS FROM THE CAMPFIRE
A fire that has died down will not respond well to an armload of large logs dumped upon it. Without flames, the logs will actually stifle the remaining embers. Small, dried twigs and extra air will have to be used to "fan the flames" back to life. Then the fire will be able to handle larger wood. A time of spiritual dryness shouldn't be treated by taking on a monumental spiritual challenge of "large logs." Instead, seek sources for spiritual rekindling:

■ Visit a motivating friend or mentor to keep you fresh and excited.
■ Look for seminars or conferences that will energize your ministry.
■ Rethink your involvement in evangelism. New, excited believers can greatly enthuse your ministry.
■ Feed daily from God's Word, complementing long-range study projects.
■ Get outside in God's creation for a few hours to recharge your spiritual life.

1:7 For God did not give us a spirit of timidity, but a spirit of power, of love and of self-discipline.[NIV] Timothy experienced constant opposition to his message and to himself as a leader. His youth (see 1 Timothy 4:12), his association with Paul, and his leadership had come under fire from believers and nonbelievers alike. Perhaps Timothy felt intimidated, angered, even helpless in face of the opposition from the false teachers. Whatever the degree of his difficulties, Paul urged Timothy to boldness by reminding him of his call, his gift, and God's provision (see 1:6).

God does *not* give *a spirit of fear,* that is, timidity or cowardice; rather God provides:

- *Power*—We do not need to have naturally powerful personalities. God gives strength of character and confidence that wins us respect when we face opposition as we speak, preach, and live the truth. God supernaturally replaces any timidity on the servant's part with boldness. The powerful minister doesn't hoard his power or lord it over others; he empowers those in his congregation. Paul experienced what he wrote: "My speech and my proclamation were not with plausible words of wisdom, but with a demonstration of the Spirit and of power" (1 Corinthians 2:4 NRSV). For Paul this power was an inseparable part of the gospel (see Romans 1:16). Such power is difficult to discredit.

- *Love*—Accompanying the power to speak the truth must be love for the listeners, believers and nonbelievers alike. Love separates Christians from the heathen world around them. Jesus promised, "By this all will know that you are My disciples, if you have love for one another" (John 13:35 NKJV). Indeed, love separated the minister of Christ from the false teachers. Such love is difficult to dismiss.

- *Self-discipline*—This can also be translated "self-control" or "sound mind." In order to lead others, the true minister must have control over himself. To put it another way, a good leader must have a cool head. Self-discipline and self-control sound like *self*-effort. But Paul explained them as divinely bestowed on his servants, resulting in soundness of mind. Such control, such "soundness" is difficult to disclaim.

All of these qualities (boldness, power, love, and self-control) are gifts of the Spirit, not just natural tendencies. They function best in harmony. Boldness and power are tempered by love and self-control. Under the pressures of leadership, people tend to gravitate toward a desire for power and boldness as the most effective tools for success. But used alone, these qualities are self-defeating. The inclusion of love and self-control clearly indicates that a leader's effectiveness comes from God's Spirit. We may be impressed by a leader who exhibits boldness and power, but without love or self-control, such a leader is little more than a bully.

Opinions differ about whether or not the word "spirit" as used here refers directly to the Holy Spirit or to some inner attitude given by God. The answer is that the Holy Spirit strengthens the human spirit. Thus, the expression *a spirit of timidity* is probably another way of saying "a timid disposition," which Timothy probably had by nature. But the Holy Spirit has given believers power (Acts 1:8), love (Romans 5:5), and self-control (Galatians 5:22-23). Thus, to have a spirit with these qualities is to have a human spirit that has been regenerated by the the Holy Spirit. This statement prepares the way for Paul's later direction to Timothy to rely on the Holy Spirit's live-in help to guard the gospel (1:14).

SPIRITED
When we allow people to intimidate us, we neutralize our effectiveness for God. The power of the Holy Spirit can help us overcome our fear of what some might say or do to us, so that we can continue to do God's work. Paul mentions three characteristics of the effective Christian leader: power, love, and a sound mind. These are available to us because the Holy Spirit lives in us. When we follow his leading each day, our lives will more fully exhibit these characteristics. We follow the Spirit's leading by studying God's Word and using the opportunities he gives us to witness. See Galatians 5:22-23 for a list of the by-products of the Holy Spirit living in us.

1:8 So do not be ashamed to testify about our Lord, or ashamed of me his prisoner.[NIV] Because of Timothy's call, gift, and provision of power, love, and self-control, he certainly had every reason to stand against any opponents, unashamed of the gospel, and unashamed of his imprisoned mentor. In this time of mounting persecution, Timothy may have been struggling with fears as he continued to preach the gospel. His fears would have been based on fact—believers were being arrested and executed. Perhaps some viewed Paul's imprisonment and impending execution, indeed the harassment of all Christians, as God's judgment *against* the Christian movement: maybe it really wasn't true; maybe Jesus and his gospel really were lies; maybe Paul deserved to be locked up for spreading that message. Against such opposition and doubt, Paul urged Timothy to remain strong, sure, certain, unwavering as he testified about the Lord, and not to be ashamed that Paul sat in prison for his testimony. Paul was sure of God's hand in his present situation; so sure that he called himself *his* [God's] *prisoner.*

> God's soldiers must be brave and unflinching in meeting the opposition of the world. When once we realize that the stores which reside in God are at the disposal of our faith, we too shall be invulnerable and irresistible. *F. B. Meyer*

But join with me in suffering for the gospel, relying on the power of God.[NRSV] Paul told Timothy to expect *suffering for the gospel.* Eventually Timothy would be jailed for preaching the gospel (Hebrews 13:23). But Paul promised Timothy that God would give him reliable *power* and that he would be able to endure if suffering came. Paul had written to the Corinthians, "I am content with weaknesses, insults, hardships, persecutions, and calamities for the sake of Christ; for whenever I am weak, then I am strong" (2 Corinthians 12:10 NRSV). When believers undergo suffering, they need not rely on their own strength for survival and sustenance; instead, God gives power and strength to endure.

> God would not rub so hard if it were not to fetch out the dirt that is ingrained in our natures. God loves purity so well He had rather see a hole than a spot in His child's garments. *William Gurnall*

ARE YOU EMBARRASSED?
We show that we are ashamed of Christ when we
- hope no one will think we are Christians
- decide *not* to speak up for what is right
- are silent about our relationship with God
- blend into society
- accept our culture's non-Christian values.

By contrast, we testify about him when we:
- live moral, upright, Christ-honoring lives
- look for opportunities to share our faith with others
- help others in need
- take a stand for justice
- love others
- acknowledge our loyalty to Christ
- use our lives and resources to carry out his desires rather than our own.

1:9 Who has saved us and called us to a holy life.NIV Paul mentioned that he was suffering for the gospel (1:8) and, in verses 9-10, summarized some important points of the gospel. Continuing from verse 8, "relying on the power of God," Paul writes that God *saved us.* Salvation forms the core of the gospel, the Good News. There would be no gospel without the sacrifice that Jesus Christ made for our sins so that we could be "saved."

Moreover, God *called us* with a holy calling:

- *"And we know that all things work together for good to . . . the called. . . ."* (Romans 8:28 NKJV)
- *"Moreover whom He predestined, these He also called; whom He called, these He also justified; and whom He justified, these He also glorified."* (Romans 8:30 NKJV)

- *"God is faithful, by whom you were called into the fellowship of His son, Jesus Christ our Lord."* (1 Corinthians 1:9 NKJV)
- *"I am astonished that you are so quickly deserting the one who called you in the grace of Christ. . . ."* (Galatians 1:6 NRSV)
- *"I therefore, the prisoner in the Lord, beg you to lead a life worthy of the calling to which you have been called."* (Ephesians 4:1 NRSV)
- *"Urging and encouraging you and pleading that you lead a life worthy of God, who calls you into his own kingdom and glory."* (1 Thessalonians 2:12 NRSV)

Why did God save us and call us? His purpose in salvation was to redeem people for himself—people who lived to glorify him. He saves people *from* sin and calls them *to* holiness. Each believer is called to a *holy life.* Holy living seeks God's view instead of the self-centered view. Holiness expects to find God involved in every facet of life. Holiness consistently turns away from self-pleasing answers in order to please God. As opposed to the pagans who often tried to please their gods through good works or self-abasement, believers can live truly holy lives because holiness is **not according to our works, but according to His own purpose and grace which was given to us in Christ Jesus before time began.**NKJV Salvation and holiness rely on the Giver alone, not on the receiver. We cannot live holy lives *according to our works*: "For by grace you have been saved through faith, and that not of yourselves; it is the gift of God, not of works, lest anyone should boast. For we are his workmanship, created in Christ Jesus for good works, which God prepared beforehand that we should walk in them" (Ephesians 2:8-10 NKJV).

Our works cannot save us nor empower us to please God with our lives. Instead, our salvation and holiness occur because of God's *purpose and grace* (see Titus 3:4). God's sovereign choice alone, through his planned purpose and his astounding grace, allowed sinners to receive salvation and the right to stand holy before him. Everything fits into the framework of God's sovereignty. We create neither the opportunity nor the possibility of our salvation. God graciously allows us to simply respond to his plan.

Salvation *was given to us in Christ Jesus.* We are saved only because of Jesus' death on the cross in our place. Only because he took the punishment we deserved does God offer salvation and holiness. Jesus said, "I am the way, the truth, and the life. No one comes to the Father except through Me" (John 14:6 NKJV).

This incredible offer to human beings did not occur as God saw the world spin out of control; rather, it was planned *before time began,* or literally "before time eternal." God's sovereignty extends from eternity to eternity, enveloping the history of humanity. God knew that people would require a Savior, and from the beginning he planned to give his only Son. "From everlasting to everlasting, You are God" (Psalm 90:2 NKJV).

UNDESERVING
God loves us, called us, and sent Christ to die for us. We can have eternal life through faith in him because he broke the power of death with his resurrection. We do not deserve to be saved, but God offers us salvation anyway. What we must do is believe in him and accept his offer.

1:10 **But it has now been revealed through the appearing of our Savior, Christ Jesus.**[NIV] That purpose and grace "given to us in Christ Jesus" was planned since eternity, but has been *revealed* to people *through the appearing of our Savior, Christ Jesus.* This "appearing" (Greek *epiphaneia*) was in human form—Christ Jesus on earth, in a human body, preaching, teaching, healing, dying, and rising again. His becoming visible and touchable allowed humans access to him in a way that had not been available before the Incarnation. But the use of "revealed" (*phanerotheisan*) also implies Christ's preexistence before the Incarnation. Jesus' life did not begin at conception in Mary but has always been. He was present and active in creation (see Colossians 1:15-17). Though "appearing" usually refers to Christ's expected return (see 2 Thessalonians 2:8; 1 Timothy 6:14; 2 Timothy 4:1, 8; Titus 2:13), here Paul used the word to describe Christ's incarnation.

Paul called Jesus Christ "our Savior." Paul may have used this particular Greek word, *soter,* because at the time, the cruel emperor Nero was applying it to himself. Paul brought his readers back to the true Savior—not any human leader, but Jesus Christ.

Who has destroyed death and has brought life and immortality to light through the gospel.[NIV] Through his death and resurrection, Christ *destroyed death.* He ended death's claim of invincibility and mortally wounded this terrible foe. All human beings still must die, but death is not the end. There is hope beyond the grave; and that hope counteracts any fear of death:

> ■ *Listen, I will tell you a mystery! We will not all die, but we will all be changed, in a moment, in the twinkling of an eye, at the last trumpet. For the trumpet will sound, and the dead will be raised imperishable, and we will be changed. For this perishable body must put on imperishability, and this mortal body must put on immortality. . . . Then the saying that is written will be fulfilled: "Death has been swallowed up in victory. Where, O death, is your victory? Where, O death, is your sting?"*
> *(1 Corinthians 15:51-55* NRSV*)*

Believers are given eternal life beginning at the moment of salvation. Believers are immortal—of necessity dying physically, but not forever. They will rise again. This is the mystery our Savior, Jesus Christ, brought to light through the gospel. The *gospel,* the Good News of salvation in Jesus Christ, reveals and illuminates these promises. Paul had been commissioned to proclaim this Good News.

1:11 For this gospel I was appointed a herald and an apostle and a teacher.NRSV Verses 9-10 summarized the *gospel* to which Paul was divinely appointed "by the will of God" (1:1). God appointed Paul to be a *herald (kerux,* "one who announces and proclaims"), and an *apostle (apostolos,* "one who is sent"), and a *teacher (didaskalos,* "one who imparts knowledge and gives instruction"). Timothy obviously already knew this information. It seems that Paul added these words as he marveled at the wonder of his own call to such a tremendous responsibility.

Paul's words for his job description mirror his actual performance. Though the title of apostle was the weightiest of the three, Paul listed it second. Top billing went to "herald." A herald has little importance apart from his or her message, and Paul's practice was to proclaim God's message, the gospel, even to strangers. In new settings where he was not known, he would proclaim the gospel and allow it to speak for itself (see Acts 17:16-34). Paul had reminded the Corinthians (1 Corinthians 2:1-5) that his arrival among them was not at all impressive except for the power of the gospel itself. His message was of such value that Paul, the herald, had insisted on being heard!

Paul also maintained he had been made an "apostle" the same way the original Twelve had been commissioned—by Jesus himself (see 1 Corinthians 15:8; 9:1; Galatians 1:11–2:10). Yes, they had spent three years with Jesus, but the final proof of apostleship was not that they had chosen to be with Christ, but that Christ had chosen them (John 15:16). As a herald, Paul had been entrusted with a message; as an apostle, he had been entrusted with an authority. Paul represented Jesus Christ.

Third among Paul's credentials was his role as teacher. Timothy was a product of his work, and he expected Timothy not only to pass on what he had been taught but to also find others who could carry on the process (see 2:2). Paul was describing himself not only as the conductor of the message and a representative of Christ; he was also declaring his function in communicating and applying the truth of the gospel. As a teacher, Paul was a tenured herald!

1:12 **That is why I am suffering as I am.**NIV Because Paul had traveled the empire announcing and teaching the gospel, he was suffering in prison. His faithfulness to God's call had led him to suffering as a common criminal. But Paul had no doubts, no apologies, and no fear for the future.

Nevertheless I am not ashamed, for I know whom I have believed and am persuaded that He is able to keep what I have committed to Him until that Day.NKJV Paul knew he had put his confidence in the right Person; he knew he had given his life for the right cause; thus, he was *not ashamed*. A lifetime of experience with the Lord—joys, sorrows, pain, frustration, persecution, prayer, ministry, guidance, sustenance—had taught Paul about God in whom he believed.

KNOWING CHRIST
In spite of the suffering that might have caused Paul to despair, he affirmed his confidence in God's protection. This was not a claim to strong faith; rather, it was a trust in one so powerful that even a weak faith was sufficient. Paul based his confidence in Christ on his intimate relationship with him. Paul's "knowledge" was personal; he "knew" Christ so well that no earthly experience could break the bond of love by which Christ held him. How would you explain to someone what it means to you to "know Christ?"

The phrase *keep what I have committed to Him* (literally, "my deposit") has been taken to mean: (1) Paul knew that God would guard the souls of those converted through his preaching; (2) Paul trusted God to guard his own soul until Christ's second coming; or (3) Paul was confident that, though he was in prison and facing death, God would carry out the gospel ministry and guard the teaching through others such as Timothy. The word for "deposit" carries the meaning of placing valuables in the hands of a friend who would keep them safe while you are on a journey. This meaning supports view 3 just mentioned, that the deposit was Paul's message and ministry. If we relate the deposit to verse 14, guard "the good deposit," or to 1 Timothy 6:20, "guard what has been entrusted to your care," the deposit implies protecting the teachings.

Paul may have expressed his confidence to encourage Timothy, who was undoubtedly discouraged by the problems in Ephesus and fearful of persecution. Even in prison, Paul knew that God was still in control. No matter what setbacks or problems we face, we can trust fully in God. Paul had written to the Romans: "For I am persuaded that neither death nor life, nor angels nor principalities nor powers, nor things present nor things to come, nor height nor depth, nor any other created thing, shall be able to separate us from the love of God which is in Christ Jesus our Lord" (Romans 8:38-39 NKJV).

SAFE AND SECURE
Paul was in prison, but that did not stop his ministry. He continued it through others like Timothy. Paul had lost all his material possessions, but he would never lose his faith. He trusted God to use him regardless of his circumstances. If your situation looks bleak, give your concerns to Christ. He will guard your faith and safely guard all you have entrusted to him until the day of his return. For more on our security in Christ, see Romans 8:38-39.

1:13 What you heard from me, keep as the pattern of sound teaching, with faith and love in Christ Jesus.[NIV] Timothy did not need to wonder about the content of sound teaching—he could always recall Paul's teaching and read Paul's letters as his *pattern.* The Greek for *sound teaching* refers to an outline or sketch. Rather than a rote repeating of Paul's teaching, Timothy was to use Paul's teaching as his outline or pattern. It was a foundation upon which Timothy could preach and teach. And, like a sure foundation, Paul's pattern would keep Timothy from straying from the truth. Timothy had every resource needed to carry on his ministry, and it boiled down to teaching only the truth, *with faith* in Christ and *love* for all people. Sound teaching requires both faith in the heart and genuine love for the Lord. Sound teaching also helps people remain true to the tenets of the Christian faith because it refers to orthodox teaching (see 1 Timothy 1:10; 6:3).

The phrase *keep as the pattern* (or "hold to the standard" NRSV), conveys a double intent that can be lost in translation. The ideas of both (1) preserving the integrity of the truth that Timothy learned from Paul and (2) modeling that truth in his life are included. This expression joins several in this letter to emphasize Paul's concern for Timothy's spiritual survival and effectiveness (see 2:2, 14-15; 3:10-14; 4:1-2).

1:14 Guard the good deposit that was entrusted to you—guard it with the help of the Holy Spirit who lives in us.^{NIV} Paul had been entrusted with the Good News (Acts 9:15-19; 1 Thessalonians 2:4; Titus 1:3). This call by Jesus became his life's mission as he preached the gospel across the Roman Empire. All who hear, believe, and accept the *good deposit* ("treasure," NRSV) of sound doctrine have also been *entrusted* with it. The words "deposit that was entrusted to you" are a single compound word in Greek (*paratheken*) that Paul also used verse 13. There the object of the verb ("to him") is implied by the context. The same is true here, though the object of the verb is "you." The language throughout this letter creates a strong sense of Paul writing his "last wishes" and disposing of his treasured goods. Paul has just affirmed (1:13) his confidence in God's ability to keep what he has deposited with him. Next Paul conferred on Timothy the ongoing duty to preserve what he had deposited with him. That "deposit" included all the good that had flowed to Timothy through Paul: not only his own conversion, but the teachings, experiences, as well as the duties conferred on him by Paul.

Timothy was to guard that treasure—not by burying it and keeping it hidden, but by entrusting it to faithful men and women, who would teach it to others, who in turn would teach it to others, and on through the centuries. Because men like Timothy "guarded the treasure" as Paul had commanded, two thousand years later we too have the true gospel, the sound doctrine, that we are commanded to entrust to others. Only *with the help of the Holy Spirit* could the truth remain untainted, guarded, and protected as it passed through the centuries.

ON YOUR GUARD
Paul was concerned both for the correct teaching (transmission) of the gospel and for the solid content of the gospel. As we try to reach new people by means of felt needs they have, we must not abandon our sacred trust to teach and preach the full content of the gospel.

Note the shared responsibility emphasized in this passage. Timothy could be charged to *guard* the good deposit, but he must do

so counting on divine help. The live-in Holy Spirit will assist
those intent on being trustworthy of the gospel. The ongoing existence of the body of Christ, as well as the availability of the
Scriptures, simply cannot be explained as the product of faithful
people throughout the ages. Supernatural help has been involved!
Both human agents and divine guarantees have had a part in fulfilling Jesus' words, "Heaven and earth will pass away, but my
words will not pass away" (Matthew 24:35 NRSV).

Paul intentionally changed grammatical persons in this verse.
By locating the Holy Spirit as living *in us* when the expected person would be "you," Paul included a powerful binding effect in
his statement. Not only does the verse emphasize the shared presence of the Spirit in Paul and Timothy, it also reminds us of his
active indwelling in us.

USING THE GIFTS
Timothy was in a time of transition. He had been Paul's bright
young helper; soon he would be on his own as leader of a
church in a difficult environment. Although his responsibilities
were changing, Timothy was not without help. He had everything he needed to face the future if he would hold on tightly to
the Lord's resources. When you are facing difficult transitions, it
is good to follow Paul's advice to Timothy and look back at your
experience. Who is the foundation of your faith? How can you
build on that foundation? What gifts has the Holy Spirit given
you? Use the gifts you have already been given.

**1:15 You know that everyone in the province of Asia has deserted
me, including Phygelus and Hermogenes.**[NIV] Ephesus was the
leading city in the province of Asia, if not all of Asia Minor (see
the map in the introduction of this commentary). By saying *everyone . . . has deserted me,* Paul may have been referring to a general lack of concern or support for him in his difficult time of
need. Many had refused to stand up for him or at least stay at his
side during his trial. This occurred not accidentally, but apparently on purpose. This caused Paul much pain. The "everyone"
was not literal, but was used by Paul as a sweeping generaliza-
tion. Those who were resisting Timothy were, in the same action,
abandoning Paul. The fact that just a few had remained faithful
heightened Paul's sense of having been deserted.

Nothing more is known about Phygelus and Hermogenes, who
evidently opposed Paul's ministry and/or his authority; the fact
that Paul named them could mean that he least expected their
desertion or that he knew they were in Ephesus. They may have
held leadership positions. Apparently Timothy knew the situa-

tion, for Paul added no further details. In any case, these men
serve as a warning that even leaders can fall.

TRANSPARENCY
Paul provided Timothy a clear example of how to face real difficulties in life with practical faith. Paul did not present himself as
some kind of superhuman. Rather, he described his all-too-
humanness in ways that highlighted the saving and keeping
grace of Jesus in him. So he could speak of suffering and abandonment in the same context with confidence in God's safe-
keeping.
   We can expect opposition, but we should not look for it. We
should not pretend to be unaffected by struggles and trials, but
share our concerns with younger people in the ministry to help
prepare them for what they might face.

**1:16 May the Lord show mercy to the household of Onesiphorus,
because he often refreshed me and was not ashamed of my
chains.**^{NIV} In contrast to those who deserted him, Paul mentioned
Onesiphorus as a true and loyal friend. His name means "help-
bringer." Unashamed of Paul's imprisonment, Onesiphorus
refreshed Paul. The stigma attached to Paul's chains and any concern about being identified as a friend of this prisoner did not
faze this faithful brother and his *household,* who continued to
minister to Paul in prison. Paul prayed for mercy on his friend
and his friend's family here and in verse 18.

There are two ways to understand Paul's prayer for Onesiphorus:

(1) Onesiphorus was dead at the time of Paul's writing. This
may be understood by the verb "show mercy" in this verse and to
"on that day" in verse 18. This view is uncertain because of the
mention of his household.

(2) Onesiphorus was separated from his family at Ephesus for
quite a while as he did missionary work. Paul wished God's blessing and mercy on his family.

Paul's strong prayer in verse 18 seems to indicate that Onesiphorus had died (see comments on verse 18).

**1:17 On the contrary, when he was in Rome, he searched hard for
me until he found me.**^{NIV} Onesiphorus lived in Ephesus, but for
some reason had been in Rome and, while there, had gone out of
his way to search for Paul until he had found him. If Paul had
been largely "abandoned" by others, Onesiphorus may have had
difficulty finding anyone who would even admit to knowing
Paul's location. Besides, a stranger to the city may simply have

had problems getting through the red tape and bureaucracy of the Roman penal system. In any case, the aging apostle saw in Onesiphorus a brother who allowed neither inconvenience nor potential embarrassment to keep him from tracking Paul down. Onesiphorus's visits had refreshed the lonely prisoner.

1:18 May the Lord grant that he will find mercy from the Lord on that day.^{NIV} Paul prayed that his friend would receive mercy from the Lord on that final day of judgment. He was certain that there would be an accounting of each person's life, and that unrewarded service for Christ in this life would be openly proclaimed.

And you know very well how much service he rendered in Ephesus.^{NRSV} Timothy was familiar with Onesiphorus and his service in Ephesus. The service Onesiphorus rendered to Paul in faraway Rome was not isolated; Onesiphorus had a record of service in Ephesus as well. Paul's statement to Timothy gives us a beautiful insight into the character of this otherwise unknown servant of God.

Some scholars have suggested that Onesiphorus was dead at this writing, and the evidence from this passage makes that assumption possible. Because Paul hoped Onesiphorus's family would be granted mercy in the present (1:16), while his subsequent request (1:18) was that his friend would *find mercy from the Lord on that day,* it can be inferred that Onesiphorus was no longer around. Paul's expression "mercy from the Lord on that day" conveys deep appreciation to Onesiphorus, rather than a formal request to God for his fate in eternity. Attempts to find support here for the idea that the church should pray for the dead could be called an "application from silence." Paul was not telling Timothy to pray for the dead, but to imitate those, like Onesiphorus, who were faithful to Christ and unashamed to be associated with servants of Christ who were suffering or who were in prison.

2 Timothy 2

Good parents want their children eventually to leave home and succeed on their own. But after the good-byes and the well-wishes, parents wonder, *Did we teach them well enough to survive?* So parents continue to offer advice. Paul's last letter to Timothy sounds like wise parental counsel. After affirming Timothy for the good character he had already demonstrated (see 1:5), Paul hinted at Timothy's "debt" of faith to his mother and grandmother (see 1:5). Then he expressed his confidence in Timothy as the right choice to carry on the ministry in Ephesus.

Like a father discussing his son's future choices, Paul used three vocations to illustrate what it is like to serve God: military service, athletic training, and farming. Each vocation showed Timothy that he, and all Christians, must work hard and trust God for the long-range results.

2:1 You therefore, my son, be strong in the grace that is in Christ Jesus.^{NKJV} Many of Paul's associates had deserted him, but at least one had remained (1:15-16). Paul challenged his "beloved son" to be like Onesiphorus, unashamed of the gospel, unashamed of his standing as a leader in the Christian church, unafraid of the false teachers, courageous through hardship and persecution. How? Through the *grace that is in Christ Jesus.*

How can someone *be strong* in grace? The term is *endunamou,* "be empowered" or "be strengthened" and implies being helped by someone else, in this case God. Paul was telling Timothy to draw strength from God as he focused on the grace that he would receive through his relationship with Christ Jesus. And he should use this strength in God's service. *Grace* means "undeserved favor." The greatest experience of God's grace is having one's sin pardoned. Once we have been pardoned by grace (Ephesians 2:8-9), we should live by grace, daily motivated and encouraged, remembering that our sins are forgiven (Colossians 2:6). Paul reminded Timothy that strength comes not from himself but from Christ and *his* power. The grace available through Christ to Paul

BE STRONG!
Scripture gives us many ways to understand the strength God
offers to his people. We must daily draw on his resources.

Reference	Meaning
Romans 4:20	We have examples to follow (such as Abraham) who were leaders of faith.
2 Corinthians 12:9	We receive strength at our point of weakness. When we acknowledge our limitations, God can use us.
Ephesians 6:10-11	God strengthens us by giving us armor to combat Satan—faith, knowledge, and truth.
Philippians 4:13	God's strength equips us for his service.
1 Timothy 1:12	Our thankfulness to God for the strength he gives enables us to be more receptive.

and to Timothy is also available to every believer today. We have
God's grace *in Christ Jesus* by living in close relationship with
him day by day.

**2:2 And the things you have heard me say in the presence of
many witnesses entrust to reliable men who will also be qualified to teach others.**^{NIV} Timothy heard Paul preach to many
diverse groups of people. The message Paul wanted Timothy to
"guard" (1:14) was not a privately shared secret, but the accumulation of public teaching. Here Paul reminded Timothy that his
essential role as guardian meant ensuring that the message was
delivered to others intact, so that they might in turn "guard" it.
Paul was not teaching apostolic succession of administrative leadership, but faithful teaching of correct doctrine. Timothy was to
keep the process of teaching going. This is a pattern for discipleship. It requires leaders to have a program for developing new
leaders who can carry on the ministry. Since Paul, there has been
a link from disciple to disciple, from generation to generation.
We must keep that link intact.

Having accompanied Paul on his second and third missionary
journeys, Timothy had heard Paul preach, argue the gospel,
and/or bring encouragement

- to the women who gathered by the river just outside Philippi
  (Acts 16:13)
- to the believers in Philippi (Acts 16:40)
- to the Jews in Thessalonica (Acts 17:1)
- to devout Greeks and women in Thessalonica (Acts 17:4)
- to the Bereans, who searched the Scriptures to see for them-

selves if Paul's words were true (Acts 17:11); Greek women
and men of high standing in Berea became believers
- to the Epicurean and Stoic philosophers in Athens (Acts
  17:18)
- to the Jews and Greeks in Corinth (Acts 18:4)
- to the Jews in Ephesus (Acts 18:19)
- to the believers in Galatia and Phrygia (Acts 18:23)
- to disciples of John the Baptist who had not heard the full
  gospel (Acts 19:1-7)
- to many Jews and Greeks in the lecture hall of Tyrannus in
  Ephesus over a two-year period (Acts 19:9-10)
- to the believers in Macedonia (Acts 20:1-2)
- to the believers in Troas, where Paul spoke until midnight;
  Eutychus fell asleep and out the window to his death; Paul
  raised the young man back to life, then continued to speak to
  the believers until dawn (Acts 20:7-12)
- to the elders of the church in Ephesus (Acts 20:17-38)

To all these different groups, Paul's message, while perhaps
changing in format, never changed in content. Almost echoing
his words of 1:13: "What you heard from me, keep as the pattern
of sound teaching, with faith and love in Christ Jesus" (NIV).
Paul's words *in the presence of many witnesses* may also refer to:
(1) others besides Paul who taught Timothy the truth: for example, his mother and grandmother (1:5), the elders (1 Timothy
4:14), and others, like Barnabas, who had seen or known Jesus
Christ; or (2) those who were present at his ordination and baptism and helped him develop. Paul realized that, although called
specially by God, the preaching of the truth also came through
many others. Paul was telling Timothy to pass on what had
proven to be true.
  Paul told Timothy to entrust that truth to reliable people who
were both loyal to the faith and able to teach. The stress was on
reliability more than position (see v. 21). Like ripples from a
stone thrown into a pool of water, the gospel would spread across
the world. When Paul wrote these words to Timothy, he realized
that the transmission of the gospel truth to the next generation
was passing into the hands of second-generation believers. Up to
this point, the Good News was being spread solely by word of
mouth and the lives of believers. The Gospels and various letters
written by Paul and others may have just begun to be circulated,
but they were not gathered into a book called the New Testament
until years later. For a while, Timothy had the only copy of 2 Timothy in existence. Part of entrusting the gospel to others was

accomplished when painstaking, handwritten copies of the precious letters were made.

If today's church consistently followed Paul's advice, there would be an incredible spread of the gospel as well-taught believers would teach others and commission them, in turn, to teach still others. Disciples need to be equipped to pass on their faith; new believers must be taught to make disciples of others (see Ephesians 4:12-13).

THE CARE AND FEEDING OF TEACHERS
Teachers in a local church ensure that the gospel is passed from one generation to another. God's truth must be taught and modeled; therefore, teachers must be respected and not taken for granted. Teaching must not simply be left to the pastor.

Every church ought to have a program to identify and train faithful and effective teachers. The following guidelines may be helpful:

- Identify those willing to teach. They may not be immediately qualified but can be trained to serve because they are motivated.
- Screen out and redirect those who are gifted in ways other than teaching or whose spiritual lives render them unsuitable as teachers.
- Train teachers in core doctrinal issues.
- Make training opportunities, books, and materials available to teachers. This will build them up and affirm them in their ministry.
- Find places of service for teachers as they become ready. Give them special teaching opportunities—new member classes, Sunday school, etc.
- Affirm teachers in the church. Let all teachers know they are appreciated.

2:3 Share in suffering like a good soldier of Christ Jesus.^{NRSV} The NIV translates this "endure hardship," stressing the fatigue and deprivation that soldiers face. The NRSV is better. This same word is used in 1:8: "Join with me in suffering for the gospel." Paul had given this warning in Lystra, Iconium, and Antioch (Acts 14:22-23). Thus Paul was returning to a theme that he knew would test the mettle of his disciple—suffering. Paul wanted young Timothy to have no illusions: Being faithful to the truth, unwilling to twist it for personal gain (unlike many of the false teachers, 1 Timothy 6:3-5), and constantly preaching it even against threat of persecution would inevitably lead to suffering. As Paul had suffered, so Timothy would share in that suffering (he was eventually imprisoned, see Hebrews 13:23). Jesus had warned his followers, "If the world hates you, you know that it hated Me before it hated you. If you were of the world, the world would love its own. Yet because you are not of the world, but I chose you out of the world, therefore the world hates you. . . . If they persecuted Me, they will also persecute you" (John 15:18-20 NKJV).

Paul followed with three examples to illustrate the attitude that Christ's followers must have through suffering (for the same three examples, see 1 Corinthians 9:7, 24). Each example encouraged Timothy in a different aspect of his ministry.

First, Paul wrote of the *soldier.* Paul often used military metaphors (see, for example, Romans 7:23; 2 Corinthians 6:7; 10:3-5; Ephesians 6:10-18; Philippians 2:25; 1 Timothy 1:18; Philemon 2). From the military model, Timothy should learn endurance, purpose, bravery, and obedience. Every soldier expects to lose personal autonomy and to experience adverse conditions; so Timothy should expect both hardship and suffering in his ministry of the gospel.

SHARE THE PAIN
The body of Christ contains all believers who have ever lived, not just those who are alive now. When we suffer, we share in a common experience, not just with those alive today, but with all those who have ever suffered for the sake of the gospel. All the martyrs, missionaries, and pioneers of the faith had to face what we face. Let us have the same courage, commitment, and willingness to renounce worldly pleasure in order to serve God. Can you face the challenge?

2:4 No one serving as a soldier gets involved in civilian affairs— he wants to please his commanding officer.[NIV] Paul instilled a sense of purpose and obedience in Timothy. A good soldier obeys the commanding officer. The soldier's call to service takes precedence over *civilian affairs,* referring to any business or distraction that gets in the way of the mission. Paul was not prohibiting marriage, as some have thought.

The phrase *gets involved* (*empleketai*) could also be rendered "gets entangled, gets absorbed." While civilian affairs are not wrong in themselves, they become a problem if the Christian gets so entangled in them that his or her ministry suffers. Christian workers, whether pastors or laymen, must watch their outside involvements carefully. Business ventures, serving on committees or boards, volunteer assignments, and/or home projects can eat up valuable time and energy. Paul wanted Timothy to understand that a good minister of the gospel must have a single-minded purpose—to preach the truth and, if necessary, to suffer for it.

There are limits to the instruction to not get involved in civilian affairs. Some have taken Paul's advice to mean that Christians should do nonstop Christian work. While the image of the soldier presents helpful insights about endurance, even soldiers need rest. Wise commanders know their soldiers need breaks from the action. Even when there have been no wounds, the soldier needs relief from the stress of the battle.

We must maintain a healthy balance in our lives between spiritual activity and spiritual rest. Pastors, teachers, and other ministers cannot function without times of refreshment. Do you give yourself permission to take time away from work?

Renouncing whatever could entangle him or her leaves the good soldier free to obey without reservations. This in turn pleases the *commanding officer.* The effectiveness of a military unit depends on its single-minded commitment to follow the leader in the accomplishment of the mission. Christ demands unquestioning loyalty and obedience from his servants.

UNDER ORDERS
Both Paul and Timothy were seeking to be good soldiers of Christ Jesus. All who enlist in military service exchange their lives as civilians for lives as soldiers. Once enlisted, recruits are expected to loyally obey their commander and to endure the training program. As a soldier of Christ, is your single-minded purpose to please him? In what ways are you carrying out his specific orders?

2:5 And in the case of an athlete, no one is crowned without competing according to the rules.NRSV Next Paul used the athlete as an example. Paul would not have been content with the slogan: "It's not whether you win or lose, but how you play the game." Based on his words to Timothy, Paul probably would have revised the slogan to say: "Whether you win or lose depends totally on how you play the game!"

How we apply this illustration depends on whether we assume Paul used the figures of the soldier, athlete, and farmer to make three different but related points for Timothy, or to make one central point in three different ways. The structure of the passage lends strength to the idea that Paul had one lesson in mind, though the details of each illustration allow for further insights. In other words, the soldier, athlete, and farmer all teach us the same lesson—to persevere to the end—while also helping us understand other requirements for Christian service.

This section (2:1-7) begins with the pair of commands in verse 1, "Be strong in the grace that is in Christ Jesus," and verse 3, "Endure hardship." These commands represent the two-fold strategy needed in a Christ-centered life: (1) to be enabled by strength flowing out of grace to (2) endure the difficulties of life. Each vocation models this two-part strategy:

- The soldier must trust the commanding officer and desire to please him so that obeying the commander becomes central, even when difficulties are encountered. Pleasing Christ gives strength to endure hardship.
- The athlete accepts the rules of the competition in order to complete the challenge of the game, including its difficulties.
- The farmer works hard at plowing, planting, waiting, weeding, and harvesting and is entitled to enjoy the results. The soldier submits to the officer; the athlete to the code of the competition; the farmer to the laws of nature and agriculture. The believer submits to Jesus Christ. In him we have a gracious commanding officer—one who provides an example and directions for our course, and who rewards the hard and patient work of his servants.

Being *crowned* most likely referred to the Olympic games. A competitor had to know the rules of his event, train diligently with an understanding of those rules, and finally compete according to the rules. Competitors in the Olympic games also had rules regarding their training—they were required to swear that they had trained for at least ten months. Only then could a competitor be qualified to enter an event. Every event was governed by rules and boundaries; an athlete who failed to compete within those boundaries faced disqualification. But those who competed fairly were eligible to receive the victor's crown.

What *rules* did Paul have in mind—training rules or rules of the game? Opinions have differed. Both ideas fit the requirements of the Christian life. We are in training more than we are in competition, but Paul probably had both in mind. We must be careful not to give the impression that Christians are rules-oriented or legalistic. We do, however, live under the rule of Christ. We have become athletes by God's grace through faith in Christ. We have accomplished nothing to merit that status, but Christ freely made us members of his team. We must wholeheartedly enter into training and competition (ministry to the church and the world) representing Jesus Christ in every facet of our lives.

Whether or not Timothy understood this crowning to mean a heavenly reward, Paul made his intent clear (4:8) when he wrote of his own expected crown. This reference to the crown of righteousness and the present context make it clear that believers are

not in competition with each other. In
the race that Paul envisions, all who
compete in the required way will win
(see also 1 Corinthians 9:24-27 and
Hebrews 12:1-2 for similar illustrations).

> Beyond warfare is victory,
> beyond athletic effort a
> prize, and beyond
> agricultural labour a crop.
> *C. K. Barrett*

**2:6 The hardworking farmer should be the first to receive a share
of the crops.**[NIV] From the farmer, Timothy should learn that physical labor produces results. But only the *hardworking* farmer will
harvest a good crop. The farmer knows that seeds will not plant
themselves; the harvest will not walk into the barn. The farmer
must go out into the fields to sow the seed, water it, protect it, and
finally harvest the crop. The reward will be a share of the crops for
the farmer and his family to eat, and the rest to sell.

If the soldier enjoys the commander's approval, and the athlete
enjoys the victory, then the hardworking farmer can enjoy the
fruits of his or her labor. Likewise a faithful believer can enjoy
the results of his or her labor. Those results may not be received
"immediately," but most certainly the fruits will be received from
Christ in eternity.

There are three ways to interpret the *share of the crops:*

1. Spiritually—The hard work will spiritually benefit the worker.

2. Financially—The laborer is worthy of his pay.

3. Evangelistically—A harvest of new believers will be a blessing
   to the minister.

YOU CAN DO IT!
Timothy would face suffering as he preached and taught, but
he should be able to endure. Paul illustrated this point with soldiers, athletes, and farmers who must discipline themselves
and be willing to sacrifice to achieve the results they want. Like
soldiers, we have to give up worldly security and endure rigor-
ous discipline. Like athletes, we must train hard and follow the
rules. Like farmers, we must work extremely hard and be
patient. But we keep going despite suffering because of the
thought of victory, the vision of winning, and the hope of harvest. We will see that our suffering is worthwhile when we
achieve our goal of glorifying God, winning people to Christ,
and one day living eternally with him.

"Share" could mean the material benefits that come to a minister from those with whom he or she ministers. That interpretation

would be incidental to the truth Paul was teaching. His main point concerned the blessing gained by those who invest themselves spiritually to minister to others and thereby receive spiritual growth in return.

2:7 Think over what I say, for the Lord will give you understanding in all things.NRSV Either Paul was worried that Timothy was not getting the point, or he was confident that the Lord would give Timothy understanding and insight into the wisdom of Paul's words as Timothy reflected on them. Whether *what I say* referred to the three illustrations above or to all of Paul's words to Timothy, the point remains that all believers need to rely on God's wisdom as they reflect on Scripture in order to understand how to apply it to their lives.

> The virtue of obedience makes the will supple. It gives the power to conquer self, to overcome laziness, and to resist temptations. It inspires the courage with which to fulfill the most difficult tasks. *John Vianney*

INSIDE INSIGHT
Paul told Timothy to reflect on his words, and God would give him insight. God speaks through the Bible, his Word, but we need to be open and receptive to him (1 Corinthians 2:10; James 1:5). As you read the Bible, ask God to show you his timeless truths and the application to your life. Then consider what you have read by thinking it through and meditating on it. God will give you understanding.

2:8-9 Remember Jesus Christ, raised from the dead, descended from David.NIV The ultimate example of endurance, purpose, obedience, self-discipline, hard work, and victory is Jesus Christ, who was *raised from the dead* and *descended from David* (see 1 Peter 2:19-22). False teachers were a problem in Ephesus (see Acts 20:29-30; 1 Timothy 1:3-11). At the heart of their teaching was an incorrect view of Christ. Many asserted that Christ was divine but not human—God but not man. These days we often hear that Jesus was human but not divine—man but not God. Both views destroy the good news that Jesus Christ has taken our sins on himself and has reconciled us to God.

Paul's response begins with *remember Jesus Christ* (or, "keep on remembering"). Our knowledge of Jesus must be, as much as possible, firsthand. We must be related to him personally by faith. We must know the Gospels, the primary historical documents that include his own claims. In this verse, Paul firmly stated that Jesus is fully man ("descended from David") and fully God ("raised from the dead"). These phrases express a central doctrine for all Christians. They echo Paul's summary of his message recorded in Romans 1:3-4.

Paul made two emphases about Jesus Christ. First, that Jesus Christ is risen from the dead. Because Christ alone has conquered death, he alone can be our Lord. His resurrection encourages any who suffer that they can be hopeful in him. Second, that Jesus Christ is the royal Messiah, the descendant of David. Christ alone has the messianic qualification, and he alone fulfills the promises of God to David that he would rule forever. So Paul stressed Jesus' humanity, showed how Jesus is connected with the Old Testament promises to David, and encouraged all believers to endure hardship because of what Christ has done for us.

This is my gospel, for which I am suffering even to the point of being chained like a criminal.NIV Paul was in chains in prison because of the gospel he preached. He was being treated *like a criminal.* (The only other location of the same Greek word is in Luke 23:32, 39 describing the men crucified with Jesus.) Such was the persecution against believers—they were considered criminals by the Roman authorities.

The truth about Jesus still faces opposition, but it also still reaches receptive hearts. When Paul said that Jesus is God, he angered the Jews who had condemned Jesus for blasphemy; but many Jews became followers of Christ (1 Corinthians 1:24). He angered the Romans who worshiped the emperor as a god; but even some in Caesar's household turned to Jesus (Philippians 4:22). When Paul said Jesus was human, he angered the Greeks who thought divinity was soiled if it had any contact with humanity; still many Greeks accepted the faith (Acts 11:20-21). The truth that Jesus is one person with two united natures has never been easy to understand, but it is believed by people every day. Despite the opposition, continue to proclaim Christ. Some will listen and believe. (See also the notes on 1 Timothy 2:5.)

But the word of God is not chained.NKJV By *the word of God* Paul meant the gospel truth. He had written to the Thessalonians: "And we also thank God continually because, when you received the word of God, which you heard from us, you accepted it not as the word of men, but as it actually is, the word of God, which is at work in you who believe" (1 Thessalonians 2:13 NIV). Although Paul was sitting in chains, he did not feel ashamed or worthless. He knew that the gospel message, entrusted to Timothy and other faithful people, could not be chained (Philippians 1:12-18; 2 Thessalonians 3:1). Even if the

Romans succeeded in imprisoning, even killing, every Christian leader, they could never stop the spread of the gospel. God's Word would continue to spread, despite persecution, and change lives everywhere.

2:10 **Therefore I endure everything for the sake of the elect, so that they may also obtain the salvation that is in Christ Jesus, with eternal glory.**^{NRSV} Despite Paul's imprisonment, God's Word would continue to work, calling out *the elect* or "the chosen" (those who had not yet trusted in Christ as Savior). Paul could confidently *endure*

It would be no paradise to St. Paul "to live in Paradise alone."
Newport White

everything knowing that God remained in control. Sometimes suffering has no other benefit than what others will learn from our experience of pain. A woman endures the pains of childbirth for the sake of her child. We must never think of suffering as some form of work of merit to earn our salvation or to work off our guilt, nor as some form of punishment from God. Although Paul experienced very real pain as he spread the gospel, he focused on the results of his suffering—others were finding salvation in Christ.

PAUL'S SUFFERING
Because of passages like 2 Corinthians 1:6; 4:7-15; and Colossians 1:24, some have suggested that Paul saw his own suffering as in some way directly redemptive for others. How does Paul's suffering affect the elect?

We know that Paul did not mean that Christ's suffering was inadequate to save him, nor that Paul's suffering helped his own redemption in any way. This would contradict Paul's central teaching in Romans 3:21-26, where he explained that salvation comes only from Christ. We also know that Paul's suffering was not just an inspiring example to all believers. He saw God's purpose in his suffering to be more than that.

But Paul could be referring to Christ's words to Ananias in Acts 9:16: "I will show him how much he must suffer for my name" (NIV). Paul reflected the early Christian idea that the sufferings Christ, the Messiah, experienced are carried on and jointly shared by his disciples.

Paul could have regarded his imprisonment as taking the heat of persecution away from other Christians who were persecuted by Nero.

Most likely, however, Paul meant that bringing the gospel to unbelievers creates opposition, hardship, and suffering. This Paul was willing to face because the salvation of others was at stake.

Who are "the elect" (*tous eklektous*)? While the concept of election has generated fierce doctrinal differences, most of these differences come from theological and philosophical points of view, not the Bible itself. In this context, Paul indicated that the elect are those who may "obtain the salvation that is in Christ Jesus." He makes no claim to know who they are. Their identification falls under the sovereignty of God. For Paul, God authored salvation and commissioned him to spread the word; God knows who will respond. Paul was so sure of God's purpose that he was willing to suffer to see that salvation realized.

The phrase *obtain the salvation* does not contradict salvation by grace. "Obtain" means "gaining," "finding," and "experiencing," though the action is not necessarily self-initiated. Salvation is not something that we can earn, as Paul taught in Ephesians 2:8-9. Christ is the source and provider of salvation, but Christians' suffering may also create opportunities for others to learn about Christ. Paul was referring to those elect ones who had not yet believed, knowing that his faithfulness to the gospel in the face of death would encourage them to "obtain the salvation that is in Christ Jesus." The result that Paul earnestly anticipated was *eternal glory,* our final salvation in Jesus Christ (Hebrews 9:28), the glory of God that we share through our relationship with Christ (Matthew 28:19), and the resurrection and renewal of our bodies (Romans 8:18-25). To the Corinthians Paul wrote, "For our light and momentary troubles are achieving for us an eternal glory that far outweighs them all. So we fix our eyes not on what is seen, but on what is unseen. For what is seen is temporary, but what is unseen is eternal" (2 Corinthians 4:17-18 NIV; see also Romans 5:2).

2:11 The saying is sure.NRSV Paul used this phrase several times in his letters to Timothy and Titus (see 1 Timothy 1:15; 3:1; 4:9; Titus 3:8). This "trustworthy saying" (NIV) quoted in verses 11-13 was probably an early Christian hymn or a quotation used in a Christian ceremony; though it would be equally proper to say that Paul may have provided here, under the inspiration of the Holy Spirit, another one of the early hymns of the church.

For if we died with Him, we shall also live with Him.NKJV The first couplet of this hymn contrasts death and life—the believer's death to sin at the moment of salvation and the new life begun now with Christ in the world and in eternity. This phrase echoes Paul's words in Romans 6:8. The entire passage in Romans 6:2-23 describes how believers are freed from the power of sin— "The death [Christ] died, he died to sin, once for all; but the life he lives, he lives to God. So you also must consider yourselves

dead to sin and alive to God in Christ Jesus" (Romans 6:10-11
NRSV). Paul could confidently "endure everything for the sake of
the elect" (2:10) because he knew the sure promises of God.

There are three views of "dying with Christ":

(1) The use of the past tense, "we died," indicates *martyrdom*—
there is special glory in heaven for martyrs as reflected in the
future tense "we shall also live" and "we shall also reign." But
Paul's reference to his own death avoids the martyr's language.

(2) Like Romans 6:3-6, "died with him" implies *identification*
with him. By faith, we identify with Christ in his death, recognize his death was for our sins, and thus we have spiritual life
now, not just at the future resurrection.

(3) The dying mentioned implies the sacrament of *baptism* that
Paul referred to in Colossians 2:12 and 3:1-3. Paul connected baptism with the death of Jesus.

Perhaps the best way to understand it would be that Paul
strictly means identifying with Christ in his death, as symbolized
by the sacrament of baptism. This is not to say that baptism is
only a symbol. That issue must be decided by other passages and
church bodies, but here Paul has the baptismal picture in mind of
new life in Christ.

2:12 If we endure, we shall also reign with Him.^{NKJV} This second
couplet of the hymn contrasts endurance and rewards. Those who
live for Christ may face severe difficulties that must be endured.
Christ endured and now reigns (1 Corinthians 15:25); all believers who endure to the end shall also reign with him (Revelation
3:21; 5:10; 20:4).

The phrase "if we died" (2:11) in the Greek implies a single
act; the phrase "if we endure" in this verse in the Greek implies
ongoing action. We only need salvation once; but enduring
through life is a continual action requiring constant prayer, guidance, and wisdom. But the reward is beyond imagination.

GREAT IS YOUR REWARD
God is faithful to his children, and although we may suffer great
hardships in this life, God promises that someday we will live
eternally with him. What will this involve? It means believers will
live in Christ's kingdom, and that we will share in the administration of that kingdom. This truth comforted Paul as he went
through suffering and death. Are you facing hardships? Don't
turn away from God—focus on your wonderful future with him.

If we disown him, he also will disown us.^{NIV} This third couplet
reveals that commitment to Christ must be total, no turning back;

HEAVENLY REWARDS

Reference	What It Says about Heaven
Matthew 16:24-27	To follow Christ, take up the cross. To save life, lose it. For Christ will come in glory with his angels and reward each person according to what he or she has done.
Matthew 19:28-30	If we give up material rewards on this earth for the sake of Christ and his kingdom, we are promised a hundred times as much, as well as eternal life with Christ.
Romans 6:8	If we died with Christ, we will also live with him.
Romans 8:17	If we are children of God, then we are his heirs (and coheirs with Christ) of all the riches of his glory. We share in suffering; we also share in glory.
1 Corinthians 15:42-58	We will be changed—at the sounding of the last trumpet we will receive imperishable bodies. Christ has the victory!
Colossians 3:3-4	Our lives are hidden with Christ in God. When Christ appears, we will appear with him in glory.
1 Thessalonians 4:13-18	The Lord will come down from heaven with a loud command, with the voice of the archangel, and with a trumpet call. The dead in Christ will rise first. Those who are still alive at his return will be caught up to meet him in the clouds. Then we will all be with the Lord together forever.
Revelation 3:21	To the one who overcomes, Christ will give him the right to sit with him on his throne in heaven.
Revelation 21:1–22:21	There will be a new heaven and a new earth. There will be no more death or mourning or crying or pain. The Holy City will be beautiful beyond imagination, and only those whose names are written in the Lamb's Book of Life will be allowed to enter. There will be no sun or light, for the Lord himself will be the light. And God's kingdom will remain forever and ever.

to *disown* results in being disowned. The Greek tense in the phrase "if we disown" is future. These words provided a solemn warning; but to deny Christ was unthinkable to the early Christians, even in the face of mounting persecution. True believers might be faithless and weak at times; they might falter when giving a testimony (see 2:13), but they would never disown their

Lord. While the word *deny* has been used in place of "disown" (*arnesometha* NRSV, NKJV), the meaning here implies deliberate refusal of Jesus as Lord.

Jesus had already issued the warning: "Whoever acknowledges me before men, I will also acknowledge him before my Father in heaven. But whoever disowns me before men, I will disown him before my Father in heaven" (Matthew 10:32-33 NIV). The writer of Hebrews assured the faithful believers that "we are not among those who shrink back and so are lost, but among those who have faith and so are saved" (Hebrews 10:39 NRSV).

2:13 If we are faithless, He remains faithful; He cannot deny Himself.NKJV This last couplet of the hymn reveals the depth of the relationship between believers and Christ the Lord; when we fail at times, this does not mean God will reject us forever. These words apply not to faithless unbelievers, but to believers who at times fail the Lord. Humans, by their very nature, are prone to failure; and Christians, though born again, are still human. But even when believers act faithlessly, God remains faithful.

> Three things are impossible with God—to die, to lie, and to fail the soul that trusts him. Even when we cannot muster faith enough, his word of promise cannot be frustrated. *F. B. Meyer*

Believers are secure in Christ's promises. This does not give a license for faithlessness; rather, it eases our conscience when we fail, allowing us to come back to the Father and start anew. God does not deny those for whom he died.

FAITHFULLY FAITH-FULL
Jesus is faithful. He will stay by our side even when we have endured so much that we seem to have no faith left. We may be faithless at times, but Jesus is faithful to his promise to be with us "to the very end of the age" (Matthew 28:20 NIV). Refusing Christ's help will break our communication with God, but he will never turn his back on us even though we are faithless.

Paul began this hymn with two couplets highlighting two goals of a believer's life: (1) to identify with Christ who died for us so that we are given eternal life and (2) to endure the hardships of this present life knowing that the life to come will be far better. Next he expressed the "worst-case" scenario of the one who would disown Christ and receive denial in return. But then, just when the hard edge of God's perfection had been revealed, Paul sounded a note of hope and grace: "If we are faithless, He

remains faithful" NKJV. Our future hangs, not on the strength of
our faith, but on the strength of God's faithfulness!

GOOD WORKERS ARE NOT ASHAMED OF THEIR WORK / 2:14-26

The second half of chapter 2 echoes the first letter to Timothy.
Apparently, the task of confronting wrong teaching and continuing the good work of discipling believers was not past the crisis
stage.

As he had done previously, Paul emphasized to Timothy that
his moral and spiritual conduct would provide the greatest confirmation of his teaching. No matter how others may respond to the
gospel, Timothy himself must remain a consistent "example of
what it means to be a believer" (1 Timothy 4:12).

2:14 **Keep reminding them of these things.**NIV Paul's instruction in
the previous verses was meant for all the believers, not just Timothy. These instructions would need to be given often, as indicated
by the present imperative *keep* [on] *reminding*. All believers, no
matter how many years they have believed, need to be reminded
of the basis of their faith and how to relate that faith to circumstances of life.

OVER AND OVER AGAIN
Few lessons are as difficult to swallow for a young pastor as
the importance of repetition. However well delivered, last
week's sermon did not get through to everyone. The basics
must be reviewed and repeated. Even in a small church, when
the pastor is convinced that *everyone* finally understands,
someone will make a statement showing that he or she missed
the point.
   Paul was practicing what he was preaching—he kept on
reminding Timothy to keep on reminding others. Consider what
truth needs repeating. Plan a strategy to use sermons, Sunday
school, small-group Bible studies, and personal Bible reading
to reinforce the teaching.

**Warn them before God against quarreling about words; it is
of no value, and only ruins those who listen.**NIV The phrase
before God reveals the importance that Paul placed on this command to Timothy, for a teacher's responsibility is great (see
James 3:1). Paul urged Timothy to remind the believers not to
argue over unimportant details (*quarreling about words*) or have
foolish discussions (*godless chatter,* see 2:16) because such arguments are confusing, useless, and even harmful. False teachers

caused strife and divisions by their meaningless quibbling over unimportant details (see 1 Timothy 6:3-5). Quarreling about words is a major problem today. Churches split over nonessentials. Quarrelsome people nitpick church programs, undermine productivity with criticism, and verbally attack the innocent. When someone shows a pattern of quarrelsomeness, church leaders should visit that person to deal with the issues in private.

Much of Paul's first letter to Timothy focused on dealing with false teachers: "Command certain men not to teach false doctrines. . . . These promote controversies rather than God's work—which is by faith" (1 Timothy 1:3-4 NIV). These false teachers discussed myths and genealogies (1 Timothy 1:4) and quibbled about words and details that focused not on Scripture but on their own ideas. This took valuable time away from teaching the truth of Scripture and spreading the gospel. The believers who got caught up in these "quarrels about words" wasted their time, and some even ended up "ruined" rather than being spiritually strengthened.

2:15 Be diligent to present yourself approved to God, a worker who does not need to be ashamed.NKJV The antithesis of the false teachers are ministers who work diligently for God. *Diligent* means "zealous in ethical responsibilities," not studious. The most effective silencer of the false teachers was the truth in the hands of faithful teachers. The Christians would need unity, strength, and the truth of the gospel to survive the persecutions ahead, to impart the truth to future generations. This incredible responsibility means individual teachers, ministers, and leaders must seek not the approval of people but the approval of God. An unashamed worker can present his or her life and ministry to God, knowing that God will be pleased with the quality of work.

Jesus told a parable about a master entrusting money to his servants. Two of the servants wisely invested their "talents" and gladly gave the master his money with the extra earned upon the master's return. And the master's reply: "Well done!" A diligent worker, desiring only God's approval, need not be ashamed to present himself and his work to his master. (See Matthew 25:14-30 for Jesus' parable.)

Who correctly handles the word of truth.NIV Paul rounded off the image of the laborer ("worker") by comparing effective ministry with the expert use of tools. The expression translated "correctly handles" is *orthotomounta,* meaning, literally, "to cut straight." Because the term is used only here in the New Testament, we cannot be sure of its use, but the meaning is clear enough—approval of one's ministry before God will depend on how well one has proclaimed, explained, and applied the *word of truth.* We must help the gospel cut a straight path and do nothing to hinder it.

But what did Paul mean by "word of truth"? In the Pastoral Epistles, the expression refers primarily to the gospel message (1 Timothy 2:3-7; 3:9, 15; 4:3, 6). There were certainly broader issues involved as well as the place and use of the Old Testament, but for Paul and Timothy, the handling of these areas always rested on the teaching and person of Jesus.

WILL YOU BE ASHAMED?
Because God will examine what kind of workers we have been for him, we should build our lives on his Word and build his Word into our lives—it alone tells us how to live for him and serve him. Believers who ignore the Bible will certainly be ashamed at the judgment. Consistent and diligent study of God's Word is vital; otherwise we will be lulled into neglecting God and our true purpose for living.

2:16 Avoid godless chatter, because those who indulge in it will become more and more ungodly.[NIV] In important areas of Christian teaching, believers should carefully work through disagreements. But bickering long hours over words and theories that are not central to the Christian faith and life only provokes anger and leads the "chatterers" (whether the false teachers or their "students") toward spiritual deterioration. Even if "godless chatter" reaches a resolution, it gains little ground for the kingdom (see also 1 Timothy 6:20 for the same warning). Learning and discussing are not bad unless they keep believers constantly focusing on false doctrine or unhelpful trivialities. Believers must not let anything keep them from their work for and service to God.

Paul said that the false teachers who engaged in teaching that is contrary to God's Word will get ahead, but in the wrong direction. *More and more ungodly* means to advance in ungodliness, to go the wrong way. The false teachers will progress to even worse forms of disruption and sinfulness (see 3:9).

2:17 Their teaching will spread like gangrene.[NIV] Paul understood the addictive power of false teaching as people feel the need to be in on these supposedly "intellectual" discussions. Paul compared the spiritual deterioration (becoming "more and more ungodly," 2:16) caused by this false teaching to *gangrene.* Gangrene was nearly always a fatal disease, thus the comparison was vivid to Paul's listeners. Gangrene begins in the body when tissues die from obstructed circulation. Once a limb gets gangrene, it often has to be amputated as the only way to stop the gangrene from spreading. The spread and deadly result of false teaching could not be more aptly described.

Among them are Hymenaeus and Philetus.^{NRSV} Hymenaeus is also mentioned in 1 Timothy 1:20, where he is included with a man named Alexander. Paul had handed these men over to Satan—put them out of the church. Just as a limb with gangrene must be amputated, these false teachers were "amputated" from the body of believers so they could cause no more harm. Nothing further is known about Philetus. The false teaching of Hymenaeus and Philetus about the resurrection was destroying some people's faith.

2:18 **Who have swerved from the truth by claiming that the resurrection has already taken place.**^{NRSV} The false teachers were denying the resurrection of the body. These believers in Ephesus grew up under Greek philosophy and a Greek understanding of the world. Greek philosophy viewed the spirit as immortal and the body as evil. Thus, a doctrine that taught the resurrection of the body was especially difficult to believe. So the false teachers tried to combine the doctrine of the resurrection with Greek philosophy in order to make it make sense to them. They taught that when a person became a Christian and was spiritually reborn, that was the only resurrection he or she would ever experience. To them, resurrection was symbolic and spiritual, not real and physical.

THE KEY
A heresy about the Resurrection was especially problematic because Jesus' resurrection is the key to the Christian faith. Why?

- Just as he said, Jesus rose from the dead. We can be confident, therefore, that Jesus will accomplish all he has promised.
- Jesus' bodily resurrection shows us that the living Christ, not a false prophet or impostor, is ruler of God's eternal kingdom.
- We can be certain of our own resurrection because Jesus was resurrected. Death is not the end—there is future life.
- The divine power that brought Jesus back to life is now available to us to bring our spiritually dead selves back to life.
- The Resurrection is the basis for the church's witness to the world.

The problem that Timothy faced in Ephesus was apparently

widespread. Paul addressed it at length in 1 Corinthians 15:12-57. Because the physical body decayed after death, it was tempting to think that whatever the future might hold, it would not involve reinhabiting what was rapidly turning to dust. Paul answered by appealing to God's power and pointing to the illustration of the seed that is planted in the soil and springs to life: "So it will be with the resurrection of the dead. The body that is sown is perishable, it is raised imperishable" (1 Corinthians 15:42 NIV). Denying the resurrection of believers was tantamount to denying the resurrection of Jesus himself. Paul clearly taught that believers will be resurrected after they die and that their bodies as well as their souls will live eternally with Christ (see 1 Corinthians 15:35ff.; 2 Corinthians 5:1-10; 1 Thessalonians 4:15-18). Any other teaching *swerved from the truth.* For example, cults often find a hearing by using familiar language, quoting the Bible, or appearing to agree with the teaching of the Christian church. To the casual or uninformed listener, they seem to be headed for the truth, but they swerve and miss it at the last moment. Scriptures are taken out of context and used to prove their points, though the biblical phrases used have nothing to do with the teaching they are promoting. Words like *Christian, believer, faith,* and *salvation* can all be used to set a person up for error by giving the atmosphere of familiarity.

The primary weapons against such attacks are not the accumulation of exhaustive knowledge of every cult. Instead, we must constantly increase our biblical literacy as well as consistently develop our relationship with Christ. Paul's reminder to Timothy applies to us: "Guard the good deposit that was entrusted to you—guard it with the help of the Holy Spirit who lives in us" (2 Timothy 2:14 NIV).

They are upsetting the faith of some.[NRSV] When the doctrine of the Resurrection is called into question, Christianity itself is questioned. The Resurrection is the basis of Christianity. People who believed the false teachers began questioning the bodily resurrection of Christ and thus their own resurrection. This questioning undermined their faith.

2:19 **But God's firm foundation stands.**[NRSV] *But (ho mentoi,* "nevertheless") introduces a forceful contrast. False teaching, for all its enticing qualities, will not last. Although it plagued the first-century church and still has footholds today, it cannot prevail against God's church because the church is built on a *firm foundation.* Heresies, false teachers, even persecution, cannot destroy the truth taught in God's churches. It stands and will stand until Christ returns.

There are differences of opinion regarding the identity of the "firm foundation" (*themelios*).

- The foundation could be the truth of the gospel.
- The foundation could be the faith of the Ephesian church, the deposit to be guarded (see 1:14).
- The foundation could be the church as a whole and thus include the Ephesians.

The third option seems most likely based on passages like 1 Timothy 3:15: "the church of the living God, the pillar and foundation of the truth" (NIV, see also 1 Corinthians 3:10-15 and Ephesians 2:19-22). But all three options are possible because Paul certainly had the gospel and its sure effectiveness in mind. Some might swerve from the truth, but it will remain the truth.

Bearing this inscription: "The Lord knows those who are his."NRSV These next two phrases appear as if they were written on the cornerstone of the foundation described above (for a similar use of the metaphor, see Romans 4:11; 1 Corinthians 9:2). This inscription can be compared to God's seal—a sign of authenticity and approval.

The first phrase may refer to the words of Moses at the time of Korah's rebellion. Korah and several associates challenged Moses' leadership: "They came as a group to oppose Moses and Aaron and said to them, 'You have gone too far! The whole community is holy, every one of them, and the LORD is with them. Why then do you set yourselves above the LORD's assembly?'" (Numbers 16:3 NIV). Moses replied that the Lord himself would reveal to all who were truly his: "When Moses heard this, he fell facedown. Then he said to Korah and all his followers: 'In the morning the LORD will show who belongs to him'" (Numbers 16:4-5 NIV). In a shocking display of power, God vindicated Moses' leadership.

These words should encourage all believers. False teachers may cause problems, but God knows his true followers. The Lord sees all who preach and teach in his name, and he knows those who are his.

"Let everyone who calls on the name of the Lord turn away from wickedness."NRSV This second phrase could be from Numbers 16:26 (in the same context as above); however, most commentators prefer to compare it with Isaiah 52:11, citing the use of the same verb in the Greek translation of Isaiah (Septuagint).

Those who are the Lord's, those who call on his name, must be responsible to *turn away from wickedness.*

Both inscriptions together remind the believers of God's sovereign control over his church and the believers' responsibility to turn from evil and maintain pure and holy lives. Timothy did not need to fear for the future of the church, for God was in control. Timothy's responsibility, and indeed the responsibility of every believer, was to stay free from sin and the contamination spread by the false teachers.

God does his part by helping us discern true from false believers; then we must do our part in turning "away from wickedness." We must not only repudiate the false teachers, we must also refuse to take part in their false teaching. We should not attend or sponsor meetings, purchase tapes or books, or support them in any way.

DISTORTED, DILUTED, OR DELETED
False teachers still spout lies. Some distort the truth, some dilute it, and some simply delete it by saying that God's truth no longer applies. But no matter how many people follow the liars, the solid foundation of God's truth never changes, is never shaken, and will never fade. When we follow God's truth, he will never forsake us.

2:20 In a large house there are articles not only of gold and silver, but also of wood and clay; some are for noble purposes and some for ignoble.NIV Paul changed his metaphor from a building to household utensils but continued the same theme. In a large house there are valuable utensils made of precious metal that are used only on special occasions; other utensils, made of common and less valuable materials, are for ordinary use. Again Paul makes the distinction between commonly useful and uncommonly useful workers of God, pointing out to Timothy that both will be found in the church. It doesn't work to stretch the details of the metaphor too far; Paul's point is that believers should desire to be special "utensils" ready for any special service needed by God.

There are three general views regarding the identity of the household *articles:*

(1) The items used for *noble purposes* are the faithful teachers, while those used for *ignoble* purposes are the false teachers (a view that leans heavily on Romans 9:19-24).

(2) The "articles" all refer to believers; some of whom are

assigned to special duty, while others receive "ordinary" assignments (a view that appeals to 1 Corinthians 12:21-24 for support).

(3) The *large house* itself is not a group of people but refers to
Timothy himself and the strong and weak qualities in his life (a
view that skips 2:21 and seeks its interpretation in 2:22-24).

While each of these explanations has possibilities, none of
them fully express Paul's own application of the illustration in
verse 21.

**2:21 All who cleanse themselves of the things I have mentioned
will become special utensils.**^{NRSV} Paul included every Christian
in his *all,* or literally "if anyone." How would this verse help us
understand each of the three views for the "articles" mentioned in
the comments on verse 20?

In reverse order, regarding the third view first, the general
scope of this promise, "All who . . . will," weakens the interpretation that Paul had only Timothy in mind. Regarding the second
view, the challenge, "all who cleanse themselves . . . will become
special," does not match Paul's picture elsewhere of the church
as a household in which various members have set roles (see
1 Corinthians 12:21-24). But to Timothy, Paul may have been
emphasizing the individual believer's moral purity in order to fulfill the role God has chosen him or her to play in the household.
In 1 Corinthians 12:21-24 Paul was highlighting the equal usefulness in God's plan for those who may appear to have lesser
importance in the household. Concerning the first view, the shift
in verses 14-19 from those who have "swerved from the truth" to
those who need to be warned and kept from having their faith
upset leads up to Paul's assertion in verse 19 that "the Lord
knows those who are his." This would make it unlikely that he
was referring to the false teachers. The metaphor of the household utensils communicates most consistently when used to indicate persons within the church at various stages of spiritual
development. Otherwise, the point of cleansing would be irrelevant.

There are different interpretations of the *things* that believers
are to *cleanse* themselves from or "purge" from their lives. But in
Timothy's case, Paul would provide a number of specific ideas
(see 2:22-24). The Greek verb for "cleanse" (*ekkathairo*) is used
only in one other place, 1 Corinthians 5:7, where Paul was telling
the Corinthians to "clean out" (excommunicate) an unrepentant
sinner from the fellowship. Thus, if "things" referred to persons,
this cleansing could mean that the believers should have nothing
to do with false teachers and/or to take a hard line by "cleaning"
them out of the church. The other interpretation, which fits better

with Paul's further counsel to Timothy, refers to personal inward cleansing from involvement in false teachings and "godless chatter" (2:16). In either case, a person who desires to be used by God must be cleansed from sin and then stay clean by refraining from contacts and activities that could soil him or her. This does not require a person's isolation from the world (for sin is all around); it refers more specifically to involvement with those whose goal is to lead people away from the faith. Cleansed people who stay away from corrupting influences are then **made holy, useful to the Master and prepared to do any good work.**[NIV] This utensil "for special use" (2:20) has three qualities that could also be considered privileges. They are:

1. *made holy*—set apart for God's special purposes while personally experiencing the effects of Christ's presence in their lives

2. *useful to the Master*—adjectives synonymous with "useful" include valuable, worthy, advantageous, helpful, and serviceable. What a privilege to be called by any of these terms in the service of the Master!

3. *prepared to do any good work*—ready and willing, without hesitation or reluctance, to serve the Master in any task he requires

How much more powerful the church of God would be in the world if all believers were "clean utensils" ready for the Master's use!

CLEANLINESS OUTPERFORMS CLEVERNESS
Paul's earnest counsel to Timothy was simple and straightforward. He did not encourage the young man to go back to seminary for more education. There was no appeal to professionalism. Rather, Paul's challenge was for Timothy to rededicate himself to being morally clean and consistent.
Paul was not opposed to education, but he resisted the intellectual elitism of the false teachers. Paul knew that a large collection of scholarly achievements was sometimes as much a hindrance as a help in making a man or woman right and available in God's eyes. Paul stressed clear purpose and pure motives first, educational achievements second.

2:22 Flee also youthful lusts.[NKJV] Focusing back on his beloved "son," Paul offered a few more words of advice concerning his words in verses 20-21. Paul knew Timothy very well from their years of travel together, and most likely he knew Timothy's weak spots. Timothy was a young man (1 Timothy 4:12), at least young for the responsibilities he carried, so Paul offered no-nonsense advice. The *lusts* (*epithumias*) mentioned here are not only sexual but are also the other passions characteristic of the young—impatience, contentiousness, favoritism, egotism, intolerance, etc. (see also 1 Timothy 6:11). Instead, Paul advised Timothy to **pursue righteousness, faith, love, peace with those who call on the Lord out of a pure heart.**[NKJV] As was frequently the case with Paul, when he issued a warning he followed it with an alternative positive strategy. Timothy was to flee from danger but *pursue* any number of healthy characteristics. The list that follows is similar to the one in 1 Timothy 6:11-12, but not identical. Paul was not issuing a development plan, but worthy personal objectives to pursue.

Righteousness refers to actions that are morally upright and virtuous. In a word, it expresses a way of life that seeks to model itself after God's directions. Rather than claiming perfection or settling for mediocrity, righteousness requires the pursuit of obedience.

Faith and *love* are fundamental to Christianity and basic to Paul's teaching (see 1 Corinthians 13:13).

In addition, while Timothy was to oppose the false teachers and deal strongly with those who followed them, he was to pursue *peace* with *those who call on the Lord* with *pure* hearts. In spite of the individual challenge that Paul presented, he was not permitting Timothy to function alone. He was to find strength and encouragement from those who love Christ and who seek to be in touch with him constantly. There were others for whom he was responsible, but also some who would be peers and share a deep and common desire to be faithful. The peace of which Paul spoke comes from the Spirit of God calming the hearts and minds of the believers.

A TIME TO RUN
Running away is sometimes considered cowardly. But wise people realize that removing themselves physically from temptation often can be the most courageous action to take. Timothy, a young man, was warned to flee anything that produced evil thoughts. Do you have a recurring temptation that is difficult to resist? Remove yourself physically from any situation that stimulates your desire to sin. Knowing when to run is as important in spiritual battle as knowing when and how to fight. (See also 1 Timothy 6:11.)

2:23 Have nothing to do with stupid and senseless controversies; you know that they breed quarrels.[NRSV] While peace should be the norm among believers, we should not entertain false teachings to keep people happy. Paul's language here does not forbid contact with such people, as is demonstrated by verse 25, where the guidelines for treating opponents imply some level of interaction.

There can be no doubt about the problem caused by the false teachers—Paul repeated it several times in his letters to Timothy and Titus. They got people caught up in *stupid and senseless controversies* that divided the church (see also 1 Timothy 1:4, 6-7; 4:1, 7; 6:3-5, 20-21; 2 Timothy 2:14, 16-17, 23-24; 4:2-4; Titus 1:9, 13-14; 3:2, 9). These ideas caused *quarrels (maxas, "fights")*. Paul used terms that describe extended verbal battles. Timothy's best approach was to simply *have nothing to do* with them. To argue would only make Timothy angry and draw him into the very trap being set by the false teachers.

A TIME TO TURN
While Paul did not forbid Timothy to have contact with the false teachers (he would need contact in order to rebuke them), he did advise Timothy to stay out of lengthy talks with them because they would be "stupid and senseless" discussions, as well as probably lead to "quarrels."

In the same manner, the apostle John, writing to the believers in 2 John, told church members to avoid controversy with the false teachers by refusing to show them any kind of hospitality. They should do nothing to encourage the false teachers to continue teaching their lies. If believers listened, showed hospitality, or attempted to discuss with them, that action would show approval of the false teachings.

So what does a Christian do when confronted with cult leaders who knock at your door, requesting a hearing? The best advice is often to have very limited dialogue with them. They are being trained for evangelism, will often have a "strong" and older member of their group with them, and will only waste your time should you attempt to show them that they do not have the truth. It may seem rude to cut off debate with heretical teachers, but how much better it is to be faithful to God than merely courteous to people.

2:24 And the Lord's servant must not be quarrelsome but kindly to everyone.[NRSV] The phrase *the Lord's servant (doulon, "slave")* here refers specifically to Timothy and to his responsibility as leader of a church. In addressing both Timothy's weaknesses as well as the expectations of his ministry, Paul consistently reminded him that believers are under orders of their commander, Jesus. Our natural response might be

> You will never really understand what it means to be a servant until you have been treated like one. *Gerry Fosdal*

timidity or quarrelsomeness. In either case, our "strengths" as well as our "weaknesses" must be at the disposal of Christ. Some he may make use of; others he may require that we leave unused.

The expression "the Lord's servant" alludes almost without doubt to the pictures of the suffering servant of God found in Isaiah (Isaiah 52:13-15; 53:1-12). The Christian who imitates Christ in this way will bear the experience of "wounds" as he or she attempts to relate compassionately to those who may strike out in hurt or anger. Some people are *quarrelsome* because they have never been listened to before; when we demonstrate kindness, we may find openness where before there was only a wall of arguments.

As a minister of the gospel, Timothy did not have to quarrel with the false teachers; to quarrel could be seen as a need to come to a compromise. There could be no compromise between the gospel truth and the false teachers. Instead, Timothy should promote unity by being kind (also translated "gentle") to everyone. The hard, sharp edge of the truth required the skilled hand of someone who could relate compassionately with others.

An apt teacher, patient.NRSV Timothy had already met the requirement for a church leader of having the ability to teach (see 1 Timothy 3:2). Paul exhorted him to remain confident in his teaching and to continue teaching the truth to those willing to learn. At the same time, he would need to exercise patience with those who opposed him. The Greek word for "patient" (*anexikakon*) is used only here in the New Testament; it literally means "to face ill treatment without resentment."

2:25 **Correcting opponents with gentleness.**NRSV Timothy was to have nothing to do with "senseless controversies" (2:23) and to exercise patience with everyone (2:24). But his goal was to gently lead his opponents to the correct understanding of the truth. Therefore, he needed to maintain contact that would lead to interaction with these people, while at the same time resisting their error. Instead of antagonizing opponents, he should calmly and gently correct their wrong ideas.

In the hope that God will grant them repentance leading them to a knowledge of the truth.NIV Timothy's first desire ought to be to bring them back into the church, not to punish them (see 2 Thessalonians 3:6, 15). God does not want "any to perish, but all to come to repentance" (2 Peter 3:9 NRSV), even those who openly had opposed Paul.

This presents the other side of leadership work that Paul presented in 1 Timothy 1:20, which speaks of "delivering people over to Satan"—an expression for excommunication. There are two sides of discipline: punitive and redemptive. Both are needed. Any of the false teachers could find the truth, repent, and become workmen for God (2:15). Paul could attest to that fact, for he had at one time opposed the gospel to the point of persecuting Christians (Acts 22:3-10). Now he was suffering unashamed for the faith because, as he wrote, "I know whom I have believed and am persuaded that He is able to keep what I have committed to Him until that Day" (1:12 NKJV).

ADVICE TO TEACHERS
As a teacher, Timothy helped those who were confused about the truth. Paul's advice to Timothy, and to all who teach God's truth, is to be kind and gentle, patiently and courteously explaining the truth. Good teaching never promotes quarrels or foolish arguments. Whether you are teaching Sunday school, leading a Bible study, or preaching in church, remember to listen to people's questions and treat them respectfully, while avoiding foolish debates. If you do this, those who oppose you will be more willing to hear what you have to say and perhaps turn from their error.

2:26 And that they will come to their senses and escape from the trap of the devil, who has taken them captive to do his will.[NIV] To *come to their senses* could also be translated "return to soberness." In other words, the false teachers have gotten "drunk," are "under the influence" of the devil, with the result of losing their senses. Then they were easy prey for Satan's trap (see also 1 Timothy 3:7; 6:9). Satan is at the root of all false teaching and division in the church. He knows the strength of a unified church and fears it. So he creates a "trap"—money, fame, pride of feeling intellectual—to draw people away from the faith and to false teaching. But there is hope—escape is possible.

While there are some grammatical complications in this verse, the easiest way to read it involves seeing that both the "trap" and "his will" belong to *the devil*. Some have tried to give the verse a positive turn at the end by making "will" refer to God or his servant, so that the verse would mean something like, "escape from the trap of the devil, who has taken them captive, to now do his [God's or his representative's] will." But the sense of the verse is complete as it stands.

2 Timothy 3:1–4:8

Paul's suffering left him with few illusions about his future; he would die before Christ returned. As has already been pointed out, this letter has the recurring tone of someone setting his personal matters in order.

Paul began this chapter with remarks about degenerating conditions in society. Both Paul and Timothy had witnessed how bad "the last days" would become. Paul listed a whole catalog of attitudes and behaviors typical of "last days" people. This list also described the false teachers in Ephesus. Paul characterized them as belonging to the perennial crop of "opposition" leaders who create a following for themselves. Timothy was to resist their methods and their underlying purposes.

3:1 But mark this: There will be terrible times in the last days.[NIV] This reference to the *last days* reveals Paul's sense of urgency. In his first letter to Timothy, Paul had written, "Now the Spirit expressly says that in later times some will renounce the faith by paying attention to deceitful spirits and teachings of demons" (1 Timothy 4:1 NRSV). But warnings about the last days were certainly not unique to Paul. It was a common theme among the leaders of the early church (see Acts 2:17; James 5:3; 2 Peter 3:3; Jude 18). *Terrible times* means "hard to bear, dangerous, troublesome." The same Greek word for "terrible" is used in Matthew 8:28 for the violent demoniacs. Paul's warning deserves our full attention.

The last days began after Jesus' resurrection, when the Holy Spirit came upon the believers at Pentecost. The last days will continue until Christ's second coming. Paul could speak about the last days as a future event (emphasizing conditions present at the close of the last days), or as a present reality (emphasizing the truth that the state of depravity in the world is always ripe for harvest). This means that *we* are living in the last days. It should not surprise us, then, to see the moral degeneration of society around us. Paul warned us that it would happen, as did Jesus (see Matthew 24).

LIVING IN THE LAST DAYS

If society is doomed to degeneration, what should believers do as they live in the "last days"? Paul offered advice in several of his letters:

Reference	Application
Romans 13:11-14	Keep close to the Lord.
2 Corinthians 11:13-15	Avoid those masquerading as servants of God.
Ephesians 5:11	Have nothing to do with evildoers and their wicked deeds; instead, *expose* them. Believers need not allow evil to continue unchecked, but should actively work against it.
Ephesians 5:18	Redeem the time.
Colossians 4:2, 5	Believers are to pray, be watchful, be thankful, and be wise in the way they act toward unbelievers, making the most of every opportunity to share the gospel.
2 Thessalonians 3:6-15	Church members who are lazy and idle must be warned. Christians should not be sitting around waiting for the Lord to return, but should continue working in the ministry.

3:2 For people will be lovers of themselves, lovers of money.^{NRSV} Paul used two close-sounding words in the Greek—*philautoi* and *philarguroi*. These first two characteristics of society in the "last days" (Paul's and Timothy's day, reaching to our day and into the future) provide the basis for society's downfall. When people misdirect their love—toward themselves and material pleasures—there can be no love left to direct toward others. Then moral corruption naturally results, as noted in the following characteristics.

Boastful, proud.^{NIV} A heart full of pride manifests itself in outward boastfulness. Such characteristics reveal a person's inflated self-importance and necessarily leads them to looking down on others.

Abusive.^{NRSV} Abusive people speak disrespectfully to others, including God. Not only are these people guilty of an over-inflated sense of their own importance, they also verbally abuse people around them.

Disobedient to their parents.^{NRSV} The extent of moral degeneration can be seen in the rejection of the most intimate human ties. Parents are not spared from abuse. This behavior willfully breaks

IS IT BAD ENOUGH YET?
Our concerns about the "last days" tend to be very personal. They usually arise, not because we are actually suffering, but because we dread suffering. Concerns focus not so much on the destructiveness of evil around us, but whether or not evil will affect our way of living. Such narrow concerns reveal our blindness to evil. Christians must not withdraw from the world entirely or use the wrong methods to defend themselves against it. Believers who attempt to insulate themselves from the moral degradation of the last days must not insulate themselves from God. Whenever material prosperity or pleasure are used in place of God's protection, we fool ourselves. But God loves us too much to leave us in our delusion. If it takes the loss of everything to get our attention, God has been known to allow that to happen. Does your life exhibit an awareness of the desperate condition of the world? Are you using God's methods for dealing with terrible times?

the fifth commandment to honor one's father and mother (see Exodus 20:12). The commandment was given because God understood the importance of strong families. To "honor" parents means speaking well of them and politely to them. It also means acting in a way that shows them courtesy and respect. It means following their teaching and example of putting God first. Parents have a special place in God's sight. Even children who find it difficult to get along with their parents are still commanded to honor them. When parents are not respected and honored, disobedience naturally results, and the breakdown of the family easily follows. Paul understood that when families fall apart, "terrible times" (3:1) follow.

Ungrateful.[NRSV] People are in a sad state when they cannot appreciate anything, express thankfulness, or give gratitude for small or large blessings or favors. In Romans 1:21, Paul noted that ingratitude was second only to dishonoring God as a just cause for God's judgment on humanity.

Unholy. People who set aside God in order to live only to please themselves can only go one direction—toward wickedness. They instinctively resist anyone or any ideas that would force them to measure themselves by God's standards.

3:3 Unloving.[NKJV] The same word (*astorgoi*) is used in only one other place in the New Testament (Romans 1:31), in a passage where Paul listed the characteristics of people who refuse God and follow their own inclinations. The NRSV translates this as "inhuman." Indeed, because these people love only themselves and their money (possessions), as Paul noted in verse 2, they are unloving toward everyone and everything else.

Unforgiving.^{NKJV} Unforgiving people cannot allow for other people's mistakes or weaknesses. They are unyielding, unrelenting, and often are filled with extreme bitterness and anger over their own hurts. They simply refuse to forgive, even if presented with the opportunity. Eventually, they become unable to forgive, even when they might acknowledge the need to do so.

Slanderous.^{NIV} This in Greek is *diaboloi,* which contains the root word for "devil." Here it is used as an adjective—such people are quick to spread falsehoods. Slanderers enjoy spreading gossip and malicious reports about others. Destroying another's good reputation gives them perverse pleasure.

Without self-control.^{NKJV} These people cannot restrain their actions, their feelings, or their words. The NRSV translates this as "profligates"—people who are thoroughly and shamelessly immoral. Their character is completely debased.

Brutal.^{NKJV} The opposite is tame or civilized. Brutal people ("brutes" NRSV) are like untamed animals, or "uncivilized" people. They are insensitive and crude, even savage and cruel.

Haters of good.^{NRSV} These people are so evil that they actually hate (despise, see NKJV) anything good.

CHECK THE LIST
In many parts of the world today, it's not too tough to be a follower of Christ—Christians aren't jailed for reading the Bible or executed for preaching Christ. But Paul's descriptive list of behavior in the last days describes our society—even, unfortunately, the behavior of some Christians. Every one of these can be found in churches today. Check your life against Paul's list. Don't give in to society's pressures. Don't settle for comfort without commitment. Stand up against evil by living as God would have his people live.

The next two characteristics begin with the *pro-* prefix in Greek, indicating a disposition toward some behavior or attitude.

3:4 Treacherous.^{NRSV} Treacherous people are traitors—ready and willing to betray anyone. In some cases, betrayal of another might enhance a person's standing or enrich him or her; at other times, the betrayal could be a vengeful act. Combined with slander (3:3), truth goes by the wayside.

Reckless.NRSV This characteristic can also be translated "head-strong" (NKJV) and "rash" (NIV). Such people act foolishly and carelessly, completely unconcerned about the consequences for themselves or others. The word *headstrong* includes their determination to have their own way, regardless of advice to the contrary.

Conceited.NIV Such people have a puffed up opinion of themselves. The NRSV gives the sense by translating the term *tetuphomenoi* as "swollen with conceit." People with this trait have an exaggerated opinion of their importance, intelligence, wit, appearance, etc. The idea differs from "lovers of self" in verse 2, for that trait can at least be concealed, while the very nature of conceit involves being noticed by others.

Lovers of pleasure rather than lovers of God. The list ends, as it began, with those whose love has become so misdirected that they can only think of their own desires. Those who fail to acknowledge God eventually aren't able to love God.

CHOOSING TO LOVE
Why is it so tempting to be a lover of pleasure rather than a lover of God?
- Pleasure is something we can control; God cannot be controlled. Most pleasures can be obtained easily; love for God requires effort and sometimes sacrifice.
- Pleasure benefits us now; the benefits of loving God are often in the future.
- Pleasure has a narcotic effect; it takes our minds off ourselves and our problems. Love for God reminds us of our needs and our responsibilities.
- Pleasure cooperates with pride. It makes us feel good when we look good in the eyes of others. To love God we must lay aside our pride and our accomplishments.

3:5 Having a form of godliness but denying its power.NKJV Often these evil characteristics appear in a context of respectability. Religion is not gone; in fact, these character qualities are frequently exhibited by people known for their "religiousness." However, as Paul wrote, they practice a *form of godliness*—that is, using godliness as a cloak of respectability while denying God's power over their lives. The "form" or appearance of godliness includes going to church, knowing Christian doctrine, using Christian clichés, and following a community's Christian traditions. Such practices can make a person outwardly look good, but if the inner attitudes of belief, love, and worship are lacking, the public appearance is hollow, meaningless.

Such persons deny the *power* of godliness in two ways:

1. Their lives act out denial. This *denying* was addressed by Paul in 2:12, where he described the inevitable result for those who "disown" God; they will themselves experience being disowned by God.

2. When confronted, their inability to express their faith will reveal that beneath the "form of godliness" there is only a vacuum of unbelief.

Have nothing to do with them.^{NIV} Although Paul's words in verse 1 seem to focus on future events, he obviously realized that evil was already at work in the Ephesian church. Paul warned Timothy not to be deceived by people who only appear to be Christians. It may be difficult to distinguish them from true Christians at first, but their daily behavior will give them away. The characteristics described in 3:2-4 are unmistakable. In fact, the false teachers plaguing the Ephesian church most likely exemplified many of those characteristics that Paul listed above. Paul had already advised Timothy to "have nothing to do with" these troublemakers (2:23)—which probably meant excommunication.

PLAYING SOLDIER
Imitation Christianity has dangerous consequences. Putting on an appearance of faith often leads people to believe a person is a true believer. In an actual incident during the Korean War, a lieutenant inspecting a new platoon over which he was about to take command reported that several soldiers carried rifles that had rusted shut. Yet they were scheduled to go into battle the next day! They looked like soldiers; they carried weapons. But they were unprepared and unable to fight.
    Some churchgoers rely on superficial appearances. Many people today carry Bibles, attend church, mouth the right words, yet evidence no spiritual power in their lives. They have no direct, personal, intimate connection with God.

3:6 They are the kind who worm their way into homes and gain control over weak-willed women, who are loaded down with sins and are swayed by all kinds of evil desires.^{NIV} Because of their cultural background, women in the Ephesian church had no formal religious training. They enjoyed their new freedom to study Christian truths, but their eagerness to learn made them a target for false teachers. At this time in history, there were almost no opportunities for women to be employed. Also, the church at Ephesus had a significantly large group of widows (1 Timothy 5:3-16). Thus, there were many women who may not have been fully occupied during the day. They became targets for the false teachers.

The expression *worm their way into homes* indicates the insidious methods of the false teachers. They targeted *weak-willed women* and perhaps somewhat unintelligent women. Then with all their "fascinating" and intellectual-sounding talk, the false teachers captivated these women—the word literally means "taken captive." The women lost whatever free thinking they had to these crafty men. These women were especially vulnerable because they were *loaded down with sins* (that is, their consciences were laden with guilt) and *swayed by all kinds of evil desires* (their personal appetites and aspirations, remnants from their pagan days, were so strong as to still cause them problems, probably leading to their overwhelmed consciences!). Their weakness combined with their guilt made them easy targets for the "cures" that the false teachers brought.

Paul warned Timothy to watch out for men who would take advantage of these women. His concern was not for women in general, but for certain women who were being targeted by the false teachers in Ephesus. New believers need to grow in their knowledge of the Word because ignorance and curiosity can make them vulnerable to deception (Ephesians 4:14).

SETTLING THE PAST
Sometimes the past can overwhelm us. Guilt and bad memories can cripple us as we follow Christ. If we don't find complete forgiveness through repentance and faith in Christ, we may run into these four pitfalls:
1. We may be attracted to self-help schemes and doctrines that will make us feel better temporarily but not deal with our real problem.
2. We may dredge up past memories and the shame that went with them; our guilty feelings would then render us both ineffective in Christian service and lacking in confidence.
3. We may allow low self-respect to make us feel powerless, causing our sinful desires to take control.
4. We may reject the central teaching of salvation—that our sins are forgiven and forgotten—and instead dwell on and attempt to solve our sin problem without Christ's help.

3:7 Always learning and never able to come to the knowledge of the truth.NKJV This is also translated, "never able to acknowledge the truth" (NIV). These women were always willing to listen to any teacher who came along, making them easy targets for the false teachers. But without basic knowledge of the faith that leads to repentance and forgiveness of their sins, these women would only get confused and never be able to recognize and understand the truth. Churches that have little or no biblical and theological content in their teaching program fall right into this error. People who attend this kind of church are easy targets for false teachers.

This verse is not opposing education; rather, it is warning about ineffective learning. It is possible to be a perpetual student and never graduate to putting theory into practice. But honest seekers and true students look for answers. The accumulation of seminars, classes, Bible studies, and books without specific application in our daily lives can easily become our own version of what Paul was describing here. Remember this as you study God's Word. Seek to find God's truth and will for your life.

3:8 As Jannes and Jambres opposed Moses.NRSV According to Jewish legend, Jannes and Jambres were two of the magicians who counterfeited Moses' miracles before Pharaoh (Exodus 7:11-12). Paul explained that just as Moses exposed and defeated them (Exodus 8:18-19), God would overthrow the false teachers who were plaguing the Ephesian church.

So these people, of corrupt mind and counterfeit faith, also oppose the truth.NRSV These *people* (referring to those with the characteristics listed above, and most specifically to the false teachers who embodied these characteristics) cannot "get very far" (see 3:9) because they

- have *corrupt* minds—they are depraved, perverted, and debased. Corrupt minds can lead only to corrupt words and actions.
- have *counterfeit faith*—their "faith" in God is faked; thus their teaching is false. It may be a "form of godliness," but its power, if any, is demonic.
- *oppose the truth*—they are not merely mistaken in their teaching; they are actively opposing God's truth. They are, in a fundamental spiritual way, "in denial" about reality, unable to even perceive the truth about God or themselves.

3:9 But they will not get very far.NIV While the false teachers' threat to the church was very real, both across the Roman world and in our world today (hence, Paul's advice about dealing with them in this and many other letters), the threat will never be fatal to the gospel.

Because, as in the case of those men, their folly will be clear to everyone.NIV Just as Jannes and Jambres's fake power was eventually revealed by God's power through Moses (Exodus 8:18-19;

9:11), so the *folly* (foolishness) of the false teachers' words would eventually become clear to everyone. Whatever the temporary success of the false teachers, eventually they would be completely humiliated.

Paul did not specify how and when *their folly will be clear.* There are three possible answers: (1) At the time of the false teacher's death, or at Christ's return, their success will abruptly end; (2) God will ensure that discerning believers will see through the deception, revealing to the church that the popular belief was nothing but "folly"; or (3) God will work behind the scenes in such a way that the false teachers will trip themselves up and be unmasked for who they really are. This will work in quite the opposite way to Timothy's progress, which would be clear to everyone (1 Timothy 4:15).

REVEALED SECRETS
We can hide our sin for a while, but eventually the truth will be revealed. Sooner or later, distraction, opposition, anger, or fatigue will wear us down, and our true heart will be exposed. The trials of life will conspire against our efforts to maintain a "religious front." We can't pick when and where we will be tested by adversity. Build your character carefully because it will come out under stress. Live each day as if your actions will one day be known to everyone. It is useless, in the middle of a test, to acknowledge that we should have prepared. Now is the time to change anything you wouldn't want revealed later.

PAUL'S CHARGE TO TIMOTHY / 3:10–4:8

Children remember, for better or worse, what their parents say and do over and over. A single encouragement or harsh word may be forgotten. But persistent reminders will be carried a lifetime. Paul laced his letters with encouragement, challenges, hopes, and affirmations for Timothy. For Paul, anything worth saying was worth saying several times.

In this last section before his closing remarks, Paul reflected on the significance of his and Timothy's life together. Paul gave the consistency of his own example and the trustworthiness of Scripture as two dependable guides for Timothy's future. Paul's words and actions created a seamless pattern for the younger man. Timothy did not have to choose between what Paul said and what he did; his challenge was to live out his own version of Paul's life and teaching. Timothy was with Paul when he wrote to the Thessalonians, "You became imitators of us and of the Lord;

in spite of severe suffering, you welcomed the message with the joy given by the Holy Spirit" (1 Thessalonians 1:6 NIV). Paul expected no less of Timothy.

3:10 You, however, know all about my teaching, my way of life, my purpose, faith, patience, love, endurance.^{NIV} After strongly denouncing the false teachers and their foolishness, Paul turned his attention back to Timothy (*you*). Timothy could look at Paul as an example of living out the opposite characteristics of those described in verses 2-9. That Timothy "knew" about all the activities and characteristics listed here and in verse 11 does not necessarily mean he was an eyewitness. Some of the persecutions mentioned in verse 11 happened before Paul had met Timothy. The same verb in Greek is used in Luke 1:3 where it is translated "investigate" (NIV, NRSV). Timothy had heard about some of these situations; however, undoubtedly he knew others from personal experience. Paul's words here are not proud; rather, they are a testimony to the truth of the gospel and God's faithfulness, meant to encourage young Timothy. Paul was also using himself as a model for what Timothy should be doing in his leadership role in Ephesus.

Timothy knew the content of Paul's *teaching;* it was the truth as opposed to the false teachers' lies, myths, and godless arguments. Timothy had been privileged to hear Paul preach many times, to many audiences, on a variety of topics. Paul's teaching would be of no value if it did not impact his life—but it did, as the following characteristics reveal.

Timothy knew Paul's *way of life.* This phrase refers to Paul's manner of life, his general behavior. Timothy had lived and traveled with Paul. He had seen Paul happy, sad, angry, and worried; he had watched Paul handle difficult people and problems; he had seen him study and had heard him pray. Paul's way of life should have been a shining example to Timothy. Paul could easily say to Timothy, as he had said to the Corinthians, "Be imitators of me, as I am of Christ" (1 Corinthians 11:1 NRSV).

Timothy knew Paul's *purpose* in life, his central mission, his chief aim. Traveling with the tireless missionary must have quickly convinced Timothy of Paul's single-minded focus on his mission. God had said of Paul, "He is an instrument whom I have chosen to bring my name before Gentiles and kings and before the people of Israel" (Acts 9:15 NRSV). Paul never took that calling lightly.

Timothy knew Paul's *faith, patience, love,* and *endurance.* Paul called on Timothy to exhibit these qualities, for they are basic Christian virtues (1 Timothy 6:11). The word *endurance* can also be translated "steadfastness," referring to a person's abil-

ity to remain strong under pressure. Paul expected Timothy to
model these same character traits in Ephesus.

**3:11 Persecutions, sufferings—what kinds of things happened to
me in Antioch, Iconium and Lystra, the persecutions I
endured.**^{NIV} Paul mentioned his suffering here to contrast his
experience with that of the pleasure-seeking false teachers. These
persecutions occurred during the first missionary journey. Paul
had met Timothy at the beginning of his second missionary journey, but Timothy certainly had heard about these experiences. In
2 Corinthians 11:23-33, Paul had summarized his lifetime of persecutions and sufferings for the sake of the gospel.

In Antioch (in Pisidia), "the Jews incited the devout women of
high standing and the leading men of the city, and stirred up persecution against Paul and Barnabas, and drove them out of their
region" (Acts 13:50 NRSV).

In Iconium, "the residents of the city were divided; some sided
with the Jews, and some with the apostles. And when an attempt
was made by both Gentiles and Jews, with their rulers, to mis-
treat them and to stone them, the apostles learned of it and fled to
Lystra and Derbe" (Acts 14:4-6 NRSV).

In Lystra, Timothy's hometown, "they stoned Paul and
dragged him out of the city, supposing that he was dead" (Acts
14:19 NRSV).

And out of them all the Lord delivered me.^{NKJV} At times, Paul
had been miraculously delivered (as in Philippi, see Acts 16:25-

---

PREDICTED AND EXPECTED
Persecution did not take Paul by surprise, for Jesus had predicted
it many times. Believers today can take encouragement and courage from Jesus' words and Paul's experiences.

Jesus predicted persecution . . . . Matthew 5:11-12
                                          Matthew 10:17-23
                                          Matthew 24:9-11
                                          Mark 8:34
                                          Mark 13:9-13
                                          John 15:18-19, 21
                                          John 16:33
                                          John 17:14-15

Paul expected persecution . . . . Romans 8:17
                                          2 Corinthians 12:9-10
                                          Philippians 1:29
                                          1 Thessalonians 3:4

26); at other times, Paul had to suffer through the persecution (as with the stoning in Lystra). To be delivered through persecution and suffering does not necessarily mean escaping from it; Paul knew that God would deliver him as often as needed until Paul's work on earth was done. Indeed, Paul suffered in prison and certainly realized that he would be called on to face the ultimate persecution—death. Paul did not fear death: "For to me, to live is Christ and to die is gain. . . . I am torn between the two: I desire to depart and be with Christ, which is better by far . . ." (Philippians 1:21, 23 NIV). Paul trusted God that his time had come, that his work was completed, and that he would see his Savior face-to-face.

3:12 **Indeed, all who want to live a godly life in Christ Jesus will be persecuted.**NRSV In this charge, Paul was telling Timothy that people who obey God and live for Christ can expect to be persecuted. In fact, after Paul had been left for dead outside the city of Lystra, he got up, went back into Lystra, on to Derbe, then retraced his steps back through Lystra, Iconium, and Antioch. In Antioch, Paul and Barnabas "strengthened the souls of the disciples and encouraged them to continue in the faith, saying, 'It is through many persecutions that we must enter the kingdom of God'" (Acts 14:22 NRSV). Paul knew that truth from his own recent experience! Jesus gave the same warning to his disciples: "If the world hates you, you know that it hated Me before it hated you. . . . If they persecuted Me, they will also persecute you" (John 15:18, 20 NKJV).

Today, most Christians do not face outright persecution just for being Christians (although being a Christian is still against the law in some places in the world). Those who worship freely and unhindered should be deeply grateful. However, we should not assume that this verse does not apply to us. If we stand up for Christian values, we can expect opposition and hostility from the world. Based upon the testimony of countless believers who have lived before us, we can expect to meet with some form of persecution or resistance if we persist in living in obedience to Christ. Absence of persecution may not mean unfaithfulness, but if our lives as Christians never affect the world, we may have to question the depth of our commitment.

 LOOKING FOR TROUBLE
Believers must set out to follow Jesus, rather than being on a quest to find trouble. It is possible to be persecuted for being obnoxious, rather than for being obedient. Don't go looking for trouble—obey Christ and let trouble find you!

3:13 But wicked people and impostors will go from bad to worse, deceiving others and being deceived.^{NRSV} Oddly, the Greek word translated "go from bad to worse" (*prokopto*) is actually a verb expressing the idea of making headway or advancement. So the phrase gives an ironic picture of evil people "advancing backwards," away from the truth. The same word is used the same way in 2:16, where it is translated "become more and more ungodly" (NIV). In 3:9, the same word pointed out the lack of advancement against Christianity on the part of the false teachers. These wicked people were progressing toward their wicked goal and dragging others down with them (see 1 Peter 4:2-5).

3:14 But as for you, continue in what you have learned and firmly believed, knowing from whom you learned it.^{NRSV} As in 3:10, Paul again used "but as for you" (*su de*) to set a contrast between the situation in Ephesus and what he expected from Timothy. Besieged by false teachers and the inevitable pressures of a growing ministry, Timothy might have been tempted at times to abandon his faith or modify his doctrine. Paul counseled Timothy to look to his past and to hold to the basic teachings about Jesus that he knew were eternally true. The false teachers might constantly move on to new and more exciting concepts and ideas for discussion and argument, but Timothy needed to stand secure on what he had learned and firmly believed. This did not mean that Timothy needed no further study, but that the basics that Timothy knew and believed would never change. However, Timothy should *continue in* his faith through perseverance and by constantly learning more of God's Word.

> Some people are rivers: they know where they want to go, and they confine themselves to the banks that lead to that goal. But some people are swamps: they spread over everything; their minds are so open they cannot hold a conviction; they are everything and nothing. . . . Paul could say: "This one thing I do." They can say, "These forty things I dabble in." Paul left a mark; they leave a blur.
>
> *E. Stanley Jones*

3:15 And that from childhood you have known the Holy Scriptures.^{NKJV} Timothy was one of the first second-generation Christians: he had become a Christian, not because an evangelist preached a powerful sermon, but because his mother and grandmother had taught him the Scriptures when he was a small child (1:5). For Timothy, the *Holy Scriptures* (*hiera grammata*) were primarily the Old Testament—Genesis to Malachi. However, the Greek phrase, used only here in the New Testament, is capable

HELP YOURSELF?
Newspaper articles, magazines, self-help books and talk shows all give the impression that if we are just honest about a problem, get lots of advice, and do what we really feel, we'll solve the problem. Modern opinion (not really thinking) says that an individual, not God, is in control of his or her own future. This is the heart of false teaching. We must not allow our society to distort or crowd out God's eternal truth. Spend time every day reflecting on the foundation of your Christian faith found in God's Word, the great truths that build up your life.

of several other translations ("holy Scriptures" NIV and "sacred writings" NRSV). Capitalizing both words creates an interpretive translation (frequently necessary and unavoidable) that practically limits the possible subject being mentioned to the Old Testament. Some encourage a less technical translation in order to admit that Paul might have also had in mind early records of Jesus' words and some of the apostolic writings. This does not minimize the role of the Old Testament. It merely takes into account that Timothy's upbringing was a Christian form of Judaism. The Old Testament remains important because it points to Jesus Christ. It certainly was the *primary* body of writing that Paul had in mind. At the same time, faith in Christ makes the whole Bible intelligible.

The sources for Timothy's faith could provide another encouragement to continue in the faith: Paul, his mentor and friend, who provided an unmistakable example of God's faithfulness; the inerrant Scriptures that Timothy had studied and loved since childhood; and Timothy's dear mother and grandmother who nurtured and loved him.

Which are able to make you wise for salvation through faith which is in Christ Jesus.^{NKJV} Scripture, God's Word, teaches about salvation; but knowing Scripture alone saves no one (many Jews had known Scripture from childhood, yet had opposed Jesus and the salvation he offered—see 2 Corinthians 3:15-16; Paul himself exemplified that in his early years, Acts 26:9-11). The Scriptures show people their need for salvation and point them to the person who alone can give it—Jesus Christ.

3:16 **All Scripture is given by inspiration of God, and is profitable for doctrine, for reproof, for correction, for instruction in righteousness.**^{NKJV} Timothy had known the Scriptures from childhood, so he knew that all Scripture was inspired by God. When Paul spoke of *all Scripture,* he was primarily referring to the Old

Testament, since it was complete at that time. But the scope of Paul's assertion would include any writing that was considered authoritative enough to be read in church meetings, which by the end of the first century would have included the four Gospels and Paul's writings. According to 2 Peter 3:15-16, Paul's writings were classified as "Scriptures."

LET THE CHILDREN COME
Jewish families began their moral and religious training when children reached age five. The original teaching was given by mothers until about age ten, when fathers were expected to take over. The role of the family was essential in Jewish tradition and developed from God's own instruction (see Deuteronomy 6:1-25).

God-designed parental roles cannot be easily replaced or eliminated. At home and in church, we should realize that teaching small children is both an opportunity and a responsibility. Jesus wanted little children to come to him (Matthew 19:13-15). Like Timothy's mother and grandmother, Eunice and Lois, do your part in leading children to Christ.

The Scriptures, affirmed Paul, were God-inspired. A translation closer to the original Greek would be, "All Scripture is God-breathed." This tells us that every word of the Bible was breathed out from God. The words of the Bible came from God and were written by men. The apostle Peter affirmed this when he said that "men spoke from God as they were carried along by the Holy Spirit" (2 Peter 1:21).

Paul's words here reminded Timothy that because Scripture is inspired and infallible, it is also profitable. The Bible is not a collection of stories, fables, myths, or merely human ideas about God. It is not a human book. Through the Holy Spirit, God revealed his person and plan to certain believers, who wrote down his message for his people. This process is known as *inspiration*. The writers wrote from their own personal, historical, and cultural contexts. Although they used their own minds, talents, language, and style, they wrote what God wanted them to write. Scripture is completely trustworthy because God was in control of its writing. Its words are entirely authoritative for our faith and lives. (See the discussion under 3:15 for the extent of the Scripture canon Paul may have had in mind.)

Scripture was profitable to every aspect of Timothy's ministry:

- *doctrine*—the content and teaching of truth, which must flow from and be consistent with Scripture. By calling the Bible

"God-breathed," Paul was identifying its divine source; by making it the source of doctrine, he was reminding Timothy of its authority. Doctrine that contradicted biblical doctrine was to be rejected, corrected, or replaced by accurate teaching.

- *reproof*—rebuking those in sin. The initial impact of true doctrine involves the confrontation of false teaching and understanding. The offensiveness of some who teach biblical truth may have to be excused, but the offensiveness of biblical truth to error and evil requires no apology.
- *correction*—helping people straighten out errors. In the area of correction, the Scriptures have two roles: (1) they provide a complete presentation of the teaching, where only part of the truth has been present; and (2) they provide for a right understanding and application where true doctrine may have been taught but has not taken effect.
- *instruction in righteousness* (training in righteousness)—showing people how to please and glorify God. The ideal setting for doctrine includes the kind of preparation that minimizes the need for later reproof and correction. The nature of Scripture allows us to teach it confidently to our children and to learn from it ourselves.

The Bible is not purely a record of the past—the history of the Jews and then of the church. Rather, every story, every prophecy, every teaching, every admonition, and every command points beyond to the author, God, who came to us in Jesus Christ. God confronts us in the pages of his Word—telling us how much he loves us, how we can become his children, and how we should live to please him.

INSPIRATION AND APPLICATION
Verse 3:16, known for its affirmation of inspiration also serves as a basic pattern for application of the Scriptures. We can approach every passage with the assumption that it accomplishes one or more of the four purposes of Scripture:
1. *Doctrine*—What basic truth that God wants me to know does this passage teach?
2. *Reproof*—What error in judgment, understanding, or behavior might this passage be reproving in my life?
3. *Correction*—How might this passage correct, balance, or direct me?
4. *Training*—What does this passage present to prepare me for some future spiritual challenge?

3:17 That the man of God may be complete, thoroughly equipped for every good work.^{NKJV} Timothy must never forget Scripture's *purpose*—to equip him (and all believers) to do good. Timothy carried a heavy responsibility in Ephesus, but through his faith in and reliance on God's Word, he was *complete* and *thoroughly equipped*. This means he was capable and proficient—able to meet all duties and challenges. Believers should not study God's Word simply to increase their knowledge or to prepare them to win arguments. They should study the Bible so that they will know how to do Christ's work in the world. Knowledge of God's Word is not useful unless it strengthens our faith and leads us to do good (Ephesians 2:10).

ARE YOU EQUIPPED?
The whole Bible is God's inspired Word. Because it is inspired and trustworthy, we should *read* it and *apply* it to our lives. The Bible is our standard for testing everything else that claims to be true. It is our safeguard against false teaching and our source of guidance for how we should live. It is our only source of knowledge about how we can be saved. God wants to show you what is true and equip you to live for him. How much time do you spend in God's Word? Read it regularly to discover God's truth and to become confident in your life and faith. Develop a plan for reading the whole Bible, not just the familiar passages.

4:1 In the presence of God and of Christ Jesus, who is to judge the living and the dead, and in view of his appearing and his kingdom.^{NRSV} Paul had used these words previously (see 1 Timothy 5:21), but this time he included references to judgment and to Christ's return. Perhaps thoughts of judgment could not escape Paul's thoughts as his own death neared: "For all of us must appear before the judgment seat of Christ, so that each may receive recompense for what has been done in the body, whether good or evil" (2 Corinthians 5:10 NRSV). The *appearing* of the kingdom, although still future in Paul's thought, was so certain as to be part of this charge and encouragement to Timothy. If we are convinced that Christ's return is inevitable, we too will be powerfully motivated by that fact.

I give you this charge.^{NIV} Paul's final words to Timothy in this letter carried a charge (a command or injunction) witnessed by God and Christ Jesus. The *charge* is composed of five specific commands that follow. The aged apostle knew that his death was at hand and that he might not see Timothy again (although he hoped to, see 4:9, 11, 13, 21). Therefore these words held great importance for Timothy. Paul wanted Timothy to realize how critical it was for him to obey his words. Timothy would stand before the Lord at the Last Judgment and answer for how he responded to Paul's charge.

4:2 **Preach the word!**^{NKJV} First and foremost, Timothy was to preach the message of the gospel. The word *preach* suggests vigorous proclamation! Paul wanted Timothy to be bold and passionate. It was up to Timothy to preach the gospel so that the Christian faith could spread throughout the world.

MISSION CONTROL
We believe in Christ today because people like Timothy were faithful to their mission. It is still vitally important for believers to spread the gospel. Half the people who have ever lived are alive today, and most of them do not know Christ. He is coming soon, and he wants to find his faithful believers ready for him. It may be inconvenient to take a stand for Christ or to tell others about his love, but preaching the Word of God is the most important responsibility the church and its members have been given. Be prepared for, courageous in, and sensitive to God-given opportunities to tell the Good News.

Be persistent whether the time is favorable or unfavorable.^{NRSV} Timothy must be always on duty and ready to serve, whether or not the opportunity was right. Paul, soon to die, may have looked back on his life realizing how short the time had been. Paul urged Timothy to make the most of the time he would be allotted on this earth, as Paul had written in Ephesians 5:16, "Making the most of every opportunity, because the days are evil" (NIV).

Correct, rebuke and encourage—with great patience and careful instruction.^{NIV} Timothy should *correct* those who were in error by patiently and carefully explaining the truth, helping them to understand and accept it. Timothy should *rebuke* those who were sinning by patiently and carefully explaining their sin and their need for repentance. Timothy should *encourage* those who were growing, for even those growing in the faith need patient and careful instruction and guidance. *Patience* should always characterize Timothy's attitude as he dealt with the people in his church; *careful instruction* (or doctrine) should be the basis for his words. Patience and careful instruction insure that preaching, correcting, and rebuking will be compassionate, not harsh.

4:3 For the time is coming when people will not put up with sound doctrine, but having itching ears, they will accumulate for themselves teachers to suit their own desires.^{NRSV} When Paul spoke about false teaching, he usually focused on the evil intentions of the false teachers. However, false teachers could not flourish if they had no audience. Here Paul was pointing out the fault on the part of the listeners. They would *not put up with sound doctrine* because it said what they didn't want to hear, convicting them and making demands they didn't want to follow. So these people would turn to others who would tell them what was more palatable. Like the false prophets of Old Testament times, these false teachers would teach whatever their audience wanted to hear. They had *itching ears,* which means they were seeking novel teaching and craving what satisfied their curiosity. To this end, they found teachers that suited *their own desires.*

CREATING YOUR OWN DOCTRINE
Many speakers, teachers, and writers talk about the pursuit of knowledge. But often they don't want knowledge, but power.
- *They will not tolerate the truth.* They have no interest or respect for absolute truth or any standard for judgment.
- *They reject truth for sensationalism.* They want truth that fits their situation and makes sense for them. What they feel, what works for them, what seems compelling—that is their truth and they claim an absolute right to it. No one should even attempt to tell them differently.
- *They gather viewpoints to suit their selfish desires.* Although they profess objectivity, their only defense for their viewpoints is that they suit their desires.

4:4 They will turn their ears away from the truth and turn aside to myths.^{NIV} These people would turn away from the truth taught by Timothy, wandering off into the false teachers' fascinating "myths and endless genealogies" (1 Timothy 1:4 NRSV). What they would hear made sense, seemed true, and made them comfortable. So wandering away from the difficult truth was easy.

WILLFUL IGNORANCE
At what point does a person become responsible for errors in belief? We tend to think that sincerity covers a multitude of sins, but does God look at us that way? Often he gives us warnings that we might be headed in the wrong direction, and he gives us the ability to know and understand key doctrines of our faith. If we do not follow his leading, we're guilty of more than ignorance or error. We're guilty of rebellion.

4:5 But you, keep your head in all situations.^{NIV} Once again, as in
2:1; 3:10, 14, Paul followed the mention of those who were way-
ward with a strong contrasting *but you* for his disciple. Timothy
should keep his head whenever he interacted with people by not
reacting quickly. Keeping his head would make him morally alert
to temptation, resistant to pressure, and vigilant when facing
heavy responsibility.

When Paul advised Timothy about self-control, there were
more issues involved than Timothy's ability to monitor and channel his desires and impulses. Timothy had already discovered (as
almost everyone who attempts to represent Christ discovers) that
one's best intentions are often misunderstood by others. Where
we offer instruction, some hear only narrow-mindedness; where
we offer compassionate correction, some hear only harsh judgment; where we express God's standards, some hear only legalism or arrogance. Unfortunately, their responses are based on
what they perceive rather than on what we mean. The ability to
"keep our head" in those moments makes the real difference between failure and faithfulness. We "keep our head" in at least two
significant ways:

(1) We must not retaliate against those who reject us. To
become defensive, attack the other person, or even to ignore his
or her words will not help.

(2) We must maintain the truth we have learned. We must
listen to what has been said, lest our method or timing is ill-
chosen, but we must not deviate from following Christ.

Endure suffering.^{NRSV} The same Greek verb is used in 2:3,
where Paul wrote, "Share in suffering like a good soldier of
Christ Jesus" (NRSV). The suffering, hardship, persecution, and
struggles would only intensify in the days and months ahead.
Many in Timothy's ministry would look to Timothy as their
example. Timothy would have to endure. In fact, like his mentor
Paul, Timothy did experience imprisonment (see Hebrews 13:23).

Do the work of an evangelist. That work was to proclaim the
gospel to all people at all times, calling on them to repent and be
saved. Whatever the obstacles, opposition of false teachers, problems of church administration, distractions, or discouragements,
Timothy was not to allow any of them to keep him from his
appointed task.

Carry out your ministry fully.^{NRSV} This is also translated, "Dis-
charge all the duties of your ministry" (NIV). Nothing should
deter Timothy from carrying out his duties until the day when his
ministry would be completed (that is, at his death).

How can we know when we have fully carried out our ministry? By defining ministry in terms of lifelong goals rather than temporary jobs, positions, and opportunities. Then, when life ends, we will be able to say with Paul, "I have fought the good fight, I have finished the race, I have kept the faith" (3:7).

4:6 For I am already being poured out like a drink offering, and the time has come for my departure.^{NIV} Paul told the terrible truth. *Departure* here means not release but death. A *drink offering* consisted of wine poured out on an altar as a sacrifice to God (see Genesis 35:14; Exodus 29:41; Numbers 28:24). Paul viewed his life as an offering, poured out before God. Paul had used the same comparison in Philippians 2:17, where he wrote, "Even if I am being poured out like a drink offering on the sacrifice and service coming for your faith, I am glad and rejoice with all of you" (NIV). There will be times when service seems wasted. Sometimes, being poured out will feel like being thrown out! When that happens, remember Paul's image of the drink offering and be encouraged. Even if he had to die, Paul was content. Paul's commitment was total; thus, sacrificing his life to build others' faith seemed to him a joyous reward.

Paul's words about his departure would communicate to Timothy that he would not be able to count on Paul's presence or encouragement much longer. Shared leadership was ending. Timothy must take charge.

4:7 I have fought the good fight, I have finished the race, I have kept the faith.^{NKJV} Paul's three phrases, in the perfect tense, convey finality. Paul knew this was the end. He had called Timothy to "fight the good fight of the faith" (1 Timothy 6:12 NRSV); his own *fight* was over. The fight had been worthwhile, and he had fought well.

Paul's *race* was finished, or at least the end was clearly in sight. It is important to note that Paul made no claim to having won the race; he was content with having finished it. Marathon runners know the exhilaration of finishing the grueling miles of that race—they are thankful just to cross the finish line. Completion is a significant accomplishment, revealing incredible endurance and determination. In his farewell to the elders in the Ephesian church at the end of his third missionary journey (prior to heading to possible imprisonment in Jerusalem), Paul had said, "I consider my life worth nothing to me, if only I may finish the race and complete the task the Lord Jesus has given me—the task of testifying to the gospel of God's grace" (Acts 20:24 NIV).

I have kept the faith has been taken two ways: (1) Paul had remained loyal to God even in trials and had played by God's rules; or (2) Paul had guarded and preserved the gospel message. Most likely, the second meaning is correct.

Paul had called Timothy to "guard what has been entrusted to you" (1 Timothy 6:20 NRSV). "The faith" referred to what had been entrusted to Paul; this also had been entrusted to Timothy. Paul had never wavered in his faith and trusted that soon he would experience all the promises on which he had based his life and ministry.

WHAT'S IT WORTH?
As he neared the end of his life, Paul could confidently say that he had been faithful to his call. Thus he faced death calmly, knowing that he would be rewarded by Christ. Is your life preparing you for death? Do you share Paul's confident expectation of meeting Christ? The good news is that the heavenly reward is not just for giants of the faith, like Paul, but for all who are eagerly looking forward to Jesus' second coming. Paul gave these words to encourage Timothy, and us, that no matter how difficult the fight seems keep fighting. When we are with Jesus Christ, we will discover that it was all worth it.

4:8 **Finally, there is laid up for me the crown of righteousness, which the Lord, the righteous Judge, will give to me on that Day.**NKJV In Roman athletic games, a laurel wreath was given to the winners. A symbol of triumph and honor, it was the most coveted prize in ancient Rome. This is probably what Paul was referring to when he spoke of a crown. Waiting for Paul, laid up for him, was a reward—*the crown of righteousness.* This phrase could be taken to mean that righteousness itself is the reward (as in James 1:12 and Revelation 2:10, where the "crown of life" is the reward of eternal life), or that the crown is the reward for righteousness (see 3:16). In either case, Paul knew that a reward awaited him.

Paul would receive his reward from *the Lord, the righteous Judge.* Soon to be condemned to death for his faith, Paul would ultimately be vindicated by God himself. Paul's reward would be given on *that Day,* a reference to Christ's return. "Our citizenship is in heaven. And we eagerly await a Savior from there, the Lord Jesus Christ" (Philippians 3:20 NIV).

And not to me only but also to all who have loved His appearing.NKJV This crown of righteousness, this reward, was not for Paul alone. It is promised to all who have loved the Lord and eagerly desire his return. What an encouragement to Timothy, to the loyal believers in his church, and to all believers. Whatever we may face—discouragement, persecution, or death—we know our reward is with Christ in eternity.

2 Timothy 4:9-22

Paul was experiencing the loneliness of a leader whose team has dispersed. He was not entirely alone (4:21), but many of his working associates were on distant assignments. At least one former leader, Demas, had deserted Paul. So Paul was lonely and wanted Timothy to come and see him. He sent Tychicus to Ephesus with this letter, with the probable understanding that Tychicus would relieve Timothy of his duties there.

In describing for Timothy the various missions of their associates, Paul also revealed his passion for ministry. He was directing the efforts of many who were spreading the gospel even while he himself was on death row.

4:9 Do your best to come to me soon.[NRSV] Both here and in verse 21, Paul urged Timothy to come *soon,* preferably "before winter." We don't know what season of the year this was written, but this letter would have to be carried from Rome to Ephesus, and Timothy would then have to make the return trip. The whole process would take a few months. Paul knew his execution was imminent, but he had no idea how quickly it would be carried out. The Roman judicial system often had long delays in its processes; more likely, it was Paul's feeling of loneliness and isolation that prompted him to say "come soon." He longed to see Timothy one last time.

THEY NEED YOU
Even though Paul had the assurance of eternal life and confidence in Christ, loneliness and isolation had hit with devastating impact. Paul needed visitors, reassurance from fellow ministers, and the practical comforts of warm clothing and familiar books. Do you know Christians who are alone and isolated due to illness or the death of a spouse, in prison, or in the far outreaches of Christian ministry? Don't overlook their need for encouragement and practical help to ease their burdens. Scripture teaches believers to encourage one another (1 Thessalonians 4:18; 5:11; Hebrews 3:13; 10:25).

4:10 For Demas, in love with this present world, has deserted me and gone to Thessalonica.^{NRSV} Demas is also mentioned in Colossians 4:14 and Philemon 24. Instead of loving the Lord's appearing (4:8), Demas loved the world and so had deserted Paul. Unlike Onesiphorus (see 4:19 and 1:16-18), he probably was ashamed of Paul's chains and not willing to face the same fate for the Christian faith. Demas may not have deserted the faith, but he deserted the apostle in his time of need. Some scholars believe Demas had chosen to take an easier assignment.

ARE YOU IN LOVE?
Demas had been one of Paul's coworkers (2 Corinthians 4:18; Colossians 4:14; Philemon 24), but he had deserted Paul because he "loved this present world." In other words, Demas loved worldly values and worldly pleasures. There are two ways to love the world. God loves the world as he created it and as it could be if it were rescued from evil. Others, like Demas, love the world as it is, sin and all. Do you love the world as it could be if God's justice ruled, the hungry were fed, and people loved one another? Or do you love what the world has to offer—wealth, power, pleasure—even if gaining it means hurting people and neglecting the work God has given you to do?

Crescens has gone to Galatia, Titus to Dalmatia.^{NRSV} Mentioning Demas reminded Paul of more faithful coworkers. Paul did not criticize Crescens and Titus for leaving; apparently they had been sent to do the Lord's work in Galatia (see map) and Dalmatia (on the eastern shore of the Adriatic Sea). That Titus was dispatched from Rome to Dalmatia suggests that he no longer ministered in Crete (which was the focus of Paul's letter to Titus).

4:11 Only Luke is with me. Demas had deserted; Crescens, Titus, and Tychicus (4:12) had been sent on various missions; only Luke the doctor (Colossians 4:14) remained with Paul, possibly to help minister to his physical needs. Luke had accompanied Paul on the second and third missionary journeys, as well as the voyage to Rome (as noted by the "we" sections in Acts 16–28). This traveling companion and historian (author of the Gospel of Luke and the book of Acts) probably had to frequently use his medical expertise as Paul and his companions were injured with whips and stones in their travels. He may have even been Paul's secretary for this epistle, putting 2 Timothy into writing as the aging apostle dictated. In addition, Luke probably cared for Paul's illness, described as a "thorn in the flesh" in 2 Corinthians 12:7-8.

Luke had shared Paul's first Roman imprisonment. He is also
mentioned in Colossians 4:14 and Philemon 24.

LOVING THIS WORLD
Demas's example reminds us that each of us is vulnerable to
enticements of comfort and pleasure. To resist worldly desires,
we must
- *Remind* ourselves that the world is not our home: we are liter-
  ally just passing through.
- *Refocus* our minds on our mission in this life to represent
  Jesus Christ in all we do and say.
- *Return* to the basic truth that we have been bought with a
  price; Christ is our Savior, and we require salvation.
- *Request* the Spirit's help to restrain our self-centered
  impulses.

**Get Mark and bring him with you, because he is helpful to
me in my ministry.**[NIV] Paul missed his young helpers, Timothy
and Mark. Timothy was to pick up Mark (apparently Mark was
located somewhere along Timothy's route) and bring him along.
This statement reveals an incredible change in Mark and in
Paul's opinion of him. Mark had left Paul and Barnabas on the
first missionary journey, and this had greatly upset Paul (Acts
13:13; 15:36-41). Barnabas had wanted to give Mark another
chance, but Paul had flatly refused. This had led to the separation
of Paul and Barnabas; Paul took Silas on the second missionary
journey; but Barnabas took Mark on to Cyprus, to preach there.
Barnabas (known for being an encourager) had apparently had a
significant impact on the young Mark, for he later proved to be a
worthy minister. At some point, Paul recognized Mark as a good
friend and trusted Christian leader (Colossians 4:10; Philemon
24). Mark had also been Peter's assistant (1 Peter 5:13) and composed the Gospel named after him, based on Peter's words.

We cannot be sure if Paul felt that Mark would be helpful to
him personally, or if *helpful to me* refers to directing and facilitat-
ing the ministry outreach to the world. It's likely that both kinds
of help were needed from Mark.

The extent of Paul's activity raises some questions about the
actual nature of his imprisonment. Was he in a prison and limited
to brief visits by those who kept contact with him from the outside? Was he under some form of house arrest that allowed him
equal immobility but gave him far more access to others? In spite
of Paul's reference to "my chain" in 1:16, the evidence available
will not allow us to be exact on Paul's conditions. He was

detained; he was involved in the process of the legal system (see 4:16); he anticipated his own death, though we cannot be sure that he expected to be executed. Whether released or executed, Paul was confident of his eventual "rescue" by Christ (see 4:18).

ANOTHER CHANCE
Paul had given Mark a second chance. Now Mark would be a tremendous blessing to him. We don't have all the details in Mark's changed life or Paul's change of heart, but Paul realized that people can change. Likewise, we should allow people to grow up and not hold them back from ministry or leadership for faults in the past that have now been corrected. When we encourage someone and open our mind to the possibility that he or she has changed and matured, we may be salvaging a significant ministry.

4:12 And Tychicus I have sent to Ephesus.[NKJV] Tychicus, a trusted companion (Acts 20:4) and messenger (he delivered the letters of Ephesians and Colossians—see Ephesians 6:21; Colossians 4:7), had already left for Ephesus. The phrase here could mean that Tychicus would be delivering this letter to Timothy, being sent also to assume Timothy's role while Timothy traveled to Rome to see Paul. Tychicus was apparently useful for such ministries (see Titus 3:12).

4:13 When you come, bring the cloak that I left with Carpus at Troas, and my scrolls, and especially the parchments.[NIV] Because he was a prisoner in a damp and chilly dungeon, Paul asked Timothy to bring him his cloak, a heavy outer garment, circular in shape with a hole in the middle for the head. Paul had left it at the home of a man named Carpus, apparently where Paul stayed on one of his visits to Troas (but probably not the visit mentioned in Acts 20:6, for that was several years earlier). Troas would also have been right on Timothy's way from Ephesus to Rome (see map), so Timothy could stop and pick up the cloak.

Even more than the cloak, Paul wanted his scrolls and the parchments. Paul's arrest may have occurred so suddenly that he was not allowed to return home to gather his personal belongings. The scrolls would have included parts of the Old Testament. The parchments (Greek *membranas*) were very likely parchment or codices, frequently used in the first century for notebooks, memoranda, or first drafts of literary works. Perhaps these parchments were draft copies of some of Paul's epistles.

In our age of disposables we find it difficult to visualize that a person in Paul's day would have just one excellent, durable, and probably valuable cloak to use for a lifetime, often passing it on to children or heirs. Items like cloaks were too important, too difficult to make, to make poorly. Almost anything written was of great value as well. Paul was a scholar and would have gathered for his use a small but effective personal library. When Paul asked for scrolls and parchments, he wasn't asking for his whole library, but for a few treasured documents.

4:14 Alexander the coppersmith did me much harm. May the Lord repay him according to his works.^{NKJV} Alexander may have been a witness against Paul at his trial, thus doing Paul *much harm.* This may be the Alexander mentioned in 1 Timothy 1:20, although Alexander was a common name. Probably it was not the silversmith who had led the riot in Ephesus (Acts 19:33). In any case, Timothy apparently knew the man and the situation. Paul had no personal desire for revenge against Alexander, as indicated by his paraphrase of Psalm 62:12: "Surely you will reward each person according to what he has done" (NIV). (See also Romans 12:17-20.) However, Paul did not want Timothy to get into a confrontation and be harmed by this man, so Paul warned Timothy to stay away.

HANDLING HURTS
Paul's statement, "May the Lord repay him," is more a prediction or prophecy of what will happen than a prayer cursing Alexander. Paul exemplified one of the toughest tasks a Christian may have to do—to leave his or her hurt with the Lord. When others oppose us and undercut our authority, our leadership, or even our friendship, our natural response is to want revenge. Yet revenge and vindictiveness do the most damage to *us.* Our anger and bitterness cut us off from God's supply of power and love. Each person who hurts us must stand and give account before the Lord for his or her actions. Let go of your hurt and leave the judgment up to God.

4:15 You also must beware of him, for he strongly opposed our message.^{NRSV} Timothy should beware of, be on his guard against, and stay away from Alexander. If Timothy were to arrive in Rome after Paul's death, he would be Alexander's next likely target. The message Alexander opposed could mean the gospel message, or Paul's words at his trial, where Alexander may have been a witness against Paul (4:14). As in other instances, especially those regarding the false teachers, Paul exhorted Timothy to have nothing to do with this man (see, for example, 2:23).

4:16 At my first defense no one came to my support, but all deserted me. May it not be counted against them!^{NRSV} This *first defense* was most likely a preliminary hearing at which advocates for the accused were usually heard. The Roman legal system allowed for several steps in the prosecution of an accused criminal. Clearly, the mention of a "first" indicates an expectation of a second defense. Perhaps the inconclusiveness of the first hearing was causing a lengthy delay.

In any case, no one had come to speak in Paul's defense or to stand by in his support; everyone had *deserted* him (compare 1:15). Although sorely disappointed, Paul seemed to understand, for he hoped that this would not be held against them (compare this to Jesus' words from the cross, Luke 23:34). Paul realized the fear the Christians were feeling; it had become extremely dangerous to be identified as a Christian in Rome. Emperor Nero had blamed the Christians for starting a great fire in Rome (A.D. 64). He had decreed that the Christians should be persecuted through torture and death as punishment. Three or four years later, when this letter was written, fear was still very present, causing Paul's fellow believers to be unwilling to defend him before the Roman authorities.

REACH OUT AND TOUCH
Each person has opportunities to encourage those whom God has called to serve in lonely, isolated, or even dangerous areas on his behalf. We certainly can pray for them! But there are also other significant ways we can support them. Telecommunications makes it possible, for relatively little expense, to talk with almost anyone in the world. Have you ever called a missionary that your church supports? Have you ever written a letter? Are there books or other special items you could send? Have you ever asked how you could help rather than waiting to be asked?

4:17 But the Lord stood by me and gave me strength, so that through me the message might be fully proclaimed and all the Gentiles might hear it.^{NRSV} Although no human being had come to support Paul at his hearing, the Lord had been with him. (See Mark 13:9-11 and Matthew 10:17-19, where Jesus promised help to those arrested for preaching the gospel.) Paul had sensed both the presence and the power of Christ. Paul used the word *endunamai,* meaning that God "infused" Paul with strength. Christ had helped Paul not just for Paul's benefit alone. He had supplied Paul with spiritual power, wisdom, and preaching skills in order to carry the message of the gospel to the listening Gen-

tiles in the far corners of the earth (compare Philippians 1:12-14).
Whatever would happen to Paul at his trial, Paul was confident
that God's purposes would once again be fulfilled through him.

GIVE ME STRENGTH!
With his mentor in prison and his church in turmoil, Timothy
probably was not feeling very brave. Paul may have been sub-
tly saying that the Lord had called Timothy to preach and would
give him the courage to continue to do so. God always gives us
the strength to do what he has commanded. This strength may
not be evident, however, until we step out in faith and actually
begin doing the task.

Even at the trial before the Roman authorities who were ready
to execute this Christian leader, Paul had proclaimed the gospel!
Paul regarded his ministry as complete and the gospel message as
fully proclaimed after giving the message in Rome, because from
Rome, the capital of the empire, all the world would eventually
hear it. Whether Paul was thinking of the gospel fully proclaimed
within the immediate context of his trial or the extended context
of his ministry, both would have been his clear intention. In other
instances (see the trial before Agrippa, Acts 26:1-28), Paul had
been much more eager to proclaim the gospel than to defend himself.

On this occasion in Rome, no one else had appeared brave
enough to be identified with Christ, but Paul's courage remained
unhindered. He continued to live out his faith to the very end: "I
can do all things through Christ who strengthens me" (Philippians 4:13 NKJV).

So I was rescued from the lion's mouth.NRSV Some have seen
this as a reference to Nero throwing Christians to the lions in the
Coliseum, or perhaps to Satan (for a parallel, see 1 Peter 5:8).
More likely, Paul used a common biblical metaphor describing
deliverance from extreme danger (see, for example, Psalm 22:21;
Daniel 6:22). Paul knew he wouldn't get out of prison alive,
though he was experiencing a temporary reprieve due to a delay
in the Roman judicial system.

**4:18 The Lord will rescue me from every evil attack and will bring
me safely to his heavenly kingdom.**NIV Although rescued from
certain death at the first hearing (and certainly at many times
over the years of his ministry), Paul realized that the end was
near. He was prepared to die, confident in God's power and sovereignty. The Lord's *rescue* mentioned here would not be physical

this time, but spiritual. Here Paul was affirming his belief in eternal life after death. Anyone facing a life and death struggle can be comforted and encouraged knowing that God will bring each believer safely through death to heaven.

To Him be glory forever and ever. Amen!^{NKJV} Just as Paul praised God in life (see, for example, Galatians 1:5; Ephesians 3:21), he also praised God in the face of death.

4:19 Greet Priscilla and Aquila and the household of Onesiphorus.^{NIV} Priscilla and Aquila were fellow Christian leaders with whom Paul had lived and worked (see Acts 18:2-3, 18, 26; Romans 16:3; 1 Corinthians 16:19). While in Corinth, Priscilla, Aquila, and Paul had made tents together. Priscilla and Aquila were an itinerant couple who used the freedom and the money provided by their tentmaking skills to carry out a ministry of hospitality and teaching in various places. They had lived in Rome and Corinth. This time they were in Ephesus, undoubtedly helping Timothy with his work.

Onesiphorus had visited and encouraged Paul in jail during this final imprisonment (see discussion 1:16-18). Paul ended the final chapter in his book and in his life by greeting those who were closest to him.

CIRCLE OF FRIENDS
Although Paul had spent most of his life traveling, he still was able to develop close and lasting friendships. Too often we rush through our days, barely touching anyone's life.
- Do you have a Paul? Each of us needs a mentor, a teacher, or a counselor to provide leadership, instruction, correction, and encouragement.
- Do you have a Priscilla or Aquila? Each of us needs a coworker, a peer, to listen and to pray with us in times of stress, to love us, and to support us.
- Do you have a Timothy? Each of us needs a younger leader we can help along, encourage, and disciple.
Like Paul, take time to weave your life into others through deep relationships.

4:20 Erastus stayed in Corinth.^{NIV} Erastus was one of Paul's trusted companions and Timothy's close friend (Acts 19:22). Timothy would be interested in his whereabouts.

And I left Trophimus sick in Miletus.^{NIV} The same would be true of Trophimus, another companion and friend of both men (Acts 20:4; 21:29). Perhaps Trophimus was to have accompanied Paul from Asia to Rome on this last visit, but had to be left in

Miletus because of illness. Commitment to ministry does not mean immunity to diseases, discouragement, or death. Paul experienced in himself and in his closest associates the realities of serving God in frail human frames under difficult circumstances. Hope, health, and security in this life are always temporary.

Timothy might not have been aware of Trophimus's illness and would have been glad to know the location of this friend from Ephesus.

PASSING THE TORCH
As Paul reached the end of his life, he could look back and know he had been faithful to God's call. Now it was time to pass the torch to the next generation, preparing leaders to take his place so that the world would continue to hear the life-changing message of Jesus Christ. Timothy was Paul's living legacy, a product of Paul's faithful teaching, discipleship, and example. Because of Paul's work with many believers, including Timothy, the world is full of believers today who are also carrying on the work. What legacy will you leave behind? Whom are you training to carry on your work? It is our responsibility to do all we can do to keep the gospel message alive for the next generation.

4:21 Do your best to come before winter.NRSV Paul certainly wanted to see his friend as soon as possible (4:9). The request that Timothy try to arrive *before winter* probably included that desire— Paul knew that sailing on the Adriatic Sea was shut down for several weeks during winter because of extreme danger. This also gives insight into Paul's desire to have his cloak (4:13) before cold weather set in.

Eubulus sends greetings to you, as do Pudens and Linus and Claudia and all the brothers and sisters.NRSV Nothing further is known of the four men listed by name. Paul sent greetings from *all the brothers and sisters,* even though most had deserted him at his trial (4:16). Paul's spirit of forgiveness in including greetings from them must not be missed.

4:22 The Lord be with your spirit. Grace be with you.NRSV The first sentence was directed personally to Timothy. The second includes the plural *you* and gives a final good-bye to all the believers.

TITUS

INTRODUCTION TO TITUS

AUTHOR

Paul, the great apostle and missionary of the church.

Paul is known for his extensive missionary travels, his powerful preaching and teaching, and his courageous witness for Christ. Undoubtedly most Christians today would characterize him as a hard-line champion of the truth, who rejected compromise and accepted no excuses. Certainly that describes Paul as we read his story in Acts and in his powerful epistles. Speaking to Galatian believers about the false teachers among them, he stated: "If anybody is preaching to you a gospel other than what you accepted, let him be eternally condemned!" (Galatians 1:9 NIV). He also confronted these same believers about their wavering faith: "You foolish Galatians! Who has bewitched you?" (Galatians 3:1 NIV). Paul opposed venerable Peter over the issue of associating with Gentiles (Galatians 2:11-14), and he wanted nothing to do with Mark because Mark had "deserted" Paul and Barnabas on the first missionary trip (Acts 13:13; 15:37-39). Paul stood strong for the gospel and against all who would twist it or undermine his ministry.

We must also remember, however, that Paul was a loving, compassionate man. He genuinely cared for people and built many solid relationships wherever he traveled. In fact, Paul concluded most of his letters with personal greetings to close friends and fellow ministers (see especially Romans 16:1-16).

The Pastoral Epistles (1 Timothy, 2 Timothy, Titus) testify to Paul's tender and loving nature. Paul considered Timothy and Titus to be his "sons" in the faith, and he treated them as such, leading, mentoring, guiding, and counseling them in their ministry and personal lives.

As with 1 and 2 Timothy, the very first line in the letter to Titus clearly establishes Paul as author: "Paul, a servant of God and an apostle of Jesus Christ . . . " (1:1 NIV). Although certain scholars in the past several decades have tried to disprove Paul's authorship of this book, the balance of the historical evidence continues to favor Paul. In fact, much of the anti-Paul sentiment seems to be based on the difficulty of placing the writing of the letter to Titus within the narrative in Acts. (See the discussion under "Date" in the introduction to 1 Timothy.) Some critics have also remarked that the writing style and content of Titus differs from Paul's other letters, but these doubts can be easily resolved by recalling the occasion and purpose of the book. The needs and problems of the church in Crete differed greatly from those in Corinth, Ephesus, and Thessalonica. When Paul wrote to Titus (and Timothy), the churches were much more established than when he wrote his earlier letters (see the discussion under "Date" on page 243). In fact, it would be too simplistic to expect the style and content to be the same when the recipients, occasions, and purposes were so different.

Paul addressed this letter, "To Titus, my true son in our common faith" (1:4 NIV). We don't know the circumstances of Titus's conversion to Christ—the epistles reveal little about his background, and he is not mentioned in Acts—but Titus probably came to faith under Paul's ministry (Paul presented him to the church leaders in Jerusalem as an example of a Gentile believer, Galatians 2:1-3, and Paul calls him "son.")

SETTING

The island of Crete.

Crete lies southeast of Greece in the Mediterranean Sea, just south of the Aegean Sea. At 160 miles long and 35 miles wide, Crete is one of the larger islands in the Mediterranean. It is quite mountainous but with very fertile valleys. The highest mountain is Mount Ida, the traditional birthplace of the Greek god Zeus. Crete has an ancient history, having been the center of the great Minoan culture that developed during the Middle and late Bronze Ages.

This Roman province had a hundred cities, many of which were scattered along the coast. These coastal towns were heavily populated and fiercely independent.

Cretans had a dubious reputation in the Mediterranean world. Epimenides (600 B.C.) called them "liars, evil beasts, slow bellies" (quoted by Paul in 1:12), and Leonides (488 B.C.) said Cretans were "always brigands and piratical, and unjust."

Crete is not mentioned in Acts as a stop on Paul's missionary journeys; thus scholars surmise that the gospel must have come to that island by way of Jerusalem and Pentecost. Crete had a large Jewish population, so each year many Cretan Jews would travel to Jerusalem for the Feast of Weeks (Pentecost). At the celebration recorded in Acts 2, Cretan Jews witnessed the power of the Holy Spirit (Acts 2:11), heard the gospel in their native language, and responded. When they returned home, they brought the Christian faith with them. The churches on Crete, therefore, were begun in much the same way as those in Rome.

Evidently the character flaws of Cretans in general had been brought into the churches (1:10-16), so Titus had to contend with an unruly and self-centered group of believers. But Paul knew that Christ could change them into people who "devote themselves to doing what is good" (3:8 NIV).

You may think that your church is filled with "Cretans." Remember, Christ can transform individual lives and churches.

AUDIENCE

Titus and the church at large.

Little is known about Titus because he is not mentioned by name in Acts. But Titus must have been a remarkable man, because Paul trusted him and assigned him great responsibility. Galatians 2:3 states that Titus was an uncircumcised Gentile, a Greek—most likely he had come to faith in Christ under Paul's ministry. It seems amazing that such a faithful and trusted partner and leader of the church would not appear in Acts, so some scholars surmise that Titus may have been Luke's brother and that Luke omitted his name from the account.

Titus and Paul enjoyed a special relationship. Paul called him "my true son" (1:4), "my brother" (2 Corinthians 2:13), and "my partner and fellow worker" (2 Corinthians 8:23). Paul felt close to both of his protégés. Titus appears to have been stronger physically than Timothy, however, since Paul expressed more concern for Timothy's health (1 Timothy 5:23) and resolve (2 Timothy 1:5; 1 Corinthians 16:10-11).

Titus's faith must have been strong, for Paul presented him to church leaders in Jerusalem as a prime example of a Gentile convert worthy of acceptance by the church. Paul related this incident in Galatians 2:1-5. Tension had been building in the church over whether to accept Paul's practice of baptizing Gentiles without insisting that they first become circumcised and submit to Jewish laws and rituals. So Paul traveled to Jerusalem to fight for the truth that salvation is by grace through faith alone. He won this test case—Titus was not compelled to be circumcised. This issue finally was resolved at the Jerusalem council (Acts 15:1-35).

Titus became Paul's key troubleshooter. First Paul sent him to the church at Corinth, an undisciplined and struggling body of believers in a pagan environment. Titus's first assignment was to resolve the tensions between Paul and the Corinthians (2 Corinthians 7:6-16; 12:18), something that Timothy had been unable to do (1 Corinthians 4:17; 16:10-11). Titus was so successful there that Paul sent him back to collect money from the Corinthians for the church in Jerusalem (2 Corinthians 8:6, 16-24). Here, in the letter to Titus, we find that Paul had sent Titus to Crete, an area known for violence and immorality. Titus's task was to "straighten out what was left unfinished" (1:5 NIV). Later, we discover that Titus visited Paul in Rome during the second imprisonment and then was sent to Dalmatia (a region on the eastern coast of the Adriatic Sea), another difficult area (2 Timothy 4:10). Paul trusted Titus to be his representative, to resolve conflicts, to collect money, and to organize churches. According to ancient tradition, Titus returned to Crete in old age. He died and was buried there at the age of ninety-four.

Titus kept a low profile—we know much less of him than of Paul and other first-century Christian leaders. And Titus was an unlikely leader—a Greek, not an eyewitness to Christ's life; a Gentile convert, not a Jewish student of the Scriptures. Yet Titus had a profound ministry and impact on church history. God can use a person, regardless of his or her background, nationality, sex, or education, to make a difference in the world. God can use you.

OCCASION

The threat of disorder and false teachers to the local congregations and the need for the churches to be organized.

It seems that after Paul's release from the Roman prison in about A.D. 62, he traveled with Titus to Crete, where they ministered together. When Paul continued his travels, he left Titus behind as his representative, to help organize and strengthen the churches there (1:5).

Paul wrote this letter at about the same time as his first letter to Timothy. Having placed these two protégés in strategic locations, Paul wanted to encourage them and counsel them about carrying out their responsibilities. Paul knew through reputation (1:12) and firsthand experience (1:5) that the ministry in Crete would be difficult, so he wanted to give Titus information and ammunition for dealing with the problems he would encounter. Paul's location is unknown, but he may have written from Corinth or Nicopolis (on the western coast of Greece), where he had decided to spend the winter (3:12). Evidently when Paul heard that Zenas and Apollos were traveling to Crete (3:13), he decided to send this letter to Titus with them.

PURPOSE

To bolster Titus's authority as Paul's apostolic representative in Crete and to give Titus clear instructions about each aspect of his work in the churches there.

Titus was not a pastor of a single congregation on Crete, nor was he the leader or "bishop" of the churches there. Titus was Paul's representative, with apostolic authority to preach, teach, and organize the churches. This letter from Paul surely would bolster Titus's standing in the eyes of believers and would underline his authority to make necessary changes.

The most important task given to Titus was to instruct and organize the churches on the island. Cretans had the earned reputation of being lazy and immoral (1:12); therefore, sound theology and church discipline were imperative. Already Judaizers were influencing many with their false teachings (1:10-16); these divisive individuals needed to be stopped (3:9-11). And because people seemed to be easily swayed and turned from the truth, each church needed dedicated and spiritual leaders.

Although this letter is addressed to an individual (Titus), Paul also meant for it to be helpful for the churches in Crete.

DATE

About A.D. 64 or 65, just after 1 Timothy, possibly from Corinth or Nicopolis.

As explained earlier, dating the Pastoral Epistles is not an easy task because they don't seem to correspond with the chronology of the other New Testament books, and they contain no references to events in Acts. Evidently Paul wrote these letters during the few years between his two Roman imprisonments. For more on Paul's travels during those years, see the discussion under "Date" in the introduction to 1 Timothy.

MESSAGE

Character; church relationships; a good life; citizenship.

Character (1:5-16). Paul had left Titus in Crete to "straighten out what was left unfinished and appoint elders in every town" (1:5 NIV). So Paul gave Titus a list of qualities for "elders" or "overseers." These church leaders must be of the highest character, as evidenced by a strong family life (1:6) and a good reputation in the community (1:7-8). They also must be firmly grounded in their faith and able to teach others (1:9). These qualifications were important because of the sinful world surrounding the church (1:12) and because of the potential for heresy and divisions within the church (1:10-11, 13-16). As Paul's representative, with apostolic authority, Titus was to make sure that church leaders exhibited strong moral character and spiritual maturity.

Importance for Today. Churches need leaders who are totally committed to Jesus Christ and who are living the way God wants them to live. It is not enough to be educated, have special abilities and gifts, or to have a loyal following to be Christ's kind of leader. Church leaders must have self-control, spiritual and moral fitness, and Christian character. God wants Christians to aspire to leadership in his church, but they must be the right kind of leaders. Who you are is more important than what you can do.

Church relationships (2:1-10, 15; 3:9-11). Part of Titus's responsibility during his stay on Crete was to teach believers how they should act in the world and with each other (2:15). Paul encouraged Titus to teach with integrity and seriousness and to set a good example for all the believers, especially the new church leaders (2:7-8). Paul emphasized the importance of sound doctrine (2:1), and he told Titus to rebuke all who would steer believers astray (3:9-11). Paul explained to Titus how his teaching should relate to the various groups in the church. Older Christians should teach younger men and women and be good examples to them (2:2-5). Young people should be self-controlled (2:6), and slaves should be trustworthy (2:10). People of every age and group have a lesson to learn and a role to play in the church, and all should be positive witnesses for Christ in the world (2:2, 8, 10).

Importance for Today. Christians who truly believe "sound doctrine" (2:1) live out what the Bible teaches in their relationships. A local church is a collection of old, young, male, female, rich, and poor, so a church in which believers love each other and get along will draw people to Christ (2:10). Pride and self-indulgence can divide any church, but the antidote is submission to Christ and to each other, as well as self-control. Treat your relationships with other believers as an outgrowth of your faith and part of your witness to the world.

A good life (3:3-8; 12-15). Paul reminded Titus that before trusting Christ they had been disobedient to God and enslaved to sin

(3:3), but Christ had transformed them (3:4-7). The gospel message is that a person is saved by grace through faith (3:5-7), not by living a good life. But the gospel changes people's lives, so that they eventually perform good deeds (3:8) and become totally devoted to serving others (3:14).

Importance for Today. A good life is a witness to the gospel's power. Christians must have commitment and discipline to serve. When we remember what Christ has done for us, we will be motivated to share his love with others. In what ways are you putting your faith into action by serving others?

Citizenship (2:11–3:2). Paul told Titus to instruct believers that how they live outside the church was very important. Christians must say *yes* to God and *no* to ungodly living in the world (2:12-14). Believers also should be good citizens in society, obeying the government (3:1) and working honestly (3:2).

Importance for Today. How a Christian fulfills his or her duties is a witness to the watching world. A believer's community life should reflect Christ's love as much as his or her church life does. Your neighbors should know that you are a faithful church member *and* a good citizen.

VITAL STATISTICS

Purpose: To advise Titus in his responsibility of supervising the churches on the island of Crete

Author: Paul

To whom written: Titus, a Greek, probably converted to Christ through Paul's ministry (he had become Paul's special representative to the island of Crete), and all believers everywhere

Date written: About A.D. 64, around the same time 1 Timothy was written; probably from Macedonia when Paul traveled between his Roman imprisonments

Setting: Paul sent Titus to organize and oversee the churches on Crete. This letter tells Titus how to do this job.

Key verse: "The reason I left you in Crete was that you might straighten out what was left unfinished and appoint elders in every town, as I directed you." (1:5 NIV)

OUTLINE

1. Leadership in the church (1:1-16)
2. Right living in the church (2:1-15)
3. Right living in society (3:1-15)

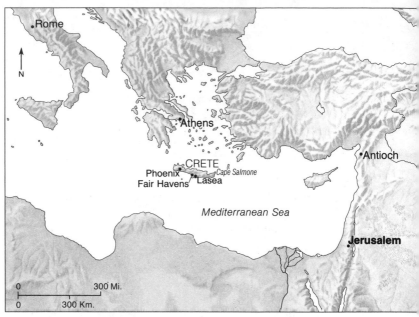

TITUS GOES TO CRETE
Tradition says that after Paul was released from prison in Rome (before
his second and final Roman imprisonment), he and Titus traveled
together for a while. They stopped in Crete, and when it was time for Paul
to go, he left Titus behind to help the churches there.

Titus 1

Paul wrote this letter between his first and second imprisonments in Rome (before he wrote 2 Timothy) to guide Titus in working with the churches on the island of Crete (see map). Paul had visited Crete with Titus and had left him there to minister (1:5). The island of Crete was a tough mission field for three reasons:

(1) Pagan influence on this small island was strong because Crete was a training center for Roman soldiers, as well as a major stopping-off point for ships crossing the Mediterranean.

(2) A large population of Jews existed on the island, according to the ancient historians Philo and Josephus. The Judaizers (those who insisted that Gentiles must convert to Judaism before they could follow Jesus) from this community caused problems for the believers (1:10).

(3) The Cretans had a bad reputation—certain character flaws developed the stereotype that Cretans were "always liars, vicious brutes, lazy gluttons" (1:12 NRSV).

> [Titus] is a short epistle, but it contains such a quintessence of Christian doctrine, and is composed in such a masterly manner, that it contains all that is needful for Christian knowledge and life.
> *Martin Luther*

Christian tradition suggests a missionary visit by Paul and Titus shortly after the first trial. Paul planted the church and left Titus to look after the early organizational phase and to oversee the new congregations. Because the gospel had only recently been preached on the island, believers were susceptible to a number of strong influences. So Titus needed to be on guard. Also the church in Crete needed strong Christian leaders; Titus was responsible to choose and prepare them.

1:1 Paul, a servant of God and an apostle of Jesus Christ.NRSV As at the beginning of 1 and 2 Timothy, Paul identified himself by name and by authority. In one short phrase, Paul gave insight into his reason for living. He called himself a *servant* of God—that is, one who was committed to obeying God. (This is the only place where Paul used this particular phrase to describe himself.) This obedience led him to spend his life as an *apostle* (meaning messenger or sent one) of the Good News about Jesus Christ. Even though Paul was not one of the original twelve disciples (later called apostles), he had been specially called by God to bring the Good News to the Gentiles (see Acts 9:1-16 for an account of his call). Paul's twofold reference to himself combines humble obedience with confident authority on his part.

For the faith of God's elect and the knowledge of the truth that leads to godliness.^{NIV} As a servant and apostle, Paul focused his life on two main concerns: *faith* and *knowledge*. God chose (elected) the believers who make up his church. The church exists because God chose its members and called them to serve him as his body in the world. God sent Paul to call many to faith, to strengthen their faith, and to further their knowledge (literally, "recognition") of the truth of that faith.

As he did once in 2 Timothy (2:10), Paul referred to his target audience as the *elect*. God's elect are those chosen or "called out" who have responded to the gospel. Although we can't totally understand the doctrine of election, it gives us tremendous insight into God's love and wisdom. Although our calling is based totally on God's wisdom and initiation, we who are called still must respond and choose to follow him. God is the author and provider of salvation; human response is in no way a good work that earns salvation. Jesus spoke of the elect in Matthew 22:14; 24:22, 24, 31; Luke 18:7; John 6:37-44; 10:27-29. Paul taught about election in Romans 8:28-39; 9:10-16; Ephesians 1:4-14; 2:4-10; 1 Thessalonians 1:4-5; as did Peter in 1 Peter 1:1-5; 2:9; 2 Peter 1:3, 10-11.

God's choice of each believer is based on:

- all of his gracious mercy so there is no room for our pride
- his decision in eternity past so there is no room for us to doubt
- his sovereign control so there is no room for fatalism
- his love for us as provided in Christ so there is no room for apathy.

God's people are not meant to be ignorant and blind followers of a blind faith. Rather, faith and knowledge go hand in hand. As opposed to the worthless "faith" and "knowledge" of the false teachers (see 3:9; 1 Timothy 1:3-7; 2 Timothy 2:14-16), faith in and knowledge of the truth have a worthwhile outcome. They lead to *godliness,* right living, and a God-honoring life-style.

Paul's view of ministry was always long-term. He was not content to aim at people merely responding to the gospel. His goal was to bring people to spiritual maturity in Christ. As he told the Colossians, "We proclaim him, admonishing and teaching everyone with all wisdom, so that we may present everyone perfect in Christ. To this end I labor, struggling with all his energy, which so powerfully works in me" (Colossians 1:28-29 NIV).

THE ULTIMATE
Paul described a process that he wanted to carry out in his ministry. The process began with *faith,* developed in *knowledge,* and exercised itself in *godliness.* He wanted men and women to be mature in Jesus Christ. This was his ultimate objective by which he evaluated all he did.

How would your church evaluate its ultimate objectives? What specific goals does it desire to accomplish? Do the programs, ministries, and service opportunities bring believers to spiritual maturity? Do established members reflect good Christian conduct and desire for Christian service? Are the smaller groups in church reaching out, or are they closed in on themselves? Consider how you can be involved in clarifying and implementing the ultimate objectives of your church.

1:2 faith and knowledge resting on the hope of eternal life, which God, who does not lie, promised before the beginning of time.[NIV] Continuing his thought from verse 1, the *faith* and *knowledge* that lead to godliness rest *on* (the word for "on" is *epi* and can also be translated "with a view toward") the *hope of eternal life.* The Greek text of verses 1-3 contains a long and complex sentence that does not repeat the words "faith" and "knowledge" as the NIV does for clarity. Although Paul described eternal life as a "hope," he does not mean it is a "maybe" but a certainty. We "hope" for or anticipate what we already know will be ours. Our hope is based on the reality that one day our salvation will be realized—final and complete—when Christ returns for us.

The power of hope depends on its basis, just as the power of faith does. Hoping that a house built on quicksand will remain standing would be false hope, for there is no basis for it. We rest our hope of eternal life on a good foundation. We have dependable authority for our faith, for God himself has promised it to us, and God *does not lie* (other versions say "cannot lie"). Apparently lying was commonplace in Crete (see 1:12). Paul made it clear at the start that God does not lie. Trust in God's character forms the foundation of our faith. (See Hebrews 6:17-20, where God's

> The Christian is strong or weak depending on how closely he has cultivated the knowledge of God.
> *A. W. Tozer*

unchanging nature reveals itself in his truthfulness.) Because God *is* truth, he is the source of all truth, and he cannot lie. This puts him in complete contrast to Satan, who is the father of lies (John 8:44). The eternal life that God has promised will be ours because he keeps his promises.

ROCK SOLID
Jesus spoke with authority. He concluded the Sermon on the Mount (Matthew 5–7) by pointing out to his listeners two ways to use his teaching. On one hand, those who listen and put his words into practice are wise. They build on a rock-solid foundation. On the other hand, those who refuse to listen and obey are foolish, like people who build a house on sinking sand. Although storms, winds, and floods may hit both houses, only the one with a solid foundation will remain standing (Matthew 7:24-27). Jesus taught that we must have hope in *something*— God's Word—not just hope itself. Build your faith on the foundation of a trustworthy God who never lies.

God made this promise *before the beginning of time.* The promise did not come at a point when sin entered the world or even at the moment that God sent Christ to deal with the problem of sin; rather, Christ's coming and the promise of eternal life had been planned by God from the beginning (literally, "before eternal times"). God has been and always will be in supreme control of the universe, world events, and the future of his people. (See Romans 16:25-26 and Colossians 1:25-27 for more on God's purposes.)

1:3 And at his appointed season he brought his word to light through the preaching entrusted to me by the command of God our Savior.^{NIV} The promise came before time began. The manifestation (revelation) of that promise, God's *word,* the hope of eternal life, came *at his appointed season.* That is, God sent his Son at the proper time, the time of his own choosing (see Romans 5:6; Galatians 4:4; Ephesians 1:9-12; 1 Timothy 2:6), to bring the word of salvation to light. And Paul, at an opportune time in history, was called by God to proclaim this gospel to the Gentiles (Ephesians 3:1-11). Because Jesus rose from the dead, we can trust that we too will rise from the dead to live forever with him (see 1 Peter 1:3-4). Through Christ, God revealed his nature, will, plans, and promises to his people.

This understanding spread across the world and down through the centuries through *preaching*—the faithful retelling of the gospel to all who would listen. Paul took his commission to preach the gospel seriously. No general could have a more important command. No trustee could guard a more valuable estate. In 1 Timothy 1:1, Paul wrote that he was "an apostle of Christ Jesus by the command of God our Savior" (NRSV). God chose Paul for special work: "He is an instrument whom I have chosen to bring my name before Gentiles and kings and before the people of Israel" (Acts 9:15 NRSV). Paul did not seek this missionary apostleship; rather, it was given to him by God's command.

God the Father is called *our Savior.* Paul used this phrase six times in the letters to Timothy and Titus (see 1 Timothy 1:1; 2:3; 4:10; Titus 1:3; 2:10; 3:4). Jesus did the work of salvation by dying for our sins; therefore, he is our Savior. God planned the work of salvation, and he forgives our sins; thus, he also is our Savior. God in his fullness (Father, Son, and Holy Spirit) authored salvation.

1:4 To Titus, a true son in our common faith.NRSV Titus, a Greek, was one of Paul's most trusted and dependable coworkers. As a *true son* he may have been one of Paul's converts. The term alludes both to their relationship and to the role Paul wanted the Cretans to accept from Titus. As Paul's "son," he represented what Paul would say if he had been there in person.

Although not mentioned in Acts, other epistles point out that Titus fulfilled several missions on Paul's behalf. Paul had sent Titus to Corinth several times to help the church in its troubles and bring back positive reports to Paul. Then he was sent back to Corinth with news of Paul and to gather an offering for the Jerusalem church (2 Corinthians 7:6-7, 13-15; 8:6, 16-17, 23). Titus showed that he could be trusted with money. Paul and Titus also traveled together to Jerusalem (Galatians 2:3) and Crete (1:5). Paul left Titus in Crete to lead the new churches that were springing up on the island. Titus is last mentioned by Paul in 2 Timothy 4:10, Paul's final letter. As Titus exhibited leadership abilities, Paul assigned him leadership responsibilities, urging him to use those opportunities well.

Grace and peace from God the Father and Christ Jesus our Savior.NRSV Paul repeated his standard greeting (see 1 Timothy 1:2; 2 Timothy 1:2) with a slight change. The last term repeats the thought of verse 3. Paul used the term *Savior* for both God the Father and Jesus Christ, thereby revealing his understanding of God's nature and work in salvation (see also 1:3; 2:10, 13; 3:4, 6).

QUALIFICATIONS FOR CHURCH LEADERS / 1:5-9

Unlike the pressing matter of the false teachers that was on Paul's mind when he wrote to Timothy in Ephesus, Paul's letter to Titus focused on establishing healthy churches on Crete. In both cases, identifying good leaders was a priority. But in Ephesus leaders were needed to get the church back on track, while on Crete effective leaders were needed to get the church moving in the right direction.

Paul urged Timothy to be confrontive, while Titus was to be constructive. Paul had left Titus to complete "phase one" of planting churches on Crete. Their preaching brought numerous converts. These new believers now needed the leadership of capable elders whom Titus was to appoint.

While the lists of leadership qualifications in 1 Timothy 3:1-7 and Titus 1:6-9 have similarities, the list in Titus seems more thematic. First come traits from private life, followed by public attributes. Negative traits ("he must not be arrogant") are grouped separately from positive ones ("hospitable"). Paul wanted Titus to choose the right people to lead the growing church in Crete.

1:5 I left you behind in Crete for this reason.NRSV Crete is a long (150 miles), narrow island in the Mediterranean Sea, southeast of Greece. Among its population were many Jews. The earliest con verts there were probably Cretan Jews who had been in Jerusalem at Pentecost (Acts 2:11) more than thirty years before Paul wrote this letter. Perhaps there had been some renewed contact with Paul when he was there as a prisoner on his first journey to Rome for trial. Later, he and Titus returned for an evangelistic visit. As Paul had left Timothy in Ephesus to provide leadership for the Ephesian church and to silence the false teachers, so he left Titus on the island of Crete to provide leadership for the new churches there. Titus was also to prevent the rise of Crete's own brand of false teachers.

Students of the book of Acts will wonder when this visit took place, since Acts does not record a visit by Paul to Crete. Most likely, Paul and Titus went to Crete following Paul's release from his first Roman imprisonment (Acts 28:16). Paul traveled and ministered for two or three years before again being imprisoned by Rome and ultimately executed in A.D. 66 or 67.

So that you should put in order what remained to be done, and should appoint elders in every town, as I directed you.NRSV Apparently Paul did not stay long in Crete, so he left Titus, his trusted and able fellow worker, to finish *what remained to be done.* The unfinished work refers to establishing correct teaching and dealing with false teachers, as well as appointing *elders* in every town. Paul had appointed elders in various churches during his journeys (Acts 14:23). On Paul's return from

the first missionary journey, he took extra time to revisit every
church and establish each church's leadership. He could not stay
in each church, but he knew that these new churches needed
strong spiritual leaders. The men chosen were to lead the
churches by teaching sound doctrine, helping believers mature
spiritually, and equipping believers to live for Jesus Christ
despite opposition. The following verses give the qualifications
for elders.

While various Christian traditions have developed methods
and systems for appointing and ordaining leaders in the church,
particularly clergy, such matters were still very fluid in the early
church. It is difficult to extract from Scripture a particular, exact,
and rigid organizational structure. *Elders, deacons,* and *pastors*
are terms used to name different roles in later Christian traditions. Those roles are not necessarily contradictory. Traditions are
long-held, specific applications of biblical principles. As long as
our methods are consistent with biblical principles and teaching,
we must be open-minded about differing applications.

The words *as I directed you,* with the emphatic "I," reveal
Paul's authority and endorsement of this plan for church government. It follows that Titus was given Paul's authority over these
newborn churches. Three principles seem to emerge here regarding the nature of leadership roles in the local church. Leadership
should be: (1) local, (2) multiple, (3) qualified. The exercise of
power and the style of government may differ as long as (1) the
leaders are rooted within the church, and therefore accountable to
it; (2) power and responsibility are shared by several rather than
concentrated in one; and (3) the qualifications of leaders are recognized by those they are leading.

1:6 An elder must be blameless.[NIV] Paul briefly described some
qualifications that the elders (also called overseers as in 1:7, or
bishops) should have. Paul had given Timothy a similar set of
instructions for choosing leaders in the Ephesian church (see
1 Timothy 3:1-7; 5:22). Notice that most of the qualifications
involve character, not knowledge or skill. A person's life-style
and relationships provide a window into his or her character. Consider these qualifications as you evaluate people for positions of
leadership in your church. It is important to have leaders who can
effectively preach God's Word; but even more importantly, they
must live out God's Word and be examples for others to follow.

The first qualification: to be *blameless.* The elders must have
no conduct that would be grounds for any kind of accusation.
They must be above reproach (see the notes on 1 Timothy 3:2,
10). Again, the point here is not that the leaders cannot be

blamed, but rather that when blamed, their life will prove the falsehood of the blame.

The husband of one wife.^{NKJV} When Paul explained that each church leader should have only one wife, he was prohibiting promiscuity and promoting faithfulness in marriage. This did not prohibit an unmarried person from becoming an elder or a widowed elder from remarrying (see the notes on 1 Timothy 3:2).

A man whose children believe and are not open to the charge of being wild and disobedient.^{NIV} Those chosen to lead the church must have proven that they can lead their own household. An elder's children should have received spiritual training and should be believers. This will prove that they care about teaching correct doctrine and discipling others. Obviously those whose children are rebelling, running wild, and refusing to obey would not be fit for the important position of leading God's people. How the children respond will attest to how Christianity is practiced at home.

Should a pastor with rebellious or unbelieving children resign? Paul probably did not have that in mind. Rather, he was encouraging Christian leaders to examine their relationships with their children and take more time for them. However, if all a pastor's children were rebellious, he probably should resign and spend as much time as possible helping his own children back onto the right path.

Paul added the note (not found in 1 Timothy) that a leader's children should *believe*. In Crete, many had only recently converted from paganism to Christianity. So the family's response would be a gauge of the reality of a person's conversion. A leadership appointment would need to wait until that person had dealt effectively with his or her own family.

1:7 **Since an overseer is entrusted with God's work, he must be blameless.**^{NIV} Paul used the word *overseer* instead of *elder* here, although he was clearly referring to the same role within the church. He repeated the qualification of blamelessness, emphasizing that this quality is essential in any person who is *entrusted with God's work.* Church leaders who act unworthily and bring blame and reproach on themselves also damage God's work.

Paul's guidelines take on added significance in the Cretan setting, for Cretans were known as having disreputable character (see 1:12). Sometimes the leadership guidelines from Scripture will harmonize with the prevailing standards for mature leaders in a culture, and, at other times, they will conflict. Apparently, Titus was to be careful with the Cretans.

He must not be arrogant.NRSV A pitfall of leadership is arrogance (pride). But pride can seduce emotions and cloud reason, making a church leader ineffective. Pride and conceit were the devil's downfall, and he uses pride to trap others.

Quick-tempered. A hotheaded person will speak and act without thinking—hurting people and damaging the church's work and reputation. James wrote: "Let everyone be quick to listen, slow to speak, slow to anger; for your anger does not produce God's righteousness" (James 1:19-20 NRSV). If this is important for "everyone" (all believers), how much more so for their leader!

Addicted to wine or violent or greedy for gain.NRSV These three prohibitions had particular significance for Titus's search for church leaders in first-century Crete. A church leader must not be addicted to wine (a drunkard) or to money (*greedy for gain*). He must not be *violent* (often the result of being quick-tempered or drunk). Furthermore, the leaders Titus chose should serve out of love, not out of a desire for money.

DISQUALIFIED
What if someone aspires to leadership but has some of these character weaknesses? That person would be wise to refrain from taking a leadership position until he or she can deal with the issue. Everyone has problems and shortcomings, but a person with a persistent character flaw should deal with the flaw first.

Character weaknesses are like broken bones. Both keep us from functioning at our fullest capacity; both need treatment and time. How should a person deal with his or her character weaknesses?

■ Consultation with the pastor and prayer support from people
■ A strategy to keep from falling down in that area
■ Insight and regular nourishment from God's Word
■ Small steps taken each day

1:8 Rather he must be hospitable.NIV After listing characteristics a church leader should *not* have, Paul lists these positive qualities. Hospitality was of primary importance in this culture. Believers were commanded to be hospitable (see 3 John), so their leaders should exemplify this characteristic, revealing devotion and concern for the welfare of others.

One who loves what is good.NIV Paul insisted that the leaders be known for loving good people and good works.

Self-controlled, upright, holy and disciplined.NIV Self-control and discipline go hand-in-hand, describing a person who, like an athlete, is constantly "in training" in his or her Christian life and service. (See note on 1 Timothy 3:2 for more on "self-control.") This person, while a lover of goodness, displays that goodness in the spiritual realm because he or she is *upright* (just) and *holy* (that is, approved of God).

TONIGHT'S ENTERTAINMENT
A Christian leader must be known for entertaining even strangers. In the early days of Christianity, traveling evangelists and teachers were helped by Christians who housed and fed them. We would benefit from inviting people to eat with us—visitors, fellow church members, young people, those in need. Giving hospitality is very important today because there are so many people struggling with loneliness. In our self-centered society, we can show that we care by being hospitable. Christians were not to entertain false teachers (2 John 10), but this prohibition did not apply to non-Christians in general. God wants us to be generous, courteous, and hospitable with non-Christians; through our friendship, some may be won to Christ.

1:9 He must hold firmly to the trustworthy message as it has been taught.[NIV] The church leader must meet moral and spiritual requirements in his or her personal life, and the person must be reliable in his or her understanding and teaching of the *message,* the gospel, *as it has been taught.* The last phrase actually occurs first in the Greek for emphasis. The message as it had been taught by the apostles was the trustworthy message that church leaders must teach their congregation. They must *hold firmly* to it, without changing it, watering it down, or demoting its importance as the false teachers were doing; they were "to fight for the faith" as an apologist, and not give in to persecution or opposition.

So that he can encourage others by sound doctrine and refute those who oppose it.[NIV] When a church leader holds firmly to the *sound doctrine,* he must both encourage adherence to the truth and refute error. Pastors must fulfill a positive and a negative function in handling the truth. They must encourage by preaching, supporting, and reinforcing people as they follow the truth. But pastors must also confront and refute false ideas. Their teaching must educate people to be able to handle the truth both positively and negatively as well. Confident leaders with backbone, courage, and an irrefutable message would stand in strong contrast with Cretan life-styles, character traits, and false teachers (described in the following verses).

WARNING AGAINST FALSE TEACHERS / 1:10-16

Titus may not have been under attack by false teachers within the church as Timothy was in Ephesus, but he was nevertheless ministering in a hostile environment. Paul expected Titus to guard against both the Judaizers and the pagans. Paul agreed with the general assessment that Cretans were con artists. It would be difficult to know when they were telling the truth and safest to assume that they weren't. Planting the gospel of truth in such soil required careful tending!

Because the reputations of Cretan believers would be hard to establish, Titus needed to be certain of his actions, his decisions, and his teaching. The challenge from the rest of the Mediterranean world was clear; other believers might be given the benefit of the doubt, but Christians from Crete would be under scrutiny. Their spiritual lives needed to be, in Paul's words, "pure" (1:15).

1:10 **There are also many rebellious people, idle talkers and deceivers, especially those of the circumcision.**[NRSV] The false teachers Paul and Titus faced were *those of the circumcision,* the Judaizers (see also 1:14). These were Jews who taught that the Gentiles had to obey all the Jewish laws, rules, and rituals before they could become Christians. This regulation confused new Christians and caused problems in many churches where Paul had preached the Good News. Paul wrote letters to several churches to help them understand that Gentile believers did not have to become Jews first in order to be Christians—God accepts anyone who comes to him in faith (see Romans 1:17; Galatians 3:2-7). Although the Jerusalem council had dealt with this issue (see Acts 15), devout Jews who refused to believe in Jesus still were trying to cause problems in the Christian churches. The ruling of the Jerusalem council may have been honored by those within the churches, but these outsiders did not recognize the apostles as having any authority.

Here Paul identified three characteristics of this brand of false teachers:

1. They were *rebellious,* flouting the authority of Paul and Titus.

2. As *idle talkers,* they spoke lots of words and said nothing.

3. Having been deceived themselves, they had become *deceivers* of others.

TRUE OR FALSE?
Paul warned Titus to be on the lookout for people who teach wrong doctrines and lead others into error. Some false teachers are simply confused—they speak their misguided opinions without checking them against the Bible. Others have evil motives—they pretend to be Christians only because they can get more money, additional business, or a feeling of power from being a leader in the church. Jesus and the apostles repeatedly warned against false teachers (see Mark 13:22; Acts 20:29; 2 Thessalonians 2:3-12; 2 Peter 3:3-7) because their teachings attack the foundations of truth and integrity upon which the Christian faith is built.

So how can you recognize false teachers? They will
- focus more attention on themselves than on Christ;
- ask you to do something that will compromise or dilute your faith;
- de-emphasize the divine nature of Christ or the inspiration of the Bible;
- divide believers with quarrelsome and contentious teaching;
- urge believers to make decisions based more on human judgment than on prayer and biblical guidelines.

1:11 **Whose mouths must be stopped, who subvert whole households, teaching things which they ought not, for the sake of dishonest gain.**^{NKJV} These false teachers must be silenced; the Greek word is *epistomizein,* literally, "to muzzle." The reason? They were ruining people's faith—*whole households* had been affected, causing confusion in the church. Perhaps these were families under the influence of the church that had been "ambushed" by these pseudoreligious people who claimed "to know God" (1:16) but who were out to promote themselves. Their efforts were to *be stopped* by Titus's sharp rebukes (1:13).

What they taught was not the trustworthy message of the gospel (1:9) but their own ideas. Their goal was not to glorify the Lord and build his church but to make money (*dishonest gain*). Naturally it was hoped that these people would respond to the truth and be united with the true body of believers.

Contrary to the situation in Ephesus, the Cretans creating problems for Titus were not recognized leaders who were betraying the faith. Instead, they were free-lance operators, taking advantage of a spiritually sensitive situation to create gain for themselves.

1:12 **It was one of them, their very own prophet, who said, "Cretans are always liars, vicious brutes, lazy gluttons."**^{NRSV} Paul quoted a line from a poem by Epimenides, a poet and philosopher who had lived in Crete 600 years earlier. Paul called him a *prophet* because other ancient writers (notably Aristotle and Cicero) did so, and because his own countrymen gave him that title. Paul was not saying he was a prophet in the biblical sense. The quotation reveals basic character flaws in the Cretans, giving them a bad reputation for lying, violence, and laziness (compare with Paul's list of qualifications for Cretan church leaders in 1:7-8). They were *liars,* "idle talkers and deceivers" (1:10). Their false teaching made them liars. *Vicious brutes* refers to their unrestrained brutality; their lives were out of control. *Lazy gluttons* identifies the false teachers as lovers of dishonest gain. Rather than make an honest living, they preferred to prosper from their false teaching. The reputation of the Cretans was so bad that the verb form of their name (*kretizo*) was used by the Greeks to indicate lying. Paul applied this familiar phrase to the false teachers.

RESPONDING TO FALSEHOOD
Whatever our roles in the local church, sooner or later we will encounter someone whose teaching or ideas contradict Scripture. What should we do when that happens?

- Personally speak to the person and gently challenge his or her viewpoint. Do not attack; instead, firmly express your perception that the teaching is unbiblical. Ask the person to clarify.
- If the teacher persists in teaching without considering your concerns, go to the pastor or another leader and ask him or her to accompany you for another conversation to help discern where the problem lies.
- If the teaching proves to be unscriptural, the church should prohibit that person from teaching within its structure until matters are settled.
- Do not act on your suspicions of falsehood by spreading rumors or innuendoes about the person. If others realize you have attacked the person without confronting a wrong teaching, they may feel compelled to stand up for the teacher, even though the teacher is wrong.

1:13 This testimony is true.[NKJV] The Cretans could hardly argue with one of their own honored prophets, so neither did Paul. Having been in Crete, Paul knew from firsthand experience the type of people with whom Titus was dealing.

Therefore rebuke them sharply, that they may be sound in the faith.[NKJV] The New Testament teaching on discipline in the church has two purposes: to purge the church of dangerous elements and to bring the perpetrators to repentance. Of the two, the redemptive purpose is given far more stress in the New Testament. In this case, Paul's recommended remedy was to rebuke, then, if possible, to restore. Titus should *sharply* rebuke the false teachers, hoping to awaken them to sound doctrine and true faith. The goal of discipline in the church is to bring the sinner to repentance. Paul hoped that this would be the case with the false teachers.

> If I speak what is false, I must answer for it; if truth, it will answer for me. *Thomas Fuller*

A forceful, direct response early would prevent utter chaos in the church later. If the first believers were to develop unhealthy spiritual lives, they would carry their "disease" into the ongoing life of the church. Better to deal with the problem right away than to let it build up. But even here, the goal demanded that even the least hopeful candidates for the church be given the opportunity to come to faith.

1:14 Not paying attention to Jewish myths.^{NRSV} Apparently, the false teaching centered on two errors: first, *Jewish myths* (probably some useless speculations on the Old Testament, see also 1 Timothy 1:4). Titus may well have been facing various shades of syncretism, in which diluted Judaism was being blended with various forms of paganism to yield a deadly brand of godless religion.

Or to the commands of those who reject the truth.^{NIV} Second, these human *commands* most likely focused on rules and rituals, especially Jewish laws regarding what was clean and unclean (as is evident from Paul's words in verses 15-16). Paul urged Titus to sharply rebuke the false teachers, hoping to bring them back to the truth so they would no longer spread their lies.

Titus faced the lethal combination of religion and falsehood. Such mixtures have always presented a challenge to God's people. In the first temptation to deceive Eve, the serpent deliberately mixed a discussion about God's requirement with an outright lie. Jesus was hounded by extremely religious people who twisted the truth for personal benefit. He asked, "Why do you break the command of God for the sake of your tradition?" (Matthew 15:3 NIV). Today the spirit of our times applauds those who create their own personal religion. Self-made rules and guidelines that come from human teaching and not God should never be the basis for Christian thought.

1:15 To the pure all things are pure. The *pure* are the opposite of the "corrupt" in the second part of this verse. Those who believe sound doctrine and live their faith do not need to worry about rules and rituals regarding what is clean or unclean. Paul had written to the Romans: "For the kingdom of God is not food and drink but righteousness and peace and joy in the Holy Spirit" (Romans 14:17 NRSV). See also Colossians 2:20-23 and 1 Timothy 4:1-5.

Phrases like this one from Paul must be understood in their immediate context, as well as within the context of Paul's wider teaching. Paul was not teaching moral relativism ("As long as I can call myself pure, whatever I choose to do is therefore pure"), but he was speaking against superficial, external legalism. Dietary restrictions or food laws presented a form of religion that people thought provided spiritual substance, but which proved to be empty of real spiritual help. Jesus addressed the futility of substituting dietary regulations for obedience to God (see Matthew 15:10; Mark 7:14-19; Luke 11:37-41). Even Peter struggled with the importance of Jewish food restrictions in God's plan (Acts 10:9-15, 28). But Paul provided no excuse for discounting the moral directives of God. Grace does not make obedience obsolete.

But to the corrupt and unbelieving nothing is pure. Their very minds and consciences are corrupted.NRSV No stronger denunciation could be made to these false teachers who taught the need for following rules and rituals in order to be clean and pure. Because of their inner corruption, *nothing is pure*—nothing they do, say, give, or teach could be pure because they were corrupted from the inside. Echoing Jesus' teaching in Mark 7:15-19 and Luke 11:39-41, Paul explained that a person who is pure on the inside cannot be corrupted by outside influences; but a person who is corrupt on the inside corrupts everything around him. There can be no purity for such a person.

PURE PEOPLE
Some people see good all around them, while others see nothing but evil. What is the difference? Our soul becomes a filter through which we perceive goodness or evil. The pure (those who have Christ in control of their lives) learn to see goodness and purity even in this evil world. But corrupt and unbelieving people find evil in everything because their evil minds and hearts color even the good they see and hear. Whatever you fill your mind with will affect the way you think and act. Turn your thoughts to God and his Word, and you will discover more and more goodness, even in this evil world. A mind filled with good has little room for what is evil (see Philippians 4:8).

1:16 They profess to know God, but they deny him by their actions.NRSV The "corrupt and unbelieving" (1:15) false teachers claimed to know and follow God ("After all, look at all the rules we follow!"), but their actions revealed their true nature. The false teachers professed knowledge of God and, with their Jewish background, may have been well versed in the Old Testament. But they based their faith on works, not on the Lord Jesus Christ, thus they denied the God they claimed to know.

Paul's charge against the false teachers is similar but even more direct than his accusation in 2 Timothy, "Having a form of godliness but denying its power. Have nothing to do with them" (2 Timothy 3:5 NIV). The Jews had a reputation for claiming *to know God,* and Paul's language throughout this section indicates that Titus's greatest difficulties would be created by the Judaizers.

They are detestable, disobedient, unfit for any good work.NRSV Paul employed strong words because the sin of these false teachers deserved strong condemnation. Paul called them *detestable,* revealing his disgust at their sin and hypocrisy; *disobedient,* because they acted against the God they claimed to know; *unfit for any good work,* because people who live in rebellion against God cannot do any works that please him.

TAKE A LOOK
Many people claim to know God. How can we know if they really do? We will not know for certain in this life, but a glance at their life-style will quickly tell us what they value and whether they have ordered their lives around kingdom priorities. Our conduct speaks volumes about what we believe (see 1 John 2:4-6). What do people know about God and about your faith by watching your life?

Titus 2

Jesus challenged his followers to be salt of the earth and light to the world (see Matthew 5:13-16). Believers are called to make an impact where they live. Subsequent events in history (for example, the spread of the gospel throughout the Roman Empire, the Reformation, the Wesleyan revivals in England, the Great Revivals in America) demonstrate that when the gospel takes root, profound spiritual and social reorientation soon follow. Conversion creates moral and ethical change.

Having people of all ages in a church can strengthen it, but it also can bring problems. Paul gave Titus counsel on how to help various groups of people. The older people should teach the younger by words *and* by example. This is how values are passed on from generation to generation. The family and the church are the two best structures designed by God to accomplish this.

In chapter 1, Paul set the primary goal for Titus's ministry in Crete: to "put in order" (1:5) what God had allowed them to begin. Titus was to teach all the new converts to become "sound in the faith" (1:13). Paul commented on the primary social relationships that were central to the growth of the church in Crete. He did not try to change the system; instead, he sought to change the persons within the systems. Marriages, homes, slavery, and work are all transformed more profoundly from within than from without. Through Titus, Paul was planting seeds of significant change in every facet of life on Crete. But it all depended on the truth of the gospel message.

2:1 But as for you, teach what is consistent with sound doctrine.NRSV The word *but* contrasts this verse with the previous verses, 1:10-16. Paul used these contrasts frequently in the Pastoral Epistles (see 1 Timothy 6:11; 2 Timothy 3:14; 4:5). Whereas the false teachers were deceivers (1:10), Titus was to teach *sound doctrine,* the "trustworthy message" of the gospel (1:9). Notice the emphasis on sound doctrine in Paul's instructions to Timothy and Titus (see 1 Timothy 1:10; 6:3; 2 Timothy 1:13; 4:3; Titus 1:9, 13; 2:2). This is the content of faith. Believers must be grounded in the truths of the Bible, then they won't be swayed by the powerful oratory of false teachers and heresy, the possible devastation of tragic circumstances, or the pull of emotions. Knowledge and acceptance of "sound doctrine" should lead to righteous living. Behavior should match belief; thus, in the following verses, Paul gave Titus examples of the right behavior expected of several types of people in the churches.

SOUND DOCTRINE
Sound doctrine rings true. It combines correct knowledge and understanding with consistent practice. How do we know if our Christian doctrine is sound?
- It is found in the Bible.
- It keeps Jesus Christ central.
- It results in consistently good behavior and actions.
- It promotes spiritual health in ourselves and others.
   Those responsible for preaching and teaching must challenge people to understand sound doctrine. We may become so caught up in relating to felt needs that we ignore their connection to sound biblical knowledge. Reaching out to people where they are should not result in theological ignorance.

2:2 Teach the older men to be temperate, worthy of respect, self-controlled.^{NIV} The *older men,* though technically not "elders," were the senior members of the community and should be examples of maturity. They were the "pool" from which elders were to be appointed.

Paul identified four objectives for Titus as he taught the older men:

(1) Because they were mature members of the community and examples to younger men, Titus should teach the older men to be *temperate,* meaning that their lives should show moderation and clearheadedness, with an absence of extravagance. Sometimes to be temperate meant the opposite of drunkenness, but here the meaning is broader. We might use the modern term *balanced,* showing that these men had placed appropriate emphasis on each of the priorities of life.

(2) Titus should teach these older men to be *worthy of respect,* meaning that they should be "serious minded." They should not act like clowns or frivolous children but as dignified and honorable adults (see also 2:3, 7). As members of the Cretan society and thus regarded as not worthy of respect, the older men needed to "live down" the stereotype of what it meant to be a Cretan (see 1:12).

(3) Paul also asked Titus to teach these Cretan older men (yet young believers) to be *self-controlled.* Having lived for years in a heathen atmosphere, they needed to monitor and restrain their passions, anger, and words. Self-control could also be translated as "prudent" or even "sensible." Paul emphasized self-control with each group of people he singled out (see 2:4-6).

REMOTE CONTROL
Self-control was an important aspect in early Christianity and is likewise vital in today's churches. The Christian community includes people from differing backgrounds and viewpoints, making conflict inevitable. Christians live and work in a pagan and often hostile world. To stay above reproach, men and women need wisdom and discernment to be discreet and to master their will, tongue, and passions so that Christ will not be dishonored. How is your self-control?

Sound in faith, in love, in patience.^{NKJV}

(4) Titus was also to emphasize that the older men should have an overall sense of "soundness" in their lives. Three key Christian virtues were to be manifested by the older men in the congregation. Sound *faith* meant that they were to have a healthy and personal faith in God by maintaining the Christian truth. Sound *love* meant that they should be loving, not bitter; their love was to be personal and outgoing (see John 13:34). Sound *patience* required endurance and steadfastness. Endurance replaces hope in the normal list of the three key Christian virtues: faith, hope, and love (1 Corinthians 13:13). Paul did this to emphasize the importance for older men to finish well (2 Timothy 4:7; see also James 5:7-8).

How do Titus's teaching objectives for Crete relate to the church today? We may be in a church where the gospel has been preached for generations. Should we use Paul's outline for Titus as our teaching plan? We must ask: Are the various age groups exhibiting the character qualities Paul told Titus to teach? If not, the pattern applies directly. We must go back to basics to teach and emphasize them. Furthermore, we must encourage older men not to give in to idleness or despair as they face years of retirement and declining activity. Lack of the feeling needed or having a meaningful role can destroy a person.

2:3 Likewise, teach the older women to be reverent in the way they live, not to be slanderers or addicted to much wine, but

to teach what is good.[NIV] The word *likewise* reveals a close comparison with the previous verse; both men and women need this

---

WAYS TO TEACH OLDER MEN
How can we help older men to exhibit the qualities Paul described in this letter to Titus?

- *Set the expectation* for proper behavior. Sermons and Sunday school classes on this passage can teach these values.
- *Reinforce the need* for temperance, respect, self-control, and soundness at men's fellowship meetings or retreats. These qualities are not always automatic by-products of the Christian life; they require prayer and effort.
- *Give feedback.* In small groups or one-on-one visitation, men should be encouraged to develop these qualities.
- *Encourage the older men to be models* for the younger men in the congregation.
- *Encourage family members to give support* by helping older men maintain their dignity and respect.

---

teaching. Paul's directive for Titus to teach women was in itself a startling departure from the way women were usually treated. The inequalities found in society were not to be brought into church relationships. We honor older people when we consider them capable of still being nurtured.

The older women must also be taught—their life-styles should be *reverent*—dignified, worthy of honor, Christlike. "Reverent" comes from a Greek word meaning "appropriate" or "suitable to the temple." It pictures a priestess carrying out her sacred duties with devotion and responsibility. Older Christian women should have a respectful attitude toward all aspects of life and toward people of all ages. Without an appropriate sense of what God reveres, their attitude will degenerate to cynicism and verbal aggression.

They must not be *slanderers* (i.e., gossipers), nor should they be *addicted to much wine* (literally, "slaves to drink"). In the Cretan environment, both excesses could develop among older women whose families were grown and who had too much time on their hands. (Perhaps too much wine and gossip went together. But gossip can be spread even at meetings where only coffee is served.) Instead, these older women could fill their time ministering to others, teaching *what is good.* This meant not necessarily public sharing, but sharing their wisdom, knowledge, and faith with their circles of family and friends.

Paul had much more in mind than simply to give honor to the older women. Older women should not regard their golden years as going on "cruise control" spiritually. Women should not regard their lives as less valuable when children have left or after retirement from a career. Nor should they capitulate to despair or loneliness. We need their wisdom, prayers, and examples.

2:4 Then they can train the younger women to love their husbands and children.[NIV] In verses 4, 5, 8, and 10, Paul uses the little word "so that" (Greek *hina*), to show the purpose behind his directions about how Titus should teach. Specifically, the older women (2:3) could teach and encourage the younger women in the church by word and by example. Paul wanted the older women to teach "what is good" (2:3), and here he explained that in detail. First, they could encourage the young women in the church to love their husbands and children. This seems obvious, but Paul may have included this because of special problems in Crete, or even because of the influence of the false teachers to disregard these responsibilities (see 1:11).

In new marriages or when children first come to a home, busyness and activity reach a high pitch as the tasks of homemaking and child care increase. Is it possible that being loving can get crowded out? Don't forget the love that motivated the marriage and the desire for children. Don't let all the tasks (even though some are very irritating) ruin the love relationship.

Within the church today, older women rarely become active role models for the younger women. In fact, the honor due our elders in the church is often absent. Age groups are isolated from each other, causing people to feel that little can be learned from one another. It is unfortunate when patterns in society become patterns for the church. The church must encourage intergenerational caring and sharing. There are times when the kitchen provides an eloquent pulpit for the application of biblical truth!

WHO'S ON FIRST?
Why did Paul stress that young Christian women should love their husbands and families? While such teaching may appear too obvious for mention, there are forces at work in today's world that undermine even that very basic part of family life. Women are being told that their interests or desires come first, that they must seek what makes them happy before they can be good wives and mothers. While women should be encouraged to use their gifts and abilities, each Christian woman must align her priorities with God's wisdom, not the world's values. She must love her husband and her children, accepting the sacrifices that love brings. God will honor those who value what he values.

FOR EXAMPLE
Women who were new Christians were to learn how to have harmony in the home by watching older women who had been Christians for some time. We have the same need today. Younger wives and mothers should learn to live in a Christian manner—loving their husbands and caring for their children—by observing exemplary women of God. If you are of an age or position where people look up to you, make sure that your example motivates younger believers to live in a way that honors God.

2:5 To be self-controlled, chaste, good managers of the household, kind, being submissive to their husbands.[NRSV] As with the older men and women, these younger women needed self-control. The next word, *chaste* (pure) helps explain what kind of self-control they needed. They should control their passions and desires, remaining true to their husbands (perhaps Paul also mentioned this because of a particular problem in Crete). These young wives and mothers should manage their household (which, as any homemaker knows, can be a challenging and diverse career in itself). They must show kindness in their relationships with husband and children.

In addition, the young women were to be *submissive to their husbands.* Submission between marriage partners is an often misunderstood concept. This text, for example, cannot be used to promote the general subjugation of all women under all men. Among Christian teachings, this one probably ranks among the least popular in society. But it is not teaching that women should become doormats. Neither does the Bible describe the process as a one-way subjection. For marriage and family relationships to run smoothly, there must be one appointed leader—God has appointed the husband and father to be this leader. The wife should willingly follow her husband's leadership in Christ, acknowledging that this is his responsibility.

Maturity provides the key to understanding submission. The husband must not be a tyrant, faithless, unloving, or impatient, as previously mentioned in verse 2. He should be worthy of respect. Likewise, the woman should not be rebellious, undermining or contradicting the man. To be "subject to" (*hupotassumenas*) does not mean to obey, but to accept the relationship that God has designed, voluntarily subjecting oneself to God's order and fulfilling the responsibilities that come with it. To Paul, submission never meant inferiority (see also Galatians 3:28; Ephesians 5:24; Colossians 3:18; 1 Peter 3:1, 5).

SUBMISSION IN ACTION
A husband should regard his leadership in the context of love, partnership, and covenant. He does not make every decision; nor are his decisions always right. A husband who doesn't consider his wife's opinions is foolish. In Ephesians 5:25, Paul tells husbands to exercise headship by means of sacrificial love. It's as much a sin for a husband to misuse his leadership as it is for a wife to refuse to submit.

The principle of submission must be worked out before marriage. The idea that two people can remain independent while married eventually fails because a couple will not agree on some decisions no matter how long they are discussed. In considering marriage, among other questions, a Christian woman must ask herself: Am I willing to submit to this man's decisions once I have told him my thoughts and we have disagreed? A Christian man ought to ask himself: Am I willing to be held fully accountable by God for any decisions I make in which I have overruled my wife's opinions? Negative answers to these questions may reveal serious weaknesses in the foundation of that marriage.

Submission should not be a problem in families where both husband and wife are believers, for both are concerned with the happiness of the other. Real leadership involves service. A wise and Christ-honoring husband will not take advantage of his leadership role but will love and serve his wife as Christ loved and served his disciples (see John 13:1-17). A wife need not fear or despise submitting to a husband who lovingly serves her in return. For more of Paul's advice about marriage, see 1 Corinthians 7:1-40; Ephesians 5:22-33.

So that the word of God may not be discredited.^{NRSV} Paul's purpose in these instructions, and every believer's purpose in following them, was to glorify God. The believers were being watched; if they lived righteous and blameless lives, there would be no ammunition for their enemies to use against them. For the believers to continue living in sin amounted to denying God's Word and God himself, who had saved them from sin and expected them to obey his commands.

2:6 Likewise, urge the younger men to be self-controlled.^{NRSV} Paul urged Titus to teach self-control, this time as his singular requirement for the younger men. Young men today, as much as in ancient times, may lack this quality. If young men exercise self-restraint, balance, and common sense, they can save themselves much trouble in all areas of life.

The parallel with verse 5 may indicate that Paul was still think-

BONDS OF FREEDOM
Christian freedom does not grant us free and unrestrained use or abuse of the following (verses quoted in NRSV):

Anger	*A fool gives full vent to anger.*	Proverbs 29:11
	Be angry but do not sin; do not let the sun go down on your anger.	Ephesians 4:26
Tongue	*Let everyone be quick to listen, slow to speak, slow to anger.*	James 1:19
	No one can tame the tongue—a restless evil, full of deadly poison.	James 3:8
Desires	*Put on the Lord Jesus Christ, and make no provision for the flesh, to gratify its desires.*	Romans 13:14
	Live by the Spirit, I say, and do not gratify the desires of the flesh.	Galatians 5:16
	Shun youthful passions and pursue righteousness, faith, love, and peace, along with those who call on the Lord from a pure heart.	2 Timothy 2:22
	Beloved, I urge you . . . to abstain from the desires of the flesh that wage war against the soul.	1 Peter 2:11
Money	*For the love of money is a root of all kinds of evil.*	1 Timothy 6:10
	Keep your lives free from the love of money, and be content with what you have.	Hebrews 13:5
Will	*For you were called to freedom . . . only do not use your freedom as an opportunity for self-indulgence.*	Galatians 5:13
	As servants of God, live as free people, yet do not use your freedom as a pretext for evil.	1 Peter 2:16

ing of marriage. If these young men were married and had children, then self-control would be doubly important. Lack of this quality creates tyrants and abusers within families. A woman attempting to practice submission in marriage to a man who lacks self-control will find that her husband may not reciprocate. All of the positive traits that a husband can contribute to a marriage—self-sacrifice, love, tenderness, compassion, listening—all flow out of self-control. Husbands who lack self-control have little right to complain about their wives' lack of submission.

In ancient Greek society, fathers were not expected to be nurturers. Many young men today have been raised in families where fathers have neglected their responsibilities to their wives and children. Husbands and fathers who are good examples of Christian living are important role models for young men who need to *see* how it is done.

> Example is the most powerful rhetoric.
> *Thomas Brooks*

2:7-8 In everything set them an example by doing what is good.^{NIV} The Greek text indicates the word *yourself* (*seauton*) in this directive. Titus, qualifying as a "younger man" himself, was urged to set an example for the young men in the churches he led (see also 1 Timothy 4:12). His authoritative words could have no impact if not backed up by a blameless life of *doing what is good*. Titus's teaching should emphasize "self-control," while his life-style should be an example of how that self-control can be applied to daily living.

Paul stressed the importance of good works often in the Pastoral Epistles:

- 1 Timothy 2:10—Women were to adorn themselves with good works.
- 1 Timothy 5:10—Widows were to be known for their good works.
- 1 Timothy 6:18—Wealthy people were to be rich in good works.
- 2 Timothy 2:21—Christian workers who cleansed themselves from sin would be "useful to the Master and prepared to do any good work" (NIV).
- 2 Timothy 3:17—Scripture thoroughly equips us for every good work.
- Titus 2:7—The young men were to set an example by doing what is good.
- Titus 3:1—Christians in society were to be ready to do whatever is good.
- Titus 3:8, 14—Paul reminded and encouraged Christians to devote themselves to doing what is good.

A GOOD IMITATION
Paul urged Titus to be a good example to those around him so that others (especially other young men) might see Titus's good works and imitate him. Titus's life would give his words greater impact. If you want someone to act a certain way, be sure that you live that way yourself. Then you will earn the right to be heard, and your life will reinforce what you teach.

In your teaching show integrity, seriousness.^{NIV} From speaking of Titus's actions, Paul turned to Titus's public ministry of teaching. That his teaching should show *integrity* would contrast him with the false teachers, who taught lies. This quality of integrity would come from careful Bible study and prayer. This would be especially important as Titus taught or confronted others about spiritual or moral issues. If he acted impulsively or unreasonably, he would more likely start arguments than convince people of the truth.

Seriousness indicates teaching with reverence so that Titus's words would be respected and taken seriously. Paul encouraged Titus, and through Titus other young men, to be reverent and purposeful. Christianity should never be intentionally boring or gloomy. The seriousness of the gospel should cause people to act, but not be repelled by a preacher's grim disposition.

Sound speech that cannot be condemned.[NKJV] Paul counseled Titus to be above criticism in how he taught. Because of his unique role in Crete, his life must display a remarkable degree of consistency. He would be constantly on display. In verse 7 above, the Greek word for "teaching" is *didaskalia,* referring to the act and/or content of teaching. The word translated "speech" here is *logos,* also translated as "word." Titus's every word must be measured so that he would remain above reproach and condemnation.

Then any opponent will be put to shame, having nothing evil to say of us.[NRSV] Titus would face opposition, but he should not provide the enemy with ammunition! His exemplary life, teaching, and speech might not stop the attacks, but the accusers would have to resort to making up accusations against him, thus putting themselves to shame; otherwise, they would have *nothing evil to say.* More likely, the meaning is that the accusers will in fact be *put to shame* when their accusations prove to be groundless.

2:9-10 **Tell slaves to be submissive to their masters and to give satisfaction in every respect.**[NRSV] Slavery was common in Paul's day. Millions of slaves occupied the empire, and many of them found their way into the early churches. Slavery was an institution and would not be changed overnight. Thus Paul did not condemn the institution of slavery in any of his letters. But Paul advised both Christian slaves and masters to be loving and responsible in their conduct (see also Ephesians 6:5-9; Colossians 3:22-25; 1 Timothy 6:1-2; 1 Peter 2:18-25).

> No one promised that Christian discipleship would be easy!
> *Gordon Fee*

Slaves were *submissive* by nature of their position, but the difference Paul hoped to teach them was in their attitude toward their masters and toward the work they performed. They should treat their masters with respect, and their work should be done to satisfy their masters. They no longer served because they had to; they served because they loved the Lord and their masters and because they took pride in their work. To the Colossian believers, Paul wrote: "Slaves, obey your earthly masters in everything, not only while being watched and in order to please them, but wholeheartedly, fearing the Lord. Whatever your task, put yourselves into it, as done for the Lord and not for your masters" (Colossians 3:22-23 NRSV).

Submission is difficult. In fact, it is possible to pretend to submit while on the inside continuing to hold tightly to our own thoughts and desires. Paul counteracted this human tendency by encouraging slaves to *give satisfaction in every respect*. Each group that Paul addressed was given a mission with serious obstacles to overcome.

WHO'S THE BOSS?
The standards set by Paul can help any employee/employer relationship. Employees should always do their best work and be trustworthy, not just when the employer is watching. Businesses lose millions of dollars a year to employee theft and time wasting. If all Christian employees would follow Paul's advice at work, what a transformation it would make! Try to give your employer complete satisfaction by the way you do your job.

Not to talk back to them, and not to steal from them.NIV If there was any doubt about the extent to which Paul taught slaves should cooperate with their masters, he removed it with these examples. That the slaves were not to *talk back* meant that they should not be stubborn, unmanageable, or resistant to authority; instead, they should act in submission as noted above. That they should not *steal* referred to any type of theft that might be classified as "petty larceny." Slaves might be tempted to take "small" needed items, but Christian slaves must resist that temptation in order **to show that they can be fully trusted, so that in every way they will make the teaching about God our Savior attractive.**NIV A person who cannot be trusted with small matters must not be trusted for large ones. If the Christian slaves refused to steal from their masters, even something minor, they would show that they could be *fully trusted,* that is, able to handle more important matters and responsibilities. But more important, they would impress their masters and other slaves with the depth of change that God had performed in their lives, making others want to know more about the Christian faith. Slaves might consider themselves of no value (indeed, their society certainly told them so), but Paul implied here an incredible opportunity for them to witness for Christ on all levels of society—to the children they cared for, the other family members, the merchants they dealt with, other slaves and their families, and the masters themselves. Being trustworthy makes the teaching about God attractive to unbelievers.

2:11 For the grace of God that brings salvation has appeared to all men.[NIV] The word *for* ties Paul's preceding words to this statement. God's salvation was offered to all the different people in the groups he had just identified. Paul referred to "God our Savior" in verse 10, followed here by a concise statement about the salvation that God brings. God, by his grace, sent Christ to earth; because of Christ's death on the cross, salvation is available to all types of people. Because he had just mentioned Christian slaves, it is apparent that Paul understood that the gospel message was offered universally to all types of people, regardless of their religious background, race, age, gender, or station in life. "For it is by grace you have been saved, through faith—and this not from yourselves, it is the gift of God" (Ephesians 2:8 NIV).

Paul's mention of the *grace of God* immediately would bring encouragement to those struggling with the difficult exhortations he had just given. We can make significant progress in our Christian growth when we know that our sins are graciously pardoned and that Christ graciously accepts us even though we don't deserve it. The grace of God makes it possible. God's offer of *salvation to all* means that salvation has been made available through Christ to everyone, without discrimination. The word "all" here refers to the universal offer, rather than implying that everyone will be saved.

The grace of God *appeared* bodily in Christ. This phrase refers to the incarnation of Jesus. That message of grace arrived in Crete with Paul and Titus. We can hardly imagine the impact! When the gospel light is turned on in a place of darkness, changes are inevitable. Those who respond are transformed; those who resist and reject the message can do so, but they must face the consequences.

2:12 It teaches us to say "No" to ungodliness and worldly passions, and to live self-controlled, upright and godly lives in this present age.[NIV] All of Paul's instructions in verses 1-10 can be summed up in these two phrases. Believers must refuse any action that lacks reverence for God. Ungodliness means lack of love or total disregard for God (Romans 1:18). We live in an age when many totally reject God's influence in any area of life. Christians must renounce that attitude. Worldly passions are desires for the pleasures and activities of this world (1 John 2:16). These are the desires of people who have an anti-God mind-set (see Romans 6:12; Galatians 5:16, 24; Ephesians 4:22). They must not only renounce *ungodliness and worldly passions;* they must also replace those desires with positive characteristics. To fight against lust, we must say no to temptation, but we must also say yes to active service for Christ. The power to live as a Christian comes from the Holy Spirit. Because Christ died and rescued us from sin, we are free from sin's control. God gives us the power and understanding to live according to his will and to do good, thus we can live a godly life.

 JUST SAY NO
We can do nothing to earn our salvation through any service we give or even by living morally upright. However, once we have accepted God's salvation, his grace makes ethical demands of us both outwardly and inwardly. Grace teaches and enables us to say no outwardly to non-Christian activities and inwardly to non-Christian desires. Some people talk as if they were hypnotized and helpless victims of their own desires. But Christians are expected and enabled to just say no.

God's salvation by grace directs our lives *in this present age.* Paul's term refers to the time inaugurated by Christ's appearing at the Incarnation that will be fully realized at his return. The grace that motivates and fortifies us to live for Christ in this present age will also be with us in the age to come—eternity. In the meantime, we are to conduct ourselves as fully devoted followers of Christ.

2:13 While we wait for the blessed hope—the glorious appearing of our great God and Savior, Jesus Christ.^{NIV} Paul gives us a wonderful motivation for all this righteous living—believers are waiting for a *hope* that is already a certainty: the second coming (or appearing, *epiphaneia*) of Jesus Christ. We can look forward to Christ's wonderful return with eager expectation and hope. Our hope makes us live each day ready morally and ethically to serve him.

What may appear to be a simple verse in English has been the cause of considerable study. Almost every word deserves attention. In the term *wait* we find the tension of an eager expectation whose fulfillment has been promised, but has not yet occurred. The term *blessed hope* means Christians are blessed and made glad by their living hope in Christ's second coming. That hope will be realized at the moment of the appearing (the term in Greek was used in 2:11 to refer to Christ's incarnation). Here Paul used it to describe Christ's ultimate glorification, his return to receive those who have trusted him.

> It is since Christians have largely ceased to think of the other world that they have become so ineffective in this. Aim at heaven and you will get earth "thrown in"; aim at earth and you will get neither. *C. S. Lewis*

The final phrase of this verse, *our great God and Savior Jesus Christ,* raises a possible ambiguity: did Paul mean to refer to two persons of the Trinity ("our great God" and "Savior Jesus Christ"), or was he extolling the divinity of Christ ("our great God and Savior, Jesus Christ")? While the phrase can be read both ways, the grammar of the sentence supports the view that this was an assertion of Jesus' deity. The same construction appears in 2 Peter 1:1, "our God and Savior, Jesus Christ." Both these verse affirm that Jesus is God (for other examples, see John 20:28; Romans 9:5; Hebrews 1:8; 1 John 5:20).

BLESSED HOPE

Paul brings out two aspects of Christian living that must be stressed today: *waiting* with anticipation and *hoping* for Christ's glorious appearing. Both are essential to our Christian sanity in this present evil age. The waiting is good for us: it builds our character, endurance, and perseverance. The hoping makes the waiting bearable. We live hopefully while we wait, anticipating three great benefits of Christ's return:
1. Christ's personal presence—we look forward to being with our Redeemer.
2. Redemption from our sinful nature—we long for the end of the battle with sin and our perfection in Christ.
3. Restoration of creation—we anticipate the complete rule of grace when the image of God will be fully realized in people and when the created order will be restored.

2:14 Who gave Himself for us, that He might redeem us from every lawless deed and purify for Himself His own special people, zealous for good works.[NKJV] The "great God and Savior, Jesus Christ" (2:13), whose return believers await, is the same Jesus Christ who came to earth and died for our sins. Christ's act of sacrifice is summed up in the words *gave Himself.* It indicates that he gave himself voluntarily. It was an act of love for us. "Gave Himself for us" indicates the substitutionary nature of his act of giving (see Mark 10:45). *For us* indicates "on our behalf"—Christ died in our place. His giving himself for us was totally effective and comprehensive, for we are redeemed "from every lawless deed."

He gave his life on our behalf with a twofold purpose. First, that he *might redeem us*. "Redeem" means to purchase our release from the captivity of sin with a ransom (see Mark 10:45; 1 Timothy 2:6; 1 Peter 1:18-21 for more on Christ as our ransom). Christ paid the ultimate price. He removed our bondage to sin that made us lawless rebels prone to do *every lawless deed*. In this statement, "redeemed from every lawless deed," Paul dispelled the arguments of the Judaizers, who wanted others to conform to petty laws and regulations. They rejected the gracious   · cleansing offered by Christ.

God's second purpose was that, through his redemption, he would set apart for himself a group of holy, special people. *His own special people* has an important Old Testament background. In Exodus 19:5, God referred to the Hebrews: "You will be my treasured possession" (NIV). (See also Deuteronomy 7:6.) The basis of the covenant was God's choosing this people and purifying them to be set apart for his special use. In Ezekiel 37:23, God reaffirmed this special relationship: "They will be my people, and I will be their God" (NIV). The apostle Peter referred to the church in this way (see 1 Peter 1:18-21).

Christ has accomplished the work required to *purify for Himself* those whom he died to save (see 1 John 1:7; Hebrews 9:12-14). This purification is a process, often called "sanctification." We are not only free from the sentence of death for our sin, but we are also purified from sin's influence as we grow in Christ. His redemption took care of the past; his purification makes the present and future an exciting and challenging prospect. As people who are cleansed and restored and who understand the awesome price paid on our behalf, we should thank God. We should also live according to God's will, *zealous for good works*. Then, when Christ returns, he will find us ready, waiting, and doing good works.

2:15 These, then, are the things you should teach. Encourage and rebuke with all authority.^NIV Paul repeated his command to Titus to be unafraid in his teaching ministry among the believers in Crete. *These things* referred to verses 1-10 above. Titus must *teach* or speak out (as opposed to being silent and thus allowing wrongdoing and sin), *encourage* (exhort, advise, commend, and/or admonish, depending on the need), and *rebuke* (express disapproval, reprimand if needed). In short, he was to persist by every means at his disposal to communicate to those in Crete what he had learned from Paul. Titus could do this on divine authority, for he had been entrusted by God with leadership gifts and with this ministry in Crete.

Let no one look down on you.^{NRSV} No doubt, as Titus exercised his God-given authority, some would *look down on* him, either because he was younger than they were or because they didn't agree with his decisions. Paul had made a similar statement with respect to Timothy's youth in 1 Timothy 4:12. The impact of the phrase communicates the idea that neither Titus nor Timothy should allow anyone else's definition of who they were to affect what they knew themselves to be. Titus should follow God's leading as he completed his mission among the Cretan churches.

NEVER FEAR
Paul told Titus to teach the Scriptures as well as to live them. We must also teach, encourage, and correct others when necessary. It is easy to feel afraid when others are older, more influential in the community, or wealthier. Like Titus, we should not let ourselves be threatened when we are trying to minister to others or provide leadership in the church.

Titus 3

Although at first glance Paul seems to have introduced the government as a new subject, his motive was to show the widest arena where the gospel could have an impact. Most of chapter 2 covers relationships and responsibilities of believers. We are not sure if the masters were Christians whom Paul instructed the Christian slaves to obey, but he was still dealing with individual relationships. In this chapter, Paul discussed Christian behavior in the context of government and society.

Paul reminded the Christians that they once shared the same "lostness" that marked the lives of those around them. But Christ came to earth to provide salvation, grace, the Holy Spirit, and mercy. He took those unable to save themselves by their righteousness and made them into a people who are "heirs according to the hope of eternal life" (3:7).

The quality of our earthly citizenship should reflect the confidence we have in our heavenly citizenship! Because we are citizens of the eternal kingdom, we can live with hope and serve people in the earthly kingdom.

3:1 Remind them to be subject to rulers and authorities, to obey, to be ready for every good work.[NKJV] In addition to speaking, exhorting, and rebuking (2:15), a Christian leader must also *remind* his congregation of their responsibility to government. As the believers awaited the return of Christ and living eternally with him in his government (2:13), they had to live under worldly authorities. So Paul explained how believers in Crete could best do that—by subjecting themselves to government rulers and authorities and by obeying civil laws. Paul may have stressed obedience to the government because of a particular problem in Crete. He did not want any trouble with the authorities that would bring the church under suspicion (see also Romans 13:1-7; 1 Peter 2:13-17).

Christians understand obedience to the government in different ways: All Christians agree that we are to live at peace with the state as long as the state allows us to live by our religious convictions. For hundreds of years, however, there have been at least three interpretations of how we are to do this:

(1) Some Christians believe that the state is so corrupt that Christians should have as little to do with it as possible. Although they should be good citizens as long as they can do so without compromising their beliefs, they should not work for the government, vote in elections, or serve in the military. Although this fulfills the principle of abstaining from evil, it prevents the Christian from being salt and light in the governmental, political, and military system.

(2) Others believe that God has given the state authority in certain areas and the church authority in others. Christians can be loyal to both and can work for either. They should not, however, confuse the two. In this view, church and state are concerned with two totally different spheres—the spiritual and the physical. Thus they complement each other but do not work together. This view is very legitimate and supports Jesus' teaching to give to Caesar what is Caesar's and to God what is God's (see Matthew 22:21), but it can lead to isolation from the political world and indifference toward state leaders.

(3) Still others believe that Christians have a responsibility to make the state better. They can do this politically, by electing Christian or other high-principled leaders. They can also do this morally, by serving as an influence for good in society. In this view, church and state ideally work together for the good of all. This view is preferred and seems to best portray the New Testament teaching. Nowhere does Jesus call laymen to leave political or social service as a requirement to discipleship. Its inherent danger would be for the Christian to get so involved in worldly affairs that the Christian mission is lost.

None of these views advocates rebelling against or refusing to obey the government's laws or regulations unless those laws clearly require believers to violate the moral standards revealed by God. Believers must be responsible citizens, as well as responsible Christians. Therefore, they ought to be active in efforts that will benefit the community in general. Genuine, caring involvement creates a platform from which believers may rightly speak in judgment if necessary. But constant criticism of others without participating in those areas needing to be improved simply isolates Christians and creates a poor atmosphere for communicating the gospel.

Besides subjection and obedience, Paul mentioned readiness for good works—in other words, a willingness to serve. "For we are His workmanship, created in Christ Jesus for good works, which God prepared beforehand that we should walk in them" (Ephesians 2:10 NKJV). No doubt Christians who obeyed the government gave a good witness for their faith among the authorities; Christians active in community service and/or government had great opportunities to witness for Christ.

But above all we must remember our true citizenship. According to Philippians 3:20, we are actually citizens of heaven rather than of the United States of America. In 1 Peter 1:1, 17 and 2:11, we are called strangers and sojourners (or tourists and resident aliens) of our own nations on earth.

I PLEDGE ALLEGIANCE
As Christians, our first allegiance is to Jesus as Lord, but we must obey our government and its leaders as well. Christians are not above the law. Obeying the civil law is only the beginning of our Christian responsibility; we must do what we can to be good citizens. In a democracy, this means being willing to serve. We should promote the welfare of the community, not just stand apart or stand in judgment. The church should be a testimony for its constructive spirit.

Are there times when we should not submit to the government? We should never allow government to force us to disobey God. Jesus and his apostles never disobeyed the government for personal reasons; when they disobeyed, it was in order to follow their higher loyalty to God. Their disobedience was not cheap: They were threatened, beaten, thrown into jail, tortured, and executed for their convictions. Like them, if we are compelled to disobey, we must be ready to accept the consequences.

3:2 To slander no one, to be peaceable and considerate, and to show true humility toward all men.^{NIV} These bridge-building characteristics revealed changed lives and made the gospel message attractive to unbelievers. All Christians should check their conduct against these traits. By the phrase *to slander no one,* Paul was forbidding Christians to spread evil rumors or gossip *about* anyone *to* anyone (see James 3:9). Believers were not to be caught making reports about others that would prove to be untrue. We should be like Christ, who did not retaliate when he was insulted (1 Peter 2:23).

"To avoid quarreling" (NRSV) conveys more directly the meaning behind the Greek words translated *to be peaceable.* Christians were to be known as peacemakers in their relationships and within the church. There may be disagreements, but the believers should actively *avoid,* not the disagreement, but quarreling about it. When disagreements degenerate into quarreling, there is little possibility of preserving peace and working toward a solution.

PASSIVE SLANDER
We don't often call it by its right name, but gossip is passive slander, and it is a massive problem in churches today. It may be even worse than slander due to its dishonesty. A slanderer actively wants to attack and hurt someone, so that person is easily identified. Gossipers don't care whether or not a person is hurt as they pass along dishonest and harmful information. Churches can save a lot of headaches and heartaches by not allowing gossip (or gossipers) to gain a foothold.

Being *considerate* (gentle, forbearing) was one of Christ's characteristics; being considerate ought to characterize our lives. In the church, we demonstrate gentleness by avoiding quarrels. Christians should not be agitators but conciliators. The considerate believer goes out of the way to "see" the other person's point of view. Believers could show gentleness to unbelievers in their neighborhoods by offering help without strings attached. When we help unbelievers, we open a door for the gospel; but our help should be offered even when the door remains closed.

Paul ended this short list of bridge builders to the world by asking believers to *show true humility* (or "display all meekness"). In a hymn about the attitude of Christ, Paul had summarized Jesus' attitude as a man: "And being found in human form, he

---

HUMILITY [AND HOW I GOT IT!]
Humility is a very elusive character trait. Yet the Bible regards it as a highly important quality. Jesus referred to himself as "humble in heart" (Matthew 11:29). Paul listed humility as a fruit of the Holy Spirit (Galatians 5:22-23). (See also Ephesians 4:2; Colossians 3:12; James 3:13.) In Romans 12:3, Paul wrote the clearest definition of humility apart from Jesus' own example: "For by the grace given me I say to every one of you: Do not think of yourself more highly than you ought, but rather think of yourself with sober judgment, in accordance with the measure of faith God has given you" (NIV).
Humility, then, boils down to having an honest estimate of ourselves before God. We show false humility when we project negative worth on our abilities and efforts. We show pride when we inflate the value of our efforts or look down on others. True humility seeks to view our character and accomplishments honestly. Recognizing that we have succeeded in an effort need not be pride.

---

humbled himself" (Philippians 2:8 NRSV). That hymn was written
to illustrate an earlier challenge to "let the same mind be in you
that was in Christ Jesus" (Philippians 2:5 NRSV). What greater
compliment could a believer ever receive than to be told that his
or her humility reminded someone of Jesus?

**3:3 For we ourselves were once foolish, disobedient, led astray,
slaves to various passions and pleasures.**NRSV The Cretans had a
reputation for certain vices (1:12), yet Paul well understood that
all believers once were sinners and had lived far from God (see
also 1 Corinthians 6:9-11; Ephesians 4:17-24). Paul never forgot
the change that God had made in his life, beginning with his
experience on the Damascus road (Acts 9:1-22). Paul included
himself, Titus, the believers in Crete, and all believers across the
world in the list of past rebels.

ENSLAVED
Following a life of pleasure and giving in to every sensual
desire lead to slavery. Many think that freedom consists in
doing anything they want. But this path leads to a slavish addiction to sensual gratification, where a person is no longer free
but a slave to what his or her body dictates (2 Peter 2:19).
Christ frees us from the desires and control of sin. Have you
been released?

Foolish is used here as it is in Proverbs for those who arro-
gantly rebel against God and go their own way. In Proverbs, fools
are proud and arrogant (Proverbs 21:24); they scorn wisdom
(Proverbs 23:9); they trust only in themselves (Proverbs 28:26);
they persist in their foolishness (Proverbs 27:22). Instead of
being submissive, obedient, and ready to do good (3:1), we were
disobedient toward God because of our sin, and *led astray,*
deceived by false teachers for the very same reason, unable to do
anything good or pleasing to God (see 1:16). Without God, all
unbelievers are enslaved to their passions and desires. This paints
a dismal picture of humanity without Christ, but it is not exaggerated. Left alone, human nature can only go from bad to worse.

**We lived in malice and envy, being hated and hating one
another.**NIV Instead of avoiding slander and quarrels, being peaceful, considerate, and humble (3:2), we lived in *malice* as people
wanting to harm one another, envious of others' possessions and
appearance. No matter how much "love" the world tries to create
without God, the overriding power of sin produces a greater

amount of hatred. Thus there is no hope for sinful humanity apart from the intervention of the holy God, our Creator.

THREE REASONS WHY WE SHOULD BE HUMBLE
1. Our past condition was shameful (3:2). We did not love God nor other people; we have no basis for pride.
2. We are unable to save ourselves (3:4). We cannot do enough good works to merit our salvation. It all depends on Christ's mercy.
3. We have the hope of eternal life by God's grace alone (3:7). It's not based on any perfection we can achieve.

3:4 But when the kindness and love of God our Savior appeared, he saved us. NIV Fortunately for us, God *did* intervene on earth for the sake of hopeless, sinful humanity. In the Greek text, the next four verses form one long sentence. The contrasting *but* that Paul used here introduces a profound summary of the gospel.

God's *kindness and love* appeared in the human form of Jesus Christ. "Love" (*philanthropia*—"love for man") is the affection God has for his created children. God's love and kindness provide the only way for us to be saved. By his death, *he saved us* from our deserved punishment for disobeying God, taking that punishment upon himself. When we become Christians, we can experience personally the kindness and love of God provided for us through the death of Christ.

His saving action was for people estranged from God (see 3:3). They needed to be saved, not theoretically, but actually. Their condition and ours ("we too") was so desperate that the only possible way we could be saved was for help to come from "the outside." By sending Christ, God did exactly that!

3:5 Not because of any works of righteousness that we had done, but according to his mercy. NRSV Why did God save us? He offered this salvation because of his mercy alone, not because we deserved it by doing righteous works; indeed, we were incapable of righteous works (3:3). Paul knew this from experience—God mercifully called Paul as he traveled to Damascus to arrest Christians. Paul wrote to other churches: "For all have sinned and fall short of the glory of God, being justified freely by His grace through the redemption that is in Christ Jesus" (Romans 3:23-24 NKJV); "For by grace you have been saved through faith, and that not of yourselves; it is the gift of God, not of works, lest anyone should boast. For we are His workmanship, created in Christ Jesus for good works, which God prepared beforehand that we should walk in them" (Ephesians 2:8-9 NKJV). (See also Romans 4:4-5; Galatians 2:16-17.)

By identifying ourselves with the lost (3:3), Paul provided clear reasons for why we should be humble in our treatment of others. After all, once we too had been lost. Paul contrasts our lost condition with the overwhelming *mercy* of God. God's mercy toward us provides the greatest reason for us to be merciful to others (see Jesus' parable of the unmerciful servant in Matthew 18:21-35).

> Works of righteousness are the fruit of salvation, and the root must come before the fruit. The Lord saves His people out of clear, unmixed, undiluted mercy and grace, and for no other reason.
> *C. H. Spurgeon*

He saved us through the washing of rebirth and renewal by the Holy Spirit.[NIV] Paul summarized what God does for us when he saves us. *He saved us* is in the aorist tense showing Christ's completed action as a historical fact. The Bible uses a number of images to describe the transformation from being lost to being saved. On this occasion, Paul chose to picture his and Titus's previous state apart from Christ as a condition of moral corruption that had to be cleansed. The direct means of salvation, then, was *washing*.

There are three views for Paul's use of the word "washing" (*loutrou*):

(1) Some take "washing" to be external water baptism only. But they hesitate to make a connection between water baptism and spiritual conversion ("spirit baptism") from this verse, because Paul would have used the term *baptizo* for water baptism. In this explanation both the "washing" and "renewal" are descriptive of the Holy Spirit's work in us to accomplish our salvation. This explanation lessens the need to define baptism; it also honors the work of God's Spirit.

(2) Others suggest that Paul referred to spiritual baptism with a stress on internal cleansing. This explanation also takes "washing" to be water baptism (or perhaps conversion) but adds a second step in the process called "renewing." This view runs into a grammatical difficulty however, because the word *through* (*dia*) is used only once before the phrase "washing and renewing." The most natural way to read the verse keeps "washing" and "renewing" as aspects of one action, not two. Further, those who support this second view are divided by how they identify these two steps: "Washing" has usually been seen by both groups as baptism or conversion; but the "renewing" has been interpreted

either as confirmation into the church or continual spiritual development, while some Pentecostal groups have defined the term as a reference to a second baptism in the Spirit. We would expect, however, that Paul would have chosen less similar words if he were indicating two entirely separate instances of the Spirit's work. Both views under number 2 also share a weakness in limiting the Holy Spirit's activity to the "renewing" action.

(3) The third view keeps "washing" and "renewing" together, seeing the "washing" as water baptism, a metaphor for the entire work of cleansing and regenerating by the Holy Spirit. Rebirth is the new creation of 2 Corinthians 5:17; renewal is the constant process started at conversion. A translation like the NRSV clearly favors this view, using *water* in the text and footnoting *washing*. But while this view may have the weight of tradition behind it, history also has shown that an overemphasis on baptism can overshadow the other matters surrounding this verse, such as salvation and the hope of eternal life. Believers have been divided over the practice of baptism. Making this verse a proof text on baptismal regeneration creates many more problems than it solves, reducing the dynamics of the Christian life to a cold formalism. (How many laity in churches that baptize infants can explain what their baptism means in biblical terms? How many laity in believer-baptism churches are guilty of uncharitable and ignorant judgments on the practice of infant baptism by genuine believers?)

As Paul explains the transaction, when believers receive this washing of rebirth, all sins, not merely some, are washed away. We gain eternal life with all its treasures. The process is complete. We can experience what we have in new ways, but we have received the whole package! We live a "new" life because of our *renewal by the Holy Spirit* (see Romans 8:9-17). The Holy Spirit is an integral and essential participant in the entire process. As Paul exclaimed to the Romans, "For all who are led by the Spirit of God are children of God" (Romans 8:14 NRSV). None of this occurs because we earned or deserved it; salvation is all God's gift.

All three persons of the Trinity are mentioned in this verse and the next because all three participate in the work of salvation. Based upon the redemptive work of his Son, the Father forgives and sends the Holy Spirit to wash away our sins and continually renew us.

3:6 Whom He poured out on us abundantly through Jesus Christ our Savior.NKJV These words remind us of the Day of Pentecost, when the Holy Spirit filled that first group of believers (the Greek verb translated "poured out," *ekcheo,* is used here and in

Acts 2:33). Paul and his associates (*us*) received the Holy Spirit
abundantly (also translated "richly," "generously"). God is not
stingy, he gives in abundance. Jesus Christ, as Mediator, came to
earth and then returned to the Father so the Holy Spirit could
come. Jesus told his disciples, "Unless I go away, the Counselor
will not come to you; but if I go, I will send him to you" (John
16:7 NIV). At the moment when they accept Christ as Savior, all
believers receive the Holy Spirit.

**3:7 So that, having been justified by his grace, we might become
heirs having the hope of eternal life.**^{NIV} As was often his style,
Paul repeated what he had just written, changing the terms for
emphasis. We were all born into sin that leads to certain death (3:3)
and clearly in need of rescue. Because of his mercy (3:4), God
"saved us" (3:5). Because we were sinners incapable of supplying
our own righteousness (3:6), God cleansed us through the Holy
Spirit's work. In this verse, the phrase *having been justified by his
grace* summarizes the same problem (needing justification) and
God's solution (justification by grace). From Adam we inherited
guilt, a sinful nature (the tendency to sin), and God's punishment.
Because Jesus took the punishment we deserved for sin and "justified" us before God, we can trade punishment for forgiveness. We
can trade our sin for Jesus' righteousness. Christ offers us the opportunity to be born into his spiritual family. If we do nothing, we will
die in our sins; but if we come to God by faith, we inherit eternal
life through Christ. (See also Romans 4:25; 5:18.)

To be *heirs* refers to our being children of God who inherit all
his riches: "And if you belong to Christ, then you are . . . heirs
according to the promise. . . . So you are no longer a slave but a
child, and if a child then also an heir, through God" (Galatians
3:29; 4:7 NRSV). In the human setting, heirs don't inherit until the
owner of the estate dies (though they may enjoy many benefits in
the meantime). But in the spiritual realm the opposite occurs: We
do not fully inherit until *we* have died; yet in this life we can
experience many joys and benefits of being "heirs" of God.
Those riches are summed up in the *hope of eternal life.* As mentioned in 2:13, this "hope" is a certainty. Eternal life began the
moment we gave our life to Christ, but there is more to come!
Our experience *now* is only a foretaste of what God has guaranteed to us in the future!

AVOID USELESS ARGUMENTS / 3:8-11

As Titus proceeded with the task of planting and nurturing the
church, Paul reminded him that he would encounter resistance.

The aging apostle Paul had summarized the key points of the faith that Titus was to communicate. Titus must lead in such a way so that the truth would not be compromised by arguments, curious teachings, or conflicts over power. Some people in the church would not listen and follow even when they were patiently and repeatedly corrected. These people would lead others astray and cause divisions in the church. Titus was not to tolerate their divisive behavior. He would have to put those people out of the church.

3:8 **This is a faithful saying, and these things I want you to affirm constantly.**^{NKJV} Paul used this phrase several times (1 Timothy 1:15; 3:1; 4:9; 2 Timothy 2:11) to indicate that what he just wrote was *faithful* or trustworthy. So Titus ought to constantly affirm (teach) it. In this verse, the *saying* referred to the basics of the gospel message—the miracle of salvation, rebirth, and eternal life given to the believers by God's mercy alone—and the lifestyle changes required of all who claimed the name of Christ. Contextually, the "saying" was probably the long sentence in verses 4-7, but Paul undoubtedly would have also meant "everything I've told you so far."

GOOD WORKS
In this chapter, Paul stressed good works. Verse 1 says, "Be ready for every good work." Verse 8 says, "Be careful to devote themselves to good works." Verse 14 says, "Our people must learn to devote themselves to doing what is good." Paul understood good works as faithful service, acts of charity, and involvement in civil affairs. While good works can't save us or even increase God's love for us, they are true indications of our faith and love for Christ. Paul did not make this aspect of discipleship "optional." Service to others is a requirement. Everyone who is a Christian should be involved. Does your church encourage everyone's involvement and service? What can your church do to help every member identify the good works he or she should be doing?

So that those who have come to believe in God may be careful to devote themselves to good works; these things are excellent and profitable to everyone.^{NRSV} The believers must show their beliefs through their conduct. They must be *careful* (or thoughtful) *to devote themselves to* (or initiate) *good works.* Sound doctrine must manifest itself in good works. Such teaching and action profits the believers as well as the unbelievers to whom the church witnesses. In Ephesians 2:8-10, Paul showed the key role good works play in the development of the life of grace. James 1:22; 2:14-25; and 3:13 show the central place of good works in the true believer's life.

3:9 But avoid foolish controversies and genealogies and arguments and quarrels about the law, because these are unprofitable and useless.^{NIV} If sound teaching and good works were "excellent and profitable to everyone" (3:8), obviously foolish arguments were *unprofitable and useless*. Paul warned Titus, as he warned Timothy, not to get involved in foolish and unprofitable arguments (1 Timothy 1:4; 6:4; 2 Timothy 2:14, 23). The false teaching in Crete apparently had Jewish roots and focused on two errors: "Jewish myths" (1:14) and *quarrels about the law*—probably some useless speculations on the Old Testament rules and rituals, especially Jewish laws regarding what was clean and unclean. These teachers were causing controversies, arguments, and quarrels about their own wholly imaginary ideas, using methods similar to those of the false teachers in Ephesus and Colosse.

Paul also referred to *genealogies* in his warning to Timothy. It might be that the false teachings in Crete, Ephesus, and Colosse had some of the same tangents (see 1 Timothy 1:4; Colossians 2:8, 18), including imaginary genealogies of angels. These were needed, so the false teachers said, because believers had to worship angels as well as God. But these speculative arguments took valuable time away from teaching the truth of Scripture and spreading the gospel. Pointless controversy does not help advance the truth.

Paul warned Titus and Timothy to *avoid* the false teachers' debates and arguments, not even bothering to answer their pretentious positions. This did not mean that the church leaders should refuse to study, discuss, and examine different interpretations of difficult Bible passages. Paul was warning against petty quarrels, not honest discussion that leads to wisdom. As foolish arguments develop, they should rebuke the false teaching (1:13) and turn the discussion back to a helpful and profitable direction. Meanwhile, the faithful minister should continue to emphasize those truths that God wants taught.

3:10 After a first and second admonition, have nothing more to do with anyone who causes divisions.^{NRSV} Paul gave a similar warning at the end of Romans 16:17-20 and follows Jesus' pattern in Matthew 18:15-17. Besides avoiding the false teachers' debates, Titus needed to take specific action toward the false teachers themselves, as with anyone who *causes divisions*. These divisive people insisted on their own opinions without proper biblical undergirding. Even more than their doctrine, their church-wrecking behavior had to be stopped. While false teachers outside the church were to be avoided, a person inside the church must be warned not to cause division or threaten the unity of the church. This warning should not be a heavy-handed action because it is intended to correct the individual's divisive nature and restore him or her to fellowship. Paul allowed for two warnings before having *nothing more to do with* the person. This step of excommunication is like Jesus saying to treat them like a pagan or a tax collector.

Paul was giving Titus a guideline for "discipline on the run" as he pursued his duties on Crete. More than two warnings to someone creating distractions and false teaching would involve Titus with them too deeply and hurt his effectiveness elsewhere.

CHURCH DISCIPLINE
In Matthew 18:15-17, Jesus gave a four-step process for church discipline that Paul uses here. Jesus said:
1. Go to the one who sins against you one-on-one.
2. If the person does not listen, take one or two others along as witnesses and try to solve the problem.
3. If the person still refuses to listen, take the matter to the church (most churches handle it by having the elders decide the issue).
4. Finally, put the person out of the church, treating him or her like a "pagan" or a "tax collector."
These guidelines are for Christians to use with Christians. They are for sins committed against us, not for us to use in order to ferret out sins others do against others. They are to be used to deal with problems within the church, not in the community at large.
Finally, believers must remember that Jesus' words are not permission to attack every person who wrongs or slights us. Nor do they permit us to find two or three others to form a gossip campaign. These guidelines must never be used to escalate conflict; they are to be used as steps to resolve problems.

3:11 Since you know that such a person is perverted and sinful, being self-condemned.[NRSV] Those who refused to be corrected should be put outside the fellowship, or at least be avoided by Titus if they were not part of the church. A person's stubborn refusal to stop teaching false doctrine and to stop causing division in the church (even after being lovingly admonished) evidenced a *perverted and sinful* mind, one that is *self-condemned;* in other words, such actions condemn the doer. (See also Matthew 18:15-18 and 2 Thessalonians 3:14-15 for help in handling such problems in the church.)

A local church cannot modify its doctrine for every new idea or accommodate every person's viewpoint. It may be better to risk having a member leave for another church that emphasizes his or her theological "hot button" than to try to be a church that caters to every conceivable theological taste. A church cannot get to the important work of evangelism and service to others if the theological base is shaky or if the church is embroiled in theological controversy.

PAUL'S FINAL INSTRUCTIONS / 3:12-15

Paul ended his letter with several personal notes. He was not entirely finished with his instructions for Titus's work, but Paul had some important duties he wanted Titus to do for him.

Unlike 2 Timothy, written when Paul was in prison, this letter to Titus came from Paul while he was still deeply involved in ministry. Paul was making plans to winter in Nicopolis and was hoping to rendezvous with Titus there. He probably intended for either Artemas or Tychicus to take over the work in Crete from Titus. Paul's helpful memo would be a written set of orders that Titus could pass on to anyone who followed him in ministry.

3:12 When I send Artemas to you, or Tychicus.[NRSV] Nothing is known about Artemas. Tychicus was one of Paul's trusted companions (Acts 20:4) and a messenger (he delivered the letters of Ephesians and Colossians to the churches in those cities—Ephesians 6:21; Colossians 4:7). Paul planned to send one of these men to Crete to fill in for Titus so Titus could go to meet Paul.

Do your best to come to me at Nicopolis, for I have decided to spend the winter there.[NRSV] We do not know Paul's location at the writing of this letter to Titus; however, he noted here that he wanted to winter in Nicopolis. Three places in the Roman Empire were named Nicopolis (literally, "city of victory"), so named after some conquest. The city mentioned here probably was on the western coast of Greece. Titus would have to leave soon because sea travel was dangerous in the winter months.

3:13 Do everything you can to help Zenas the lawyer and Apollos on their way and see that they have everything they need.[NIV] Nothing is known about Zenas the lawyer, except that he would have been an expert in the law—either Hebrew or Roman, depending on his nationality (his name is Greek, so we might assume the latter). Apollos was a famous Christian preacher. A native of Alexandria in

THE INDISPENSABLE HOLY SPIRIT

The following passages show us what an important role the Holy Spirit has in our daily lives.

Passage	Role of the Holy Spirit
John 14:15-31	When Jesus was about to leave the disciples, he told them he would remain with them. How could this be? The Counselor, Helper, Advocate, Spirit of Truth—the Spirit of God himself—would come to care for and guide the disciples after Jesus was gone. The Holy Spirit is a powerful person on our side, working for and with us.
John 20:22; Acts 2	The regenerating power of the Spirit came on the disciples just before Jesus' ascension, and the Spirit was poured out on all the believers at Pentecost, shortly after Jesus ascended to heaven. The Holy Spirit is the very presence of God within us. By faith we can appropriate the Spirit's power each day.
John 14:16	The Holy Spirit will be with us forever.
John 14:17	The Holy Spirit cannot be accepted by the world at large.
John 14:17; Romans 8:9-14	The Holy Spirit lives with us and in us. Although Jesus ascended to heaven, he sent the Holy Spirit to live in believers. To have the Holy Spirit is to have Jesus himself.
John 14:26	The Holy Spirit teaches us. As we study the Bible, we can trust the Holy Spirit to plant truth in our mind, convince us of God's will, and remind us when we stray from it.
John 14:26	The Holy Spirit reminds us of Jesus' words.
John 15:26	The Holy Spirit gives strength to endure the unreasonable hostility many have toward Christ. This is especially comforting for those facing persecution.
John 16:8	The Holy Spirit convicts us of sin, shows us God's righteousness, and announces God's judgment on evil.
John 16:13	The Holy Spirit guides into truth and gives insight into future events. The truth is the truth about Christ.
John 16:14	The Holy Spirit brings glory to Christ.
Romans 8:1-2	The Holy Spirit sets us free.
Romans 8:16; Galatians 4:6-7	The Holy Spirit assures us that we are God's children.
Romans 8:26-27	The Holy Spirit intercedes for us in our weakness and in our prayers.
Ephesians 1:13-14	The Holy Spirit seals us for eternity.

North Africa, he became a Christian in Ephesus and was trained by
Aquila and Priscilla (Acts 18:24-28; 1 Corinthians 1:12). From the
context, it appears that Zenas and Apollos were on a preaching mission in Crete. Thus Titus, as leader of the churches in Crete, should
be an example to the believers, encouraging hospitality and financial assistance in order that these missionaries would be helped *on
their way* and had *everything they need.* (For more about hospitality and help for traveling preachers in the days of the early church,
see 2 and 3 John.)

WHO CARES?
In the church's early days, traveling prophets, evangelists, and
teachers like Paul, Apollos, and Zenas were helped on their
way by believers who housed and fed them. Hospitality is a lost
art in many churches today. We would do well to invite more
people for meals—fellow church members, young people, traveling missionaries, those in need, and visitors. This is an active
and much-appreciated way to show your love. Opening our
homes will also deeply influence our children. They will learn
firsthand *from* these ministers and learn *about* hospitality in the
process. These opportunities are available to us almost continually. They provide us with a way to practice ministry to other servants of God.

**3:14 Our people must learn to devote themselves to doing what is
good, in order that they may provide for daily necessities and
not live unproductive lives.**NIV Paul repeated his words of verses 1
and 8, again stressing the importance of *doing what is good.* Speaking to the Cretan believers as *our people,* Paul urged them to focus
these good works on providing for *daily necessities* for themselves,
their families, and those in need (such as the traveling preachers
mentioned in 3:13, as well as believers who might be in dire
straits). By saying "our people," Paul was pointing out to Titus that
the principal lessons involved in being effective followers of Jesus
are for everyone. What the Cretans were learning, the rest of the
church around the Mediterranean was also trying to learn.

GET THEM STARTED
For some people, good works may be a natural by-product of
their faith; others would have to be taught what to do and how
to do it. For those not yet involved in good works, use the "Tell,
Show, Do, Review" model of instruction:
- *Tell*—Explain what good works are, give lots of options, show
why they are important.
- *Show*—Demonstrate through skits, dialogues, and examples
what each type of work entails.

■ *Do*—Arrange practice and involvement by taking church members along on assignments or give them specific, concrete service they can do.

■ *Review*—Meet with them to discuss what they did, how they felt, and how they can improve for the next time.

Taking on normal responsibilities ensured that no one would be *unproductive*. (See also Ephesians 4:28.) Paul's view of productivity differs radically with today's view. Most people think "productive" means becoming affluent, achieving notoriety, or holding a high position. But Paul emphasized good works and fruitful Christian ministry to the needs of others. We must remember that it is the Holy Spirit who makes us fruitful as we use the opportunities given us (Galatians 5:22-23).

KEEP IT GOING
The letters of Paul to Titus and Timothy are his last writings and mark the end of his life and ministry. These letters are rich treasures for us today because they give vital information for church leadership. They provide a strong model for elders, pastors, and other Christian leaders as they develop younger leaders to carry on the work—therein following Paul's example of preparing Timothy and Titus to carry on his ministry. For practical guidelines on church leadership and problem solving, carefully study the principles found in these letters.

3:15 All who are with me greet you. Greet those who love us in the faith.^{NKJV} We do not know who was included in the *all* who were with Paul; however, such a greeting occurred in many of his letters with the people listed (see for example, 1 Corinthians 1:19-20; Colossians 4:10-15; 2 Timothy 4:9-12). Paul, in turn, sent greetings to all the faithful believers in Crete.

Grace be with you all. Amen.^{NKJV} Paul used a similar closing in both his letters to Timothy. The inclusion of *all* indicates that this letter was to be read to a wider audience than just Titus.

BIBLIOGRAPHY

Barclay, William. *The Letters to Timothy, Titus, and Philemon.* Philadelphia: The Westminster Press, 1975.

Bauer, Walter, William F. Arndt, Wilbur F. Gingrich. *A Greek-English Lexicon of the New Testament and Other Early Christian Literature.* Chicago: University of Chicago Press, 1979.

Brown, Robert K., and Philip W. Comfort, trans. *The New Greek-English Interlinear New Testament.* Wheaton, Ill.: Tyndale House Publishers, 1990.

Douglas, J. D., and Philip W. Comfort, eds. *New Commentary on the Whole Bible: New Testament Volume.* Wheaton, Ill.: Tyndale House Publishers, 1990.

Earle, Ralph. "1 Timothy." In *The Expositor's Bible Commentary,* vol. 11. Frank E. Gaebelein, ed. Grand Rapids: Zondervan, 1978.

————. "2 Timothy." In *The Expositor's Bible Commentary,* vol. 11. Frank E. Gaebelein, ed. Grand Rapids: Zondervan, 1978.

Fee, Gordon D. *1 and 2 Timothy, Titus.* The New International Biblical Commentary Series. Peabody, Mass.: Hendrickson Publishers, 1988.

Greek New Testament. Third Corrected Edition. United Bible Society.

Guthrie, Donald. *The Pastoral Epistles.* Rev. ed. Tyndale New Testament Commentaries. Grand Rapids: Eerdmans, 1990.

Hiebert, D. Edmond. "Titus." In *The Expositor's Bible Commentary,* vol. 11. Frank E. Gaebelein, ed. Grand Rapids: Zondervan, 1978.

Jensen, Irving L. *1 and 2 Timothy and Titus: A Self-Study Guide.* Chicago: Moody Press, 1973.

Kelley, J. N. D. *A Commentary on the Pastoral Epistles.* Peabody, Mass.: Hendrickson Publishers, 1960.

Kent, Homer A. Jr. *The Pastoral Epistles.* Chicago: Moody Press, 1986.

Knight, George W. III. *The Pastoral Epistles.* New International Greek Testament Commentary Series. Grand Rapids: Eerdmans, 1992.

Lea, Thomas D., and Hayne P. Griffin, Jr. *1, 2 Timothy, Titus.* The New American Commentary. Nashville: Broadman, 1992.

Meyer, F. B. *Devotional Commentary.* Wheaton, Ill.: Tyndale House Publishers, 1989.

Rolston, Holmes. *The Layman's Bible Commentary: 1 Thessalonians, 2 Thessalonians, 1 Timothy, 2 Timothy, Titus, Philemon.* Atlanta: John Knox Press, 1961.

Stott, John R. W. *The Message of 2 Timothy.* Downers Grove, Ill.: Intervarsity Press, 1973.

Walvoord, John F., and Roy B. Zuck. *Bible Knowledge Commentary: New Testament Edition.* Wheaton, Ill.: Victor Books, 1983.

Ward, Ronald A. *Commentary on 1 and 2 Timothy and Titus.* Dallas: Word Books, 1974.

INDEX